FLEET OWNER'S MAINTENANCE SHOP DESIGN BOOK

Library of Congress Cataloging in Publication Data

Main entry under title:

Fleet Owner's Maintenance Shop Design Book.

Includes index.

1. Motor vehicles—Service stations—Design and
construction. I. Siegel, Stewart. II. Fleet Owner
III. Title: Maintenance Shop Design Book.

TL153.F56   629.28′6   81-15080

McGraw-Hill Publications Company ISBN 0-07-606785-8 AACR2
McGraw-Hill Book Company ISBN 0-07-021260-0   AACR2

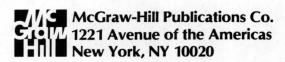

McGraw-Hill Publications Co.
1221 Avenue of the Americas
New York, NY 10020

FLEET OWNER'S MAINTENANCE SHOP DESIGN BOOK

FROM THE FLEET OWNER'S BOOK SERIES

EDITED BY STEWART SIEGEL

FLEET OWNER THE MAGAZINE

Fleet Owner magazine is edited for those involved in the management, operation and specification of truck and bus fleet maintenance and equipment. Each month it delivers news and features on maintenance, fleet operation and legislative interpretation to over 105,000 truck and bus operators. The regular edition reaches some 75,000 fleets running ten or more vehicles. The small-fleet edition is received by another 30,000 administrative, operations and maintenance executives in fleets or one to nine vehicles, at least one of which weighs 19,500 lb. GVW or over. *Fleet Owner* traces its history back to 1928, when it was conceived by Ferguson Publications Co. at Cleveland, Ohio. McGraw-Hill purchased *Fleet Owner* in 1949. At the time, McGraw-Hill had another surface transportation magazine in its fold—*Bus Transportation.* However, in 1959 it was decided to suspend publication of *Bus Transportation,* and much of the material that had been carried in that magazine was picked up by a vigorous and growing *Fleet Owner.* Today, *Fleet Owner* serves the information needs of a dynamic readership consisting of the nation's top common carriers, contract haulers and private truck fleets—as well as its transit, intercity and charter bus operators.

DEDICATION

With admiration and respect I dedicate this book to *Fleet Owner* senior editor Jack Lyndall. Beginning with his early years on the farm, and continuing as a fleet maintenance executive and editor, Jack has had an abiding interest in vehicle maintenance, shops and tools. His pioneering and innovative editorial skills inspired this volume, and many of the articles carry his byline. The instructional content of Jack's shop writings have helped distinguish *Fleet Owner* for many years. The excellence of his observations on shop design and planning is equaled only by his ability to instruct others on how to apply sound vehicle-management techniques to their new-shop plans.SS

CONTENTS

ONE

TWO

THREE

FOREWORD

There are two general aspects to motor truck and bus transportation: operations and maintenance. And it's certainly that, after a period of operational work, equipment will have to be brought in for servicing and repairs. To mount an economical, efficient maintenance effort, a fleet needs a convenient place for its mechanics to work . . . a shop that can house vehicles, tools and support equipment, yet also provide a safe, comfortable environment. In many cases, an attempt must also be made to make the shop a good neighbor that lives in harmony with nearby residents who—even the the best of circumstances—may be less than enthusiastic about being in close proximity to a fleet garage.

Over the years, *Fleet Owner* editors have visited a variety of modern truck and bus repair shops, discussed maintenance requirements with fleet management and interviewed shop designers and architects. The result of these activities is a continuing series of articles in *Fleet Owner* magazine. Taken as a group, these articles represent a unique informational tool for the fleet maintenance executive and shop designer. Virtually every one of the shop stories in this book details home-grown solutions to thorny maintenance problems. It is the editors' hope that by reading this volume, the reader can learn from experiences of others, and, in so doing, make the new or expanded shop as useful and "bug-free" as possible.

— Stewart Siegel

PART ONE

GETTING IDEAS DOWN ON PAPER

Those who work in fleet shops are judged by the results they achieve and are well aware of how much the shop itself affects their performance. They know, too, that once a shop is built they will have to live with it for a long time. A mistake made in spec'ing a new vehicle can sometimes be corrected by changing one or more vehicle components. At worst, the worker may have to live with the problem for a few years until the vehicle is depreciated on the books and can be replaced.

In contrast, a blunder made in planning a fleet shop may be extremely expensive, if not impossible, to correct. Tearing down and rebuilding walls is far more expensive and disruptive of shop operations than, say, changing an engine or transmission.

Having worked in fleet shops myself for many years, and having talked to many men who designed or modified their shops, I know how hard it can be to sell top management on the need for a new or improved shop. The best way to do that, I believe, is to use a calm, well-thought-out approach based on the cost savings and improved productivity of such a shop.

I would suggest developing a balance sheet that compares the differences in cost and time of performing fleet maintenance in a better facility with those of doing it in the old or current shop. The costs and worker-hour figures for an existing shop are, or should be, available from fleet records. Comparable figures for a new or remodeled shop, of course, have to be estimated.

A word of caution: Be conservative when making such estimates. It's better to be able to deliver on the projected savings when the shop is completed than to be discredited before management should an expensive building fall short of achieving the predicted results.

The selling job can be especially difficult when the fleet shop is in a rented building. The fleet tenant is usually reluctant to spend much money to improve the landlord's property unless the need and potential gain are overwhelmingly apparent. And the landlord, typically, would resist making expensive changes unless the fleet tenant pays the cost or agrees to a rent increase. However, it is safe to say that any improvement in shop facilities usually is a good investment.

—Jack Lyndall

SHOP SKETCHBOOK

One expert company's compilation of ideas—just to spark your own thinking—of the hows, whys, wheres (and why nots) of design

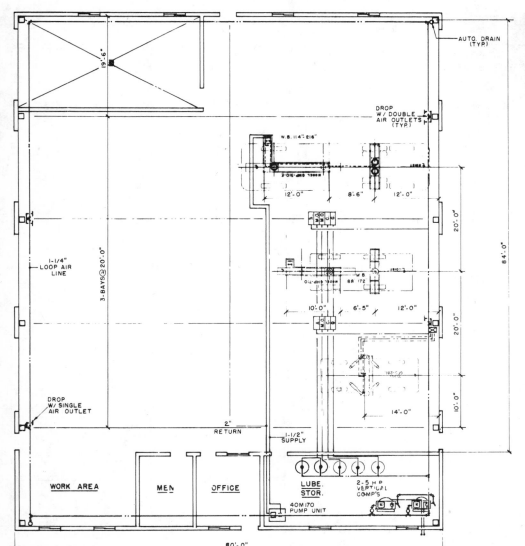

Fleet-shop needs vary as widely as do fleets. Even within a single company, shop needs will vary if there are multiple shop locations. The main shop may be a large complex, with areas for service lines, tire shops, and component-rebuild rooms.

But that fleet's satellite shop generally doesn't have to be that large. For that type of shop or for a small fleet, the four-bay shop shown here may be ideal. The 80-ft. depth allows a tractor-trailer unit to be serviced indoors without unhooking the trailer.

The pump for the five remote storage tanks is powered by two 5-hp vertical compressors. Those compressors also supply pressurized air for maintenance operations throughout the shop, and power the air-over-oil lifts.

This drawing and the one on the following page are typical of those offered as part of a free shop-design service by the Petroleum Equipment Div. of Dresser Industries, Salisbury, Md.

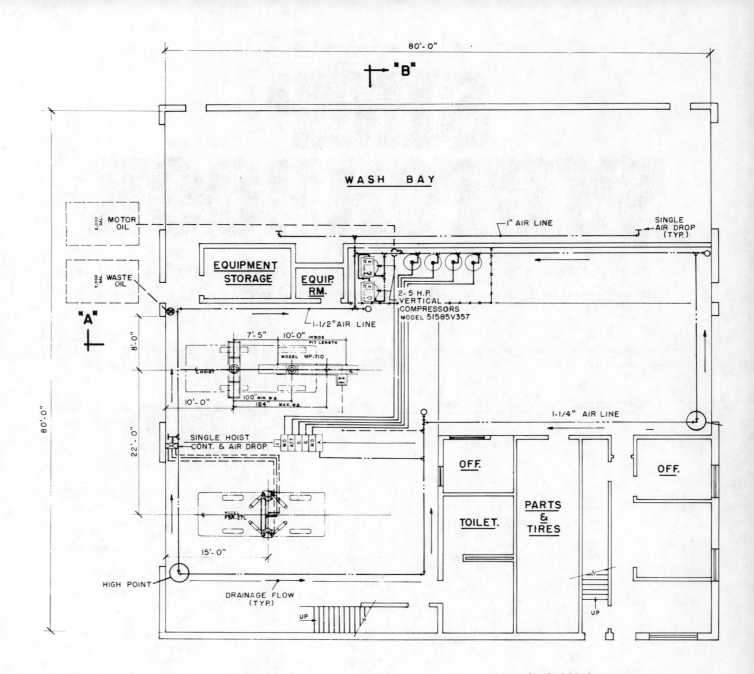

WASH BAY

80'-0"

"B"

MOTOR OIL

WASTE OIL

"A"

EQUIPMENT STORAGE

EQUIP. RM.

1" AIR LINE

SINGLE AIR DROP (TYP.)

2-5 H.P. VERTICAL COMPRESSORS MODEL 51585V357

1-1/2" AIR LINE

7'-5" 10'-0" INSIDE PIT LENGTH
MODEL MP-710

8'-0"

HOIST

10'-0" 100" MIN W.B.
184" MAX. W.B.

22'-0"

SINGLE HOIST CONT. & AIR DROP

1-1/4" AIR LINE

MODEL FSR-27L

OFF.

TOILET.

PARTS & TIRES

OFF.

15'-0"

HIGH POINT

DRAINAGE FLOW (TYP.)

UP

UP

80'-0"

2ND FLOOR PLAN

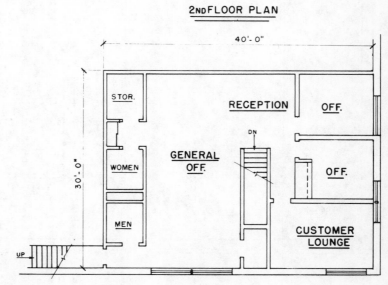

40'-0"

STOR.

RECEPTION

OFF.

WOMEN

GENERAL OFF.

DN

OFF.

30'-0"

MEN

CUSTOMER LOUNGE

UP

MAINTENANCE SHOP DESIGN

4

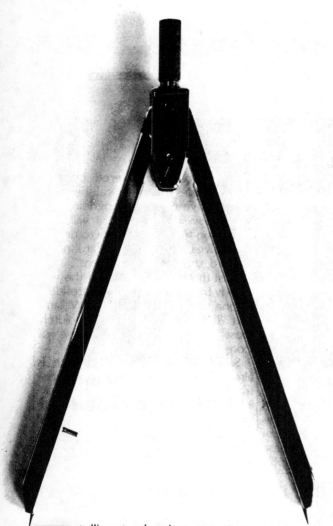

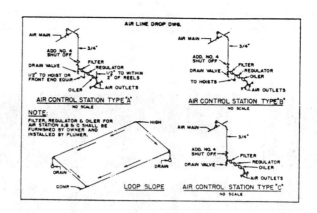

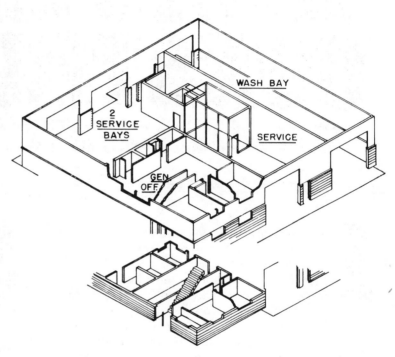

ntelligent planning can turn even a comparatively small area, such as this 80x80-ft. building, into a complete shop and office facility. The layout, shown here as it was provided by the Petroleum Equipment Div. of Dresser Industries, Salisbury, Md., is fully illustrated and indicates the full equipment package. It can be used by the fleet as a constant reference, and it can also serve as an architect's or builder's guide.

As a first step in planning a new shop, a fleet should prepare a questionnaire-type survey of its needs. From that, preliminary developmental sketches can be made. And those should be reviewed by all interested departments. After any necessary modifications, a fully dimensioned drawing can be made, and service-shop equipment can be positioned on the drawing. That equipment includes underground fuel storage tanks, lubrication systems, and exhaust units., Next, above-floor equipment can be located without possible interference problems. If a fleet plans to install front-end-alignment equipment, now is the time to do it. At this stage, it involves only a touch of the eraser.

Fleet personnel should get involved in shop planning. If they don't, the result could be poor work-flow patterns and/or traffic patterns that could cause work or safety problems.

LONGITUDINAL SECTION "A"-"A"

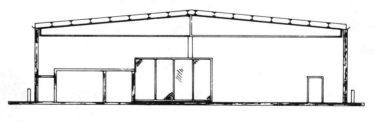

CROSS SECTION "B"-"B"

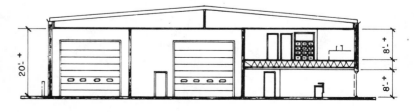

MAINTENANCE SHOP DESIGN

10 PITFALLS TO AVOID IN SHOP CONSTRUCTION

Advance planning of a new shop can help a fleet avoid ten common building mistakes that could push today's high costs even higher

1 **Inadequate planning.** Every building project must be analyzed according to its specific purpose, site, and budget. The building may very well fit your requirements now, but those requirements may change. A carefully considered, flexible building plan will pay continuing dividends.

The cost of construction and furnishing your building is important, but don't let it be the only consideration. Today's tax structure allows from 10 to 40 years' amortization. Your building must remain useful and attractive for at least such periods.

2 **Overlooking expansion.** Plan for expansion before you break ground for your building. A building designed for future growth or expansion may cost more initially, but later alterations and additions will be less expensive and, in most cases, will more than offset the original added expense.

In choosing your building site, plan for more than enough land. That will allow you to grow horizontally. Horizontal expansion allows changes in floor plans and building dimensions, requires no heavy foundation and column structures, and is more accessible than construction over a finished building. Surplus land, too, may be needed for parking, drives, shipping stations, and protection from adjacent tenants. If at all possible, avoid building on the edge of your site. Give yourself enough room to grow in any or all directions.

by Stran Div., National Steel Products Co., Houston, Texas

3 **High heating and cooling bills.** Insulation is essential in any building to be occupied by people or used for certain types of storage. A building without insulation can become as cold in winter as the temperature outside—and up to 30°F. hotter in the summer.

4 **Excessive maintenance cost.** Excessive maintenance costs usually result from the choice of interior building materials and finishes. A tight construction budget may force you to trim the initial cost of your building, but substitution of cheaper materials can mean more in maintenance and repair. If given a realistic budget, most builders will specify the material best suited for your particular job.

5 **High insurance rates.** One of the most effective ways to cut your building insurance costs is to consult a competent insurance agent during the planning stages of your shop building. He can make suggestions that will allow you to conform to the local building insurance codes during initial construction.

Three of the major mistakes that building owners most often make concerning fire insurance are: (1) Failure to make sure that plans conform to the fire-insurance-rating bureau's standard building code; (2) failure to install an automatic sprinkler system; and (3) failure to make use of other devices that can reduce fire-insurance rates.

Whatever the cause, buildings have been known to collapse. To be safe, choose a reputable builder, specify quality materials.

6 **Costly site selection.** Your building site may be the cause of increased building, operating, and maintenance costs. A talk with your builder before selecting the building site can help you avoid some of these extra expenses. Here are a few questions to ask yourself before selecting a site:

Will site-preparation costs be justified? Consider condition of soil, as well as landscaping and clearing that will be required. Investigate possible drainage and grading problems, and needed street improvements.

Are utilities readily available? Check possible utility installation costs and the utility company's ability to supply required amounts in your site area.

Will traffic circulation be convenient? Make sure you have room for an easy flow of employe, supplier, and company vehicles.

Are zoning and tax laws compatible with your business? Study the possibilities of future tax increases, or changes in zoning, air-pollution, and building laws.

Does the site complement your proposed building? The building should blend well architecturally with the natural landscaping. The site should display the building prominently, and the attractiveness of the location should lend prestige to your operation.

7 **The low-bidding contractor.** Hiring the low bidder on your building contract may cost you more in the long run. Unless you have investigated the integrity, financial stability, and experience of the builder you select, be ready for possible headaches. Delays, arguments over specifications, substitution of inferior materials, and charges for unnecessary extras are just a few of the problems that can arise.

Screen every builder you ask to bid. Inspect finished jobs. Talk to other building owners and architects who have worked with your prospective builder. Check credit rating agencies and banks for information on his financial status. It is surprising how many times these precautions are ignored. But what is not surprising is how often a finished building falls short of the quality intended.

8 **Inappropriate materials.** Some building materials are inappropriate for certain jobs. Materials vary, and so do job specifications. If you're not familiar with building materials, get help from an architect or reputable builder.

Be sure the material you choose will be attractive as well as functional. Check the price of materials in relation to the cost and quality of the building. Learn what materials will be suitable as substitutes should your first choice not be available. The specifications of the material should relate to the anticipated use and the projected life of the building. That will help control maintenance and operation costs.

9 **Lagging construction.** When planning a shop building, you lose money every day you extend the completion deadline. The unfinished building represents a substantial capital outlay that returns nothing until it is occupied. Taxes must be paid, and upkeep on your present location continues longer than you expected. There are many reasons for a delay in construction, but some can be avoided in the planning stages of your building.

Learn all you can about the type of foundation required. It may affect the cost, require moving the building, or even eliminate the possibility of building on your site. Pay particular attention to water levels.

Have a lawyer settle any special legal problems before you begin construction. Litigation can often be a time-consuming project, and the results may not be in your favor.

The most important step in on-time construction is careful planning of every facet of your building before the design stage. Decide whether steel, aluminum, concrete, or masonry will be used, and decide exactly where to use it. Consider the possiblity of long spans, the type of fireproofing that will be used, and plan intelligently for future expansion.

10 **Extra charges.** Most extra charges are a result of inadequate planning. The contractor will usually claim extra charges when plans call for unnecessary requirements, or if he has to correct an error or omission in the specifications. Additional construction costs to building owners often result from:

Changes required after the contract is let. It makes no difference to the builder whether the changes are made out of necessity or at the whim of the owner. He has bid according to the specifications.

Foundation problems because of surface conditions. Investigate the condition of your soil thoroughly. Do not speculate here.

Mistakes in your plans. Without sufficient time to draft your plans carefully, any architect or design engineer is likely to make mistakes or important omissions. Give him enough time to do a thorough job.

Poor communication between your architect, engineer, and builder. Select a construction team that can work together. Inspect their work to be sure that you get a coordinated effort.

Failure of specifications to meet requirements of local codes and regulatory boards. Any good architect should be aware of those requirements. Double check them with him before you let the contract.

Unexpected costs for required utility service. Consult the utility companies and local governments involved to be sure that adequate power, gas, water, and waste-disposal service is available.

CHOOSING THE SHAPE OF YOUR SHOP

Some basic questions of traffic flow, size of the fleet, and the available land now, and for future expansion, have to be answered

Primarily a major maintenance and rebuild center for a nationwide household-goods mover, this long, rectangular shop works well for a fleet whose rolling stock is made up almost entirely of tractors and furniture-van trailers with a few straight-truck vans.

The work bay layout allows vehicles to remain inside for extended periods of time for major repairs or ground-up rebuilding without interfering with movement or work on other vehicles. Trailers are backed in through the doors on both sides of the trailer shop; a wide aisle and generous work area is provided at the rear of the trailer. The majority of trailer work involves the axles

by Jack Lyndall, senior editor

and/or suspension and rear loading doors, which also are involved in access to ther trailer interior for floor or lining repairs.

Angled work bays in the tractor shop allow use of single doors at each end of the shop with a center traffic aisle. Adjoining supplemental tractor repair bay, with doors on both ends, can also be used for trailer repairs if necessary. In this particular shop, that bay is also partly used for tire-storage racks. The rest of the area could also be used for a tire-recapping plant.

This shop has a second floor level above the midsection for a parts room and shop supervisor's office.

If land is available, the design lends itself to easy expansion by extending either end. The center core area can be expanded, too, in both directions.

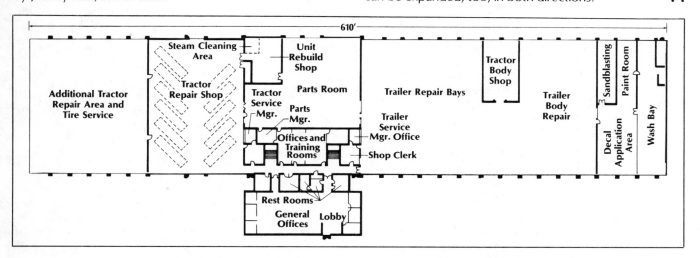

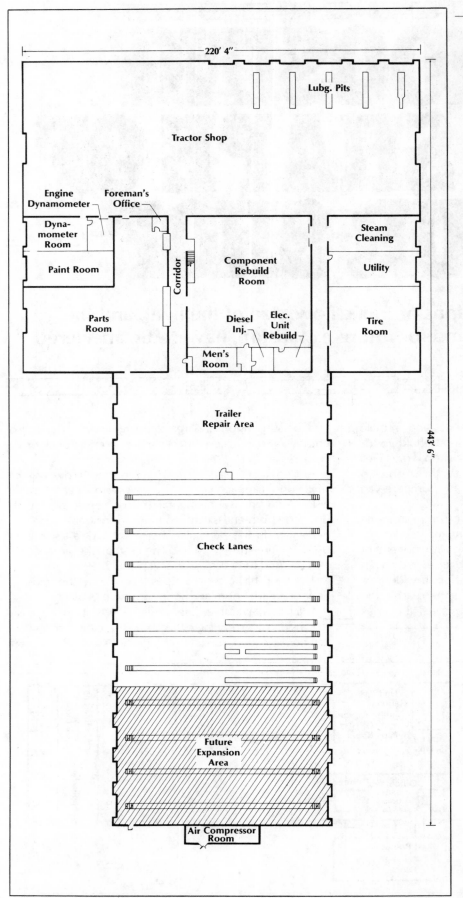

Tractor Shop

Lubg. Pits

220' 4"

Engine
Dynamometer

Foreman's
Office

Dyna-
mometer
Room

Paint Room

Parts
Room

Corridor

Component
Rebuild
Room

Diesel
Inj.

Elec.
Unit
Rebuild

Men's
Room

Steam
Cleaning

Utility

Tire
Room

Trailer
Repair Area

443' 6"

Check Lanes

Future
Expansion
Area

Air Compressor
Room

T-shaped shop plan was designed as a fleet's central overhaul and rebuild base. Combined with safety check-lanes, the shop is part of a major break-bulk terminal complex near the geographic center of the common carrier's routes.

The cross-bar of the T houses the tractor shop, with bays for major rebuilds and pits for fast-turnaround PM service. (A special extension of one pit simplifies oil changes and fork lift lube jobs.)

At the upper end of the T-leg is a trailer overhaul and rebuild shop. It's length, with exterior doors at both ends, allows individual trailers to be backed in or removed without disturbing others in the shop.

Between the tractor and trailer shops is the central service core, which decreases non-productive walking and service time. A second floor, above the central service core, contains administration offices, locker room and rest area.

On the lower end of the T-leg are safety check-out lanes with in-floor pits and centralized piped-in oil, lube, and antifreeze. For effective supervision of the checklanes, where vehicles in the lanes would block the view from ground-level foreman's office, the supervisor's office is overhead, midway in the check-lane area. A steel-grating catwalk extends from the office in both directions the length of the check-lane area, with stairs at convenient intervals.

At this facility, the truck wash lane is in a separate building. It was located so vehicles leaving the check-lanes next go to the wash building and from there to the parking area until they are dispatched. That setup prevents freshly washed vehicles from dripping water on the check-lane floor and onto mechanics working in the pits.

Future expansion was partly designed-in, with four additional check lanes "roughed in" at time of construction for finishing as need requires. The shop can also be extended outward in any one of three directions.

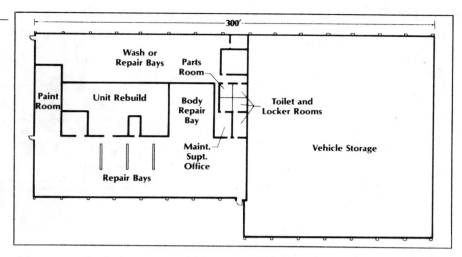

Compact rectangle is a popular shop configuration where land is limited. Shown here is a bus shop for a fleet of 48 school buses with adjoining storage garage. It is a pre-engineered steel building, which eliminated architects' fees.

Typical of fleet shops erected during the past decade, this design includes a central service core, which houses parts room, component rebuild, body and paint rooms, and supervision office. It also serves to divide the building into two distinct shop areas.

Roll-up exterior doors the length of two shop walls give easy access to vehicle bays. Bays on one side of the shop are for maintenance and repair, on the other side are individual wash bays or stalls. (In this fleet,

drivers wash their own vehicles, frequently.) Wash bays could, of course, be converted to maintenance or repair bays if other washing facilities are provided.

Adjoining storage building (unpaved in this example) helps shield vehicles from snow in winter and is

minimally heated. If such storage is not currently required, it can easily be eliminated.

Relatively easy expansion can be achieved by extending the shop lengthwise. More office or parts storage could be provided by adding a second floor.

Although a headline could say, "U-shaped layout is best bet," 25 years ago because it was "a cinch for a vehicle to get into or out of any service bay," times have changed, and the practicality of such a layout is open to serious question.

There was a major difference between that earlier shop plan and the one shown here, built by a municipal government fleet. The 1956 design had doors only along the paved yard inside the U.

"Advantages" stressed for that '56 layout were short roof spans with no columns or support posts, parking for trucks waiting to come into the shop in the paved "courtyard," maximum natural lighting, easier exhaust fume disposal through short ducts in the roll-up doors, and usage flexibility with all service bays essentially the same size.

Like the plan shown here, the old layout had the shop administration office in the base of the U. Although theoretically in a central location, it is not an ideal arrangement for work supervision in the far ends of the two shop legs.

Likewise, parts room, washroom, and component rebuild areas in the

base of the U make for extra walking and lost work time by mechanics working in the more distant shop bays.

The relatively easy expansion, by

simply extending the U, could be self-defeating as increased length compounds supervision problems and the long, narrow shop legs become more costly to heat.

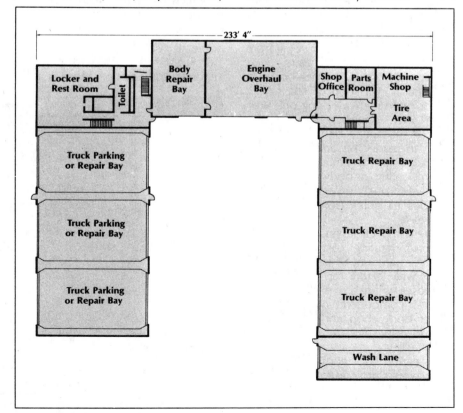

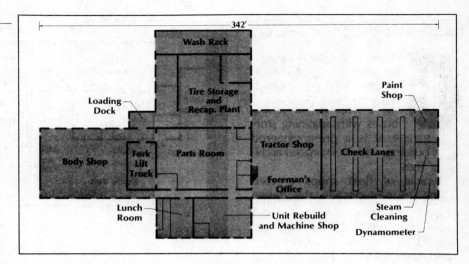

A cross or X-shaped shop offers the advantage of four wings, each of which can be devoted to a single type of work, with a central service and supervision core at the transcept. A somewhat unusual feature is a fork lift truck repair department. Fork lifts are brought in from production plants within a practical distance on the fleet's trucks.

The layout shown here is from a shop built a few years ago by a major private fleet with an almost total tractor and trailer operation. With its long haul, plant-to-plant service, similar to a common carrier, this fleet shop has several safety check-lanes with in-floor pits. A tractor shop with service bays along both walls makes good use of the floor space. One wing is wholly devoted to trailer body repairs.

Ancillary services occupy another cross leg. Those include a tire recapping shop together with tire mounting and storage facilities.

Component rebuild and diesel injection pumps and nozzle rebuild rooms occupy the fourth leg of the cross.

As with so many other modern, efficient shops, a second floor level above the central core provides space for shop or company offices, bulky-parts storage, wash-up and locker rooms and classrooms, making optimum use of ground floor space for vehicle servicing.

Expansion is flexible. Each of the four wings can be expanded outward if necessary.

The square shop offers low cost and simplified design, adaptable to pre-engineered contruction. Such was the case with this 135-vehicle fleet's shop, which handles everything from pickups to tractors and trailers.

Since a central service core is impractical in a shop of this size, it was located midway along one wall. Floor area on each side of the service manager's or foreman's office can readily be adapted to unit rebuild, engine overhaul, tire storage and mounting, or body shop.

Drive-through service bays allow vehicles to enter from either end, with ease.

The compact design, which should save on heating costs, requires a minimum amount of land. It is especially well suited for branch shop purposes where a parts back-up and central component overhaul, plus major body shop and mjor chassis rebuild services, are housed in a main facility.

A second floor above the service core would provide low-cost space for bulky-parts storage, wash rooms and/or locker rooms plus offices.

This particular shop does, in fact, have a balcony area used for its limited parts stock, for it was built as a branch, with the main parts and rebuilt-components stock room located at the headquarters shop some 20 miles away.

If substantial future expansion is required and additional land is available, this layout could be expanded by two or more service bays opposite the two existing. Then the shop office and unit overhaul rooms would be a true central service core.

This type of shop could be the nucleus of a long rectangular U-shaped, or X-shaped building as future needs dictate.

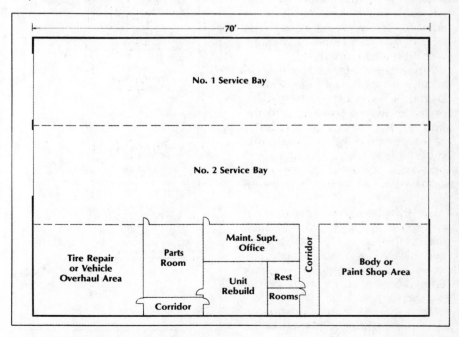

PART TWO

LEARNING FROM EXPERIENCE

"Only someone who has been 'through the agony' can tell you what it's really like," said one veteran fleetman we talked to in putting this volume of fleet shop plans together. "Every person in charge of a maintenance operation should have to design a shop—once. But no one should have to go through it twice."

So it would appear that, even in an industry where experience has almost always been a favorite teacher, there is still a lot to be learned second-hand, from those who have gone through it before. The following pages contain numerous shop descriptions, illustrations and floor plans. By learning what operations similar to yours have done, you can refine ideas for your shop. However, it should be understood that this material is not just applicable to the "design" of the facility, not at all.

You don't have to be in the middle of a shop-planning session to realize that in addition to facilities for physical work on vehicles you need a good way to control and store fuel. You certainly don't have to be reminded of the need to conserve heating fuel through better insulation and door design. Even if you are in an old building, you want to be able to make the best possible use of floor space and shop equipment.

However, if you are forging ahead with a new facility, you will, undoubtedly, want to keep numerous factors in mind. Take a good, long look at the shop solutions others have found. If you have some ideas already, answers developed by other fleets can help clarify your designing. But remember that these layouts are not intended to be perfect examples for you to follow. Only you can fully understand your fleet's needs and requirements.

—Stewart Siegel

BUS GARAGE
Layout boosts efficiency

One modern building—with shop, bus storage, and office facilities—replaces two older ones, bringing both increased productivity and flexibility to a privately owned charter and tour bus operation.

Nestled in a wooded area on a suburban Schenectady, N.Y., site is the ultramodern new headquarters and shop for Wade Tours, a privately owned bus line that operates a fleet of 23 buses over a short suburban route and in charter and tour bus service in 48 states. The fleet (see box) also includes several service vehicles and a company car.

The new headquarters and shop building replaces two outmoded facilities, says fleet owner Robert E. Wade, who took over the company at the passing of his father, who founded the company in the 1930s. One of the old facilities in the central Schenectady area accommodated six buses and was the main repair facility. The other, with a capacity of 15 buses, was used for bus storage as well as lubrication and washing. Buses had to be shuttled back and forth from one facility to another, but with the move to the new building, all operations are now under one roof. (One of the old buildings was sold; the other has been kept for storage of inactive buses and parts.)

Elegance combined with practicality

The headquarters office wing of the new facility has a modern, handsome front facing the road running past the property. The shop, a Stran-Steel pre-engineered building, was completed and occupied in December 1979; the office wing, on Oct. 15, 1980. (The architect was C.T. Male Assoc., Schenectady, N.Y.; the general contractor, Rotterdam Builders Inc., Rotterdam, N.Y.

The shop, 90x255 ft., includes a 24x120-ft. wash bay across one end (see floor-plan drawings). Completed cost of the facility was between $850,000 and $900,000, Wade reports. The shop, which operates five days a week in winter and six days a week from Easter until Nov. 1, is staffed with three mechanics, one of whom serves as a working shop supervisor and parts manager, and three bus cleaners, who also fuel and service the buses as they move through the wash bay.

by Jack Lyndall, senior editor/equipment

Because of seasonal variations in the charter and tour business, the entire shop force works on the day shift in winter. In the summer, the cleaning crew works at night, as does one mechanic, who transfers from the day shift.

Fleet participates in shop planning

Drawing on his many years with the company in driving, dispatching, and maintenance, Wade worked closely with the architect. And it shows.

The bus-cleaning bay is large enough to allow hand-washing of two buses at the same time. Fleet size does not justify an automatic brush-type washer, and Wade believes that hand washing is superior.

Buses enter the wash bay at the north end. In mild weather, they are fueled at pumps alongside the entrance driveway. In cold weather, they can be fueled in the wash bay from a hose installed on the west side wall near the entrance door. Next to that fuel hose is a motor-oil dispensing hose.

Also mounted on that wall are hoses and nozzles dispensing bus toilet chemicals, windshield-washerfluid, and premixed antifreeze.

The translucent fiberglass roll-up doors at each end of the wash bay provide improved lighting inside with the doors closed. Because of the frigid winters in the Schenectady area, Wade plans to install an additional ribbon-

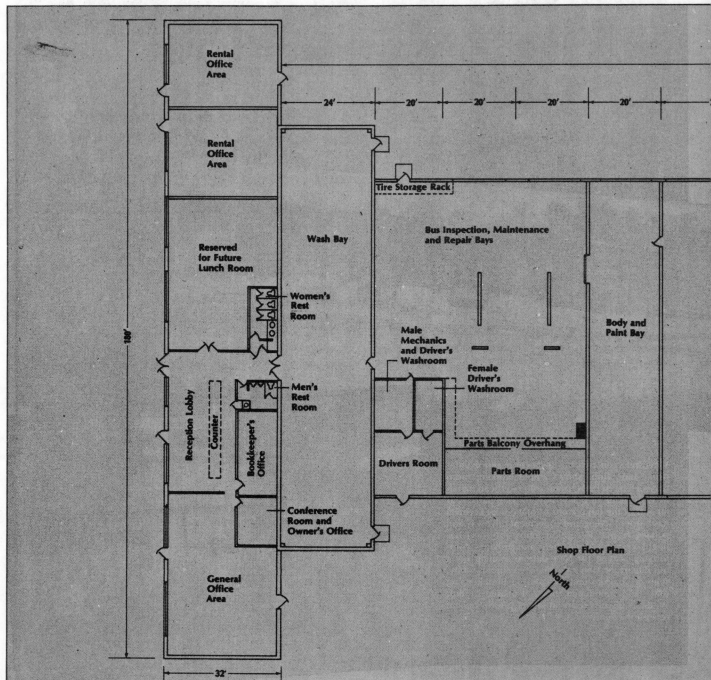

Shop Floor Plan

type, drive-through curtain at each door opening to reduce cold drafts and heat loss.

Adjacent to the wash bay is the driver's room, which has an outside entrance door and doors leading into the men's and women's restrooms. The driver's room is equipped with lockers for driver's clothes and uniforms, an automatic clothes washer and dryer for use by drivers to launder their company-provided uniforms, and two desks for use by drivers completing trip reports.

Two repair bays of the main repair and maintenance shop area have 11x14-ft. roll-up exterior doors on the south side; an additional bay near the wash bay has no exterior door. Eliminating outside doors in the north side

wall of the repair shop area (they had been shown on a preliminary shop-layout drawing) reduces heat loss and cold drafts in winter.

The two bays with the roll-up doors are equipped with Rotary AT70-8 twin-post hydraulic lifts with a capacity of 36,000 lb. Those bays are used for PM inspections, maintenance, and minor repairs. The third bay is used for major repairs that would immobilize a bus for some time. At the end of that bay is a three-tier tire rack.

Across the north end of the two service and PM bays is the parts room. A balcony, which extends out above part of the shop floor and also above the driver's room and the rest rooms, is used to store bulky and slow-

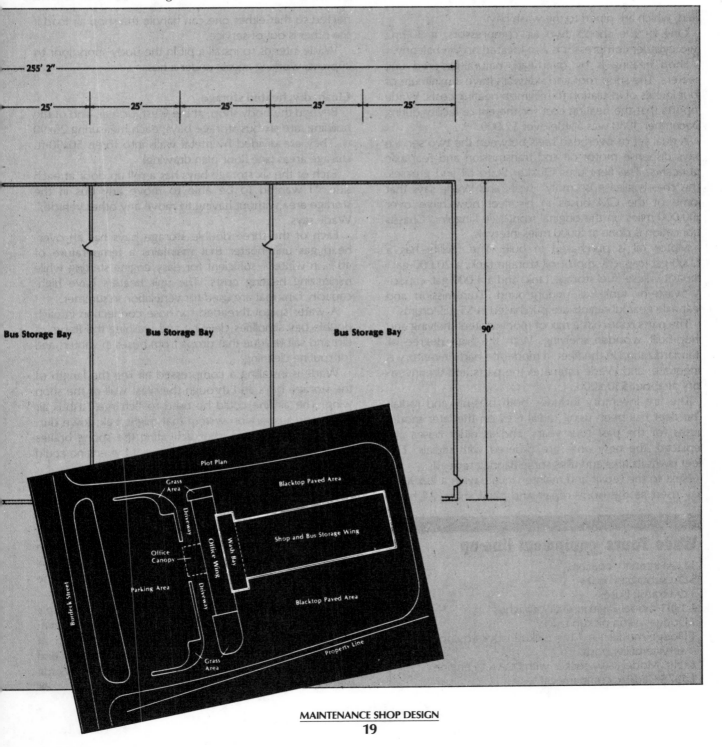

moving parts such as brake drums, body panels, and windows. Complete sets of body panels and luggage compartment doors for GM intercity coaches are stocked so that, in case of an accident, the shop can make immediate repairs without waiting for parts from the nearest parts warehouse.

The shop also stocks a spare rebuilt engine, transmission, and rear-axle differential assembly. These units are overhauled by the Wade shop, which also overhauls the automatic transmissions used in the three city transit buses. Unit rebuilding is done in the shop area nearest the parts room.

Also stored on the balcony are the drums of toilet chemicals, premixed antifreeze, and windshield washer fluid, which are piped to the wash bay.

One of the shop's two air compressors, a 10-hp., two-cylinder compressor is also located on the balcony.

Shop heating is by overhead, natural-gas-fired unit heaters. The shop roof and sidewalls have a minimum of four inches of insulation to minimize heating costs. Wade reports that the heating cost for the entire facility during December 1980 was a little over $2,000.

A dual set of overhead reels between the two service bays dispense motor oil and transmission and rear-axle lubricants. The fleet uses Quaker State oil and greases. The chassis grease is "moly" type, and Wade says that some of the GM buses in his fleet now have over 600,000 miles on the original front-axle kingpins. Chassis lubrication is done at 5,000 miles intervals.

Motor oil is purchased in bulk. The facility has a 2,000-gal.-capacity motor-oil storage tank, a 20,000-gal.-capacity diesel-fuel storage tank, and a 4,000-gal.-capacity waste-oil tank—all underground. Transmission and rear axle gear lubricants are purchased in 55-gal. drums.

The parts room has a mix of modern steel shelving and shop-built wooden shelving. With the high degree of standardization in the fleet, a moderate parts inventory is adequate, and Wade estimates the parts and tire inventory at about $100,000.

The tire inventory includes both bias-ply and radial. The fleet has been using radial tires on the later model buses for the past four years, and as older buses are replaced, the new ones are ordered with radials. The fleet owns its tires and uses some Bandag retreads.

Next to the repair and maintenance bays is a 20x90-ft. bay used as the body repair and paint shop. All body

Wade Tours' equipment line-up

11 GM intercity coaches
5 GM suburban buses
3 GM transit buses
4 1981-model Eagle intercity coaches
1 Dodge ½-ton pickup truck
1 Dodge Model 100 1-ton pickup truck equipped with
   service-utility body
1 GMC Model 860 wrecker with DDA 6-71 engine
1 1975 Cadillac company car

repairs from minor accidents or corrosion damage are done in the Wade shop. But a major wreck would be farmed out to a bus-body repair specialist.

Wade himself does much of the paint work, primarily repainting of repaired areas or replaced parts. Complete bus repainting is farmed out.

The body and paint-shop bay, like the adjacent repair bays, has no outside roll-up door on the north side but does have a small hinged door. At the north end of that bay is an elevated, overhead platform for storage of parts and tools. A 5-hp. De Vilbiss air compressor is also mounted on the platform, and its air intake is outside to assure clean incoming air and to reduce noise in the body shop. The two shop compressors are interconnected so that either one can handle the shop air load if the other is out of service.

Wade intends to install a pit in the body-shop floor to improve working access under a bus.

Clean, dry, heated storage

Beyond the body shop, at the west, or rear, end of the building, are six bus storage bays, each measuring 25x90 ft. They are divided by metal walls into three 50x90-ft. storage areas (see floor-plan drawing).

Each of the six storage bays has a roll up door at each side. "I wanted to be able to move any bus in the storage area without having to move any other vehicle," Wade says.

Each of the three double storage bays has an overhead gas unit heater that maintains a temperature of 40°F. in winter—sufficient for easy engine starting while minimizing heating costs. The unit heaters have high-capacity fans that are used for ventilation in summer.

A water spigot threaded for hose connection in each double bay simplifies cleaning and washing the floors of dirt and salt residue that drops from buses in winter, and for routine cleaning.

Wade is installing a compressed air line the length of the storage bays and through the west wall of the shop wing. The air line could be used to "charge" a bus air brake and suspension system that might leak down during extended storage, thus activating the spring brakes and preventing movement of the bus if the engine could not be started.

The entire building, both shop and offices, is circled by a black-top driveway (see site-plan drawing). A U-shaped traffic pattern provides smooth movement of vehicles to any door in the shop and exit to the street.

Consistent with the good planning, future expansion poses no problem. The new facility with its driveways and parking areas occupies about four acres of the 10-acre site.

The shop can be expanded at the west end by simply adding to the existing building and extending the driveways. Likewise, the office wing can be extended at either end. Or, rental space (two offices at the south end of the office wing) could be taken over for future Wade office expansion.

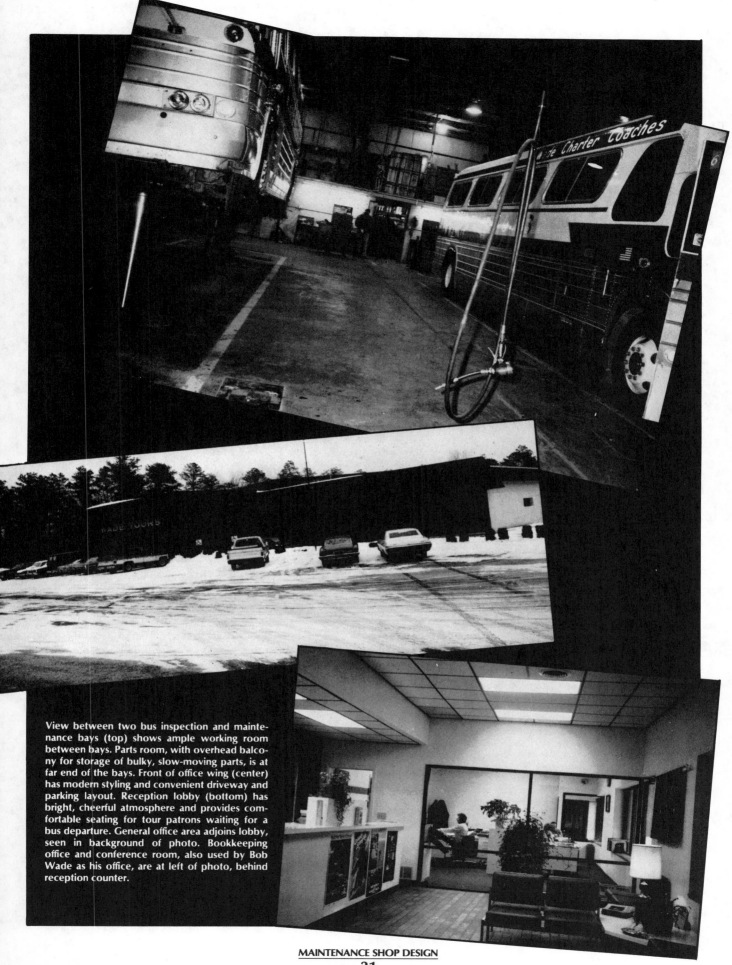

View between two bus inspection and maintenance bays (top) shows ample working room between bays. Parts room, with overhead balcony for storage of bulky, slow-moving parts, is at far end of the bays. Front of office wing (center) has modern styling and convenient driveway and parking layout. Reception lobby (bottom) has bright, cheerful atmosphere and provides comfortable seating for tour patrons waiting for a bus departure. General office area adjoins lobby, seen in background of photo. Bookkeeping office and conference room, also used by Bob Wade as his office, are at left of photo, behind reception counter.

1

Grand Rapids Area Transit Authority,
Public transit center,
Grand Rapids, Mich.
Architects: Ellis/Naeyaert/Genheimer Assoc.
General contractor: Triangle Assoc.

1. Repair bays were planned and built to provide flexibility for handling different size buses in the Grand Rapids fleet, as shown, as well as different size buses that may be added in the future.

2. View down the repair bays shows modern overhead reels for dispensing motor oil, gear oil, transmission fluid, and chassis lubricant. Each bay has its own exterior roll-up door; for security reasons, there are no outside door openers. Doors in the high-traffic-flow storage area are electronically operated; each has an outside and inside loop embedded in the concrete door ramp to activate opening and closing on a 30-sec. cycle to conserve heat. Repair-bay doors are pushbutton-controlled, but have a manual backup system.

3. Modern paint-spray booth is an important element in GRATA's program of attractive, colorful buses.

4. Front view of facility shows its clean, modern design. White glazed brick, with a large expanse of sharply contrasting gray insulating glass, gives the office a crisp, colorful, yet dignified facade. The building was designed for maximum utilization of the limited land available, with minimum social, economic, and environmental impact on nearby commercial and residential neighborhoods. And it was built on schedule and under budget.

Replacing a century-old streetcar barn, the Grand Rapids Area Transit Authority's new bus-maintenance center is the cornerstone in a revitalized public transit system for that western Michigan city and its suburbs.

Almost ideally located on a 5.2-acre site in an urban-renewal area that's just a few minutes from Grand Rapids' downtown business district, the new facility houses, maintains, and serves as operations headquarters for the GRATA fleet of 79 large diesel transit coaches (49 GMCs, 15 Flxibles, and 15 Flxible advance-design buses), 17 small gasoline-powered buses, and 10 support or service vehicles.

Those 109 vehicles serve a population of 360,000 in the 185-sq.-mi. Grand Rapids metropolitan area.

The building is of conventional rectangular design, but that shape offers several big advantages:

□ More usable floor space is available. That permits buses to move most often in a straight line, which speeds bus servicing and minimizes accident hazards.

□ Floor cleaning is simplified and can make use of a scrubbing machine.

□ The minimum number of corners eases snow removal, an important consideration for any company doing business in an area known for heavy snows.

The building consists of three major areas: bus storage/service, maintenance, and administration. Buses circulate and are stored in the same area, making maximum use of storage space. The concept of a "floating" rotation lane allows buses to be staged in the storage area. The buses are parked in the eight storage-area lanes when they come in from their runs, and one lane (the one along the exterior wall) is left vacant to serve as the rotation lane.

Buses are driven from the first staging lane to the rotation lane, then to the dual servicing lanes and through the washer, and finally parked in the rotation lane. As that lane fills, the next lane opens and becomes the rotation lane. That sequence is repeated until vehicle servicing is completed.

Such staging saves both time and money. Servicing attendants only walk the width of one lane to park a bus and pick up another. Internal turning areas eliminate the need to drive buses out of the building and back during servicing, which reduces building heat loss and saves fuel and time. Also, the number of service attendants was cut from seven to three.

Important energy savings result from the use of acrylic skylights, which usually eliminate the need for artificial lighting in the shop during daylight hours. Also, the use of gas-fired unit heaters in the shop, each with its own thermostat, permits close control of heat in work and non-work areas.

The maintenance bays, each with its own power-operated exterior door, can accommodate a variety of vehicle sizes and types—both those in the current fleet and those that GRATA expects to add to its transit fleet in the future.

The shop, which occupies 18,000 of the building's 87,000-sq.-ft. floor area, is staffed with 21 mechanics, seven utility men, and five supervisors. There are also 89 drivers, 15 clerical employes, and 31 administrative personnel.

Reflecting the facility's ultra-modern design, the office section is faced with white glazed brick, which contrasts sharply with a large expanse of gray insulating glass and spandrel glass to achieve a crisp, colorful facade.

Storage and maintenance areas have blue metal siding, set off with gray roll-up doors. And all the interior block walls and shop floors are coated with epoxy for appearance and ease of cleaning.

A two-story operations-center expansion is already being designed. And the coach storage area itself can be readily expanded by simply taking down the north wall, moving it out, and reassembling it.

Tom Inman Trucking Inc.,
Headquarters, terminal, and shop complex
Tulsa, Okla.
Architects: Wozencraft Mowery & Assoc.
General contractor: Fleming Builders

1. Administration and office building has "TI" cast into facade.

2. Fuel-pump island is covered for protection from rain and snow.

3. Pit in tractor shop is adjacent to dyno room (rear, left).

4. Modern computer provides constant watch on fleet finances.

5. Laboratory tests and analyzes fuel and used crankcase oil.

6. Artist's rendering of complete facility shows, in clockwise order, administrative building (center foreground), 150-seat subsidized cafeteria, tractor shop, body shop, fuel island with wash and paint building behind, and gate control building.

7. View inside the tractor shop shows shop offices at the left.

This complex of five new buildings comprises the headquarters and main overhaul facilities for a Class I irregular-route carrier that hauls refrigerated and dry freight in truckload shipments throughout the contiguous 48 states.

On a 23.3-acre site adjacent to a major industrial park and close to several important shippers, the complex includes the 14,346-sq.-ft. administrative and general office building, 9,100-sq.-ft. cafeteria (subsidized to serve 150 people), 99,560-sq.-ft. maintenance building, 28,125-sq.-ft. truck painting and washing building, and 150-sq.-ft. gate house, for a total of 157,531 sq. ft.

Architectural engineering costs came to $54,801, and the land cost $472,798. Site preparation added another $77,018, and construction costs amounted to $2,650,245, for a total completed cost of $3,254,862.

The maintenance and body shops as well as paint and

wash-bay building serve the Tom Inman fleet of 345 diesel tractors and 430 trailers; 285 of the trailers are reefers with mechanical refrigeration units.

These facilities are equipped to perform complete PM, overhaul, and rebuild of all the fleet equipment. The shops can handle everything "in house" except crankshaft regrinding and tire recapping.

The well-equipped facilities also include a complete fuel and lubricant analysis laboratory and a fully enclosed chassis-dynamometer room.

Communication between buildings is carried out by means of both telephone and pneumatic-tube systems. The latter transfers actual documents by air pressure between remote terminal points. Computer terminals for CRT stations are located in various buildings to permit immediate recognition of information at points of design need. (The computer is an IBM System 3, Model 15D for on-line dispatching and maintenance accounting functions as well as general accounting and data processing.)

That this fleet cares about its vehicle appearance as well as its mechanical condition is evident from some of the other equipment: a DeVilbiss 45-ft. self-contained paint spray booth, an automatic drive-through washer, and a steam cleaner—all of which are located in the paint/wash building.

Company personnel total 741, including 585 drivers, 87 mechanics, 30 supervisors, 30 clerical, 6 dockmen, and 3 shop utility men.

The modern styling for the administration building includes the company's initials, "TI," cast repeatedly into the upper-wall facade.

For future growth of an obviously progressive fleet, all of the five principal buildings of the complex can be expanded to the west side with no interference.

Commercial Carriers Inc., Terminal and maintenance complex, Dearborn, Mich.
Architects: Ellis/Naeyaert/Genheimer Assoc.
Gen. contractor: Etkin, Johnson & Korb

1., 2. The maintenance building, largest in the complex, is isolated to keep moving trucks away from the new cars and to improve traffic flow. Because of its many overhead doors, the building uses both forced air and radiant heat. It has 21 tractor, 12 trailer, and five drive-through bays.

3. The CCI multi-lane fuel island is attached to the vehicle inspection building. Each of that structure's two bays has a pit to facilitate inspection of undercarriages and wiring. Originally, minor repair work was scheduled for this facility. The idea was abandoned, however, for fear that type of maintenance would impede inspection procedures. It was also decided that in the interest of quality, no repair work should be a pass-through procedure.

4. Although simple in appearance, CCI trailers require an inordinate amount of shopwork because of their hydraulic systems.

5., 6. Superstructure design of both tractors and trailers preclude automatic washing. As a result, to be spic and span, CCI vehicles must be cleansed by hand.

In 1979 Commercial Carriers Inc., Southfield, Mich., the nation's largest highway common carrier of new automobiles and trucks, opened an $8.6-million terminal comprising several buildings, parking, and storage areas on a 50-acre site in Dearborn, Mich.

Commercial Carriers Inc. (CCI) handles Cadillac new-car production directly off the assembly line for highway shipment. That's why the new terminal complex had to be located as close as possible to the Cadillac plant, although the site that filled the bill didn't offer all that could have been desired in the way of building-construction flexibility.

The completed project included an operations building, a new-car loading dock, a fuel and inspection building, and a maintenance building that includes machine-shop areas in addition to many truck maintenance and repair bays.

Originally, architect, general contractor, and customer considered a multi-purpose structure, which could have been L, T, or U-shaped. It was decided, however, that in the interest of good production and traffic flow, sepa-

rate buildings were required. These were constructed and situated to provide the client with room for additions or modifications.

When the 50-acre project was completed it encompassed a 3,342-car-capacity vehicle-storage area, a 33,790-sq.-ft. loading-dock structure, a 5,292-sq.-ft. operations building, and a 54,696-sq.-ft. maintenance structure.

The maintenance building, which is set on steel pipe piles driven to depth of 85 ft., necessitated by the depth of bedrock at the site, houses service pits, 2- and 4-ton overhead crane systems, a carbon-monoxide discharge system, and an underground lubrication system. The building is equipped with insulated doors, and uses both forced air and radiant heat.

All of the buildings feature the use of structural steel and a metal-panel curtain-wall system. The lower section of the maintenance building is constructed of metal upper walls and lower concrete walls.

The multi-lane fuel island contains a sophisticated underground system that delivers 60 gpm with a dual card/ticket printout. The printout is computerized at the moment of dispatch and controls driver road-fuel purchases by indicating how much can be purchased at remote commercial locations and where.

Every CCI rig entering the yard passes through one of two inspection lanes in the building adjacent to the fuel island. Each inspection bay has pits for checking vehicle undercarriage wiring and the condition of tires and springs. No vehicle-maintenance work is done in the inspection area.

The 26-bay, covered loading dock is strategically placed in the new-car loading area so that cars can be driven up rear ramps, onto the dock, and then onto the carriers. The carriers back-up to the dock to receive the cars; they are never maneuvered within the confines of the new-car lot, thereby preventing any possible damage to the cars.

Outside areas in the terminal complex are illuminated by 1,000-watt, weatherproof, high-pressure sodium lights mounted on 41 poles.

Site paving consists of 15,000 sq. yd. of concrete and 143,000 sq. yd. of asphalt. Areas subjected to heavy truck traffic are "deep strength" asphalt-paved.

Lunch room (right) is located off the main aisle between the auto-and-truck maintenance wing and the heavy-equipment wing.

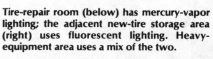

Tire-repair room (below) has mercury-vapor lighting; the adjacent new-tire storage area (right) uses fluorescent lighting. Heavy-equipment area uses a mix of the two.

**City of Winston-Salem, N.C.
Vehicle maintenance shop
Architects & engineers: Hayes, Seay,
Mattern & Mattern
Contractor: King-Hunter Const. Co.**

Replacing a shop originally designed and built for horse-drawn vehicles, a new, modern maintenance facility now provides the best in maintenance and repairs for municipal vehicles in Winston-Salem, N. C. That diversified fleet of over 800 units ranges from fleet cars and pickup trucks to 10-cu.-yd. dump trucks to back-hoes, scrapers, front-end loaders, and several motor graders.

Built entirely of brick in a modified "T," the shop has two vehicle-service and repair wings, with a central service core. One of the wings has 20 drive-through service bays with roll-up doors for car and light-truck work.

The other wing has six drive-in bays for heavy equipment. Flanking that wing are the machine shop and a two-bay lubrication department.

A wide aisle through the central core connects the two main shop wings. Bordering the aisle are the large-parts stockroom, which contains a tire-storage area, the parts-control office, a training classroom, the lunchroom,

Auto-and-truck maintenance area (below) services the city's fleet of automobiles, dump trucks, and motor scooters.

New building (left and below), which replaced one built around 1930, is constructed entirely of brick. To strengthen shop floors, metal flake was added to the concrete

and rest rooms. Adjoining the parts stockroom are a tire-repair room and a covered storage area for discarded tires. A covered loading dock, with space for outdoor storage, has a direct entrance door into the parts room.

Offices are located at the cross of the "T" for efficient management control.

Located on a completely fenced 12-acre site, the shop has 43,375 sq. ft. of floor space, and there are 392,000 sq. ft. of paved area around the shop. All repair areas, the tire shop, and the parts room have 125,000-Btu gas-fired heaters. The parts-control and administrative offices are heated and cooled by a 100-kW electric furnace/air conditioner.

Heavy emphasis was put on specification and installation of high-quality shop equipment. Included are eight 8,000-lb.-capacity hydraulic lifts, a front-end alignment machine, a welding system with underground wiring, and an in-floor exhaust system.

The fuel island can serve 12 vehicles simultaneously,

and existing fuel pumps can be readily converted into automatic dispensers.

A hallmark of good planning, the automotive shop can be expanded when necessary by simply moving the end wall. And the heavy-duty shelving in the parts room can be double-decked to expand storage capacity.

An internal communications system makes use of telephones and speakers. To assure uninterrupted service during emergencies, a stand-by generator provides power for the communications system and the fuel island.

One construction problem overcome was a 50-year-old landfill that occupied about one-third of the site. Despite the extensive grading and filling required, land-preparation costs were held to $104,000. Architectural and engineering fees came to $100,000, while construction of the shop amounted to $996,000. Grand total: $1,200,000. A $200,000 car- and truck-washing facility was started recently to round out a complete, ultra-modern maintenance complex. 🚚

Pinecrest Transit Center, located on a 13-acre site in Ottawa, has residential development on two sides. Six-foot-high berms, topped with evergreens, surround property and minimize the visible and audible effects of garage on its neighbors. Below, an OC Transpo bus is checked on a chassis dynamometer, which is located in a separate room to isolate the noise.

**Ottawa-Carleton
Regional Transit Commission
Pinecrest Transit Center
Ottawa, Ontario, Canada
Engineers: James F. MacLaren Ltd.
Contractor: Doran Const. Ltd.**

From an architect's scale model that was built for use in discussion with nearby residents and city officials, the Pinecrest Transit Center received the approval of both. Today, the new garage houses and performs all running repairs and routine servicing of 180 51-passenger transit buses of the Ottawa-Carleton Regional Transit Commission.

Two site problems had to be overcome. First, scenic berms topped with tree plantings were combined with careful placement of employe parking areas to virtually screen the new shop from view and hearing of nearby residents. Second, the building is located to allow two alternative paths for projected rapid-transit corridors with need for later building alterations. That also minimized the turning between the street entrance and the garage's main door.

To win neighbors' approval, one high-ranking goal

Control board at Pinecrest shows bus numbers and mileage intervals. Coded pins indicate target mileages, previous repairs and replacements, status of special tests, and unplanned defect repairs. Similar boards are located in each of OC Transpo's four main garages.

Buses returning from service (photos above and below, taken from berm) enter through one main door to storage or repair facilities. At left is a bus-servicing station, with blue-and-white vacuum cleaners, vault for deposit of fares and, in foreground, a 40-gpm (U.S.) diesel-fuel dispenser.

was maximum beauty within practical limits. A brown, anodized-aluminum screen or fence was constructed all around the roof, and all the ventilation hoods were located behind that screen. That preserved the simple, pleasing exterior appearance.

The plain-finished concrete facade above the ribbed concrete wall paneling adds a finishing touch and softens the effect of the 22-ft. over-all building height.

Within the 133,000-sq.-ft. area of the garage are 15,000 sq. ft. devoted to the 11-bay bus repair and service area. It is fully equipped for any and all work except major body repairs, diesel-injector overhaul, or engine and transmission rebuilding.

Heating is a major consideration in the Ottawa area. All heating at Pinecrest is by natural-gas unit heaters on the building perimeter, supplemented by combination make-up air/exhaust units in the centers of the bays.

They recover for re-use up to 70% of the heat in the exhaust air.

The personnel roster includes three shift foremen, 14 skilled mechanics, 21 utility men, and janitors and dispatchers.

Because of poor soil conditions, the building is supported on piles, and the floor is poured structural concrete rather than the usual slab on grade. That was a factor in the over-all building cost of $4,055,500 (Canadian). Architects and engineers fees were $280,000, and land preparation and landscaping amounted to $1,475,000. Those add up to a total, completed cost of $5,810,500.

The 17-bay bus shop is equipped with ten vehicle lifts, and has two component-overhaul rooms, a fuel-injector rebuild room, body shop, paint bay, and wash rack. A 9-bay garage houses fleet at night. Sodium-vapor lighting conserves energy.

The Bus Company
Fort Wayne Public Transp. Corp.
Renovated bus-maintenance shop
Fort Wayne, Ind.
Architect: Cole Mattot

In a time of near-astronomical costs for new buildings, The Bus Company achieved the benefits of a new facility through expansion and careful renovation of its existing buildings and grounds.

Serving Fort Wayne, Ind., with a fleet of 70 transit coachs and nine assorted service vehicles, The Bus Company has a main bus maintenance shop with 31,000 sq. ft. of floor space and an adjoining two-story general-office building with 83,709 sq. ft. A nine-bay bus-storage garage houses the fleet at night, and there are 148,375 sq. ft. of paved parking area.

Included in the recent renovation program were the renovation of the shop and general offices, re-roofing of all buildings, addition of new shop equipment, building a

Colorful, contemporary offices (above) in the two-story general office building adjoining the maintenance shop use carpeted walls both as a design element and to absorb noise. One result of the $783,000 refurbishing and renovation program was the spacious, well-lighted parts room shown below.

new storage garage to augment the existing garage, and paving and landscaping.

The 17-bay bus shop is equipped with ten vehicle lifts. It has two component-overhaul rooms, a fuel-injection-rebuild room, body shop, paint bay, and wash rack, and there are automatic fueling and lubrication systems. Sodium-vapor lighting helps conserve energy. Natural-gas heat is used, and there is an electric-exhaust-fan ventilation system.

In the colorful, contemporary offices, carpeted walls act to absorb sound while serving as a design element. The walls contrast with the natural oak furniture and wood finishes in the drivers' lounge, lobby, and dispatch areas.

Both daily and emergency security were high on the planning lists. The chain-link fence that surrounds the facility is planted with grape and bittersweet climbing plants for "living green walls" in the summer. All areas of the shop and offices have built-in sprinkler systems and fire alarms.

Stand-by generators provide emergency power for the telephone and communications-radio systems, and for the lights in the dispatch area.

Land and preparation costs were $249,000, including paving; architectural and engineering fees were $38,500; shop improvements and equipment came to $371,500; and office renovation cost $124,000—for a grand total of $783,000.

Modern service building has three main bays. One is a bus service and maintenance bay; the other two can store up to 30 buses each. In operation around the clock, seven days a week, garage has maintenance staff of ten skilled mechanics, six garage helpers, and a foreman.

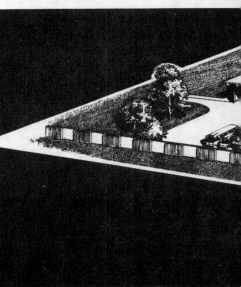

**Niagara Frontier Transit
Metro System Inc.
Operational bus garage
Niagara Falls, N.Y.
Architects & engineers: Duchscherer
Oberst Associates
Contractor: Smith Brothers Co.**

Filling a need for a central operating garage to minimize excessive deadhead mileage on bus routes, the new central Operational Bus Garage in Niagara Falls, N.Y., also pays off in beauty and improved bus maintenance for Niagara Frontier Transit Metro System.

More than a parking garage, the ultra-modern service building has three main bays. One is a bus service and maintenance bay; the other two can store up to 60 buses. The NFT-Metro fleet based there includes 30 transit buses, two service trucks and a snow plow.

The shop bay, which has one vehicle lift and four depressed work areas (formerly called pits), is fully equipped to handle all minor running inspections and repairs as well as daily bus servicing and cleaning. For the latter functions, there are two fueling lanes and an automatic bus washer.

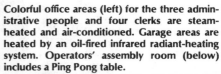

Colorful office areas (left) for the three administrative people and four clerks are steam-heated and air-conditioned. Garage areas are heated by an oil-fired infrared radiant-heating system. Operators' assembly room (below) includes a Ping Pong table.

In operation around the clock, seven days a week, the garage has a staff of 61 people: a foreman, 10 skilled mechanics, 6 garage helpers, 38 bus drivers, 3 administrative people, and 4 clerks.

Designed and built for Niagara Falls' rigorous winters, the garage has masonry and brick walls of a pleasing design. Prestressed-concrete tee roof beams, measuring 2½ ft. high, 10 ft. wide, and 72 ft. long, support the snow loads the area is famous for. (Like a 10-ft. snowfall in one storm alone during the winter of 1976-77.)

Located on a plot of approximately 164,000 sq. ft., the garage building has 39,700 sq. ft. of floor space, and there are 53,000 sq. ft. of paved parking and yard area. The balance is landscaped for esthetic value to the community. An environmental sound-barrier fence shields the neighbors from noise.

Among the problems handled in design and construction was a 30-ft.-wide underground-cable tunnel for major electric-power cables. Because the tunnel bisects the garage property, the building had to be designed and built to protect that tunnel and its right-of-way.

Reflecting the careful planning, architectural fees were $165,000. Land and its preparation cost $550,000; the garage and shop ran to $1,115,000; and the office added $170,000—for a total of $2,000,000.

Because of the severe weather emergencies that sometimes hit the Niagara area, the garage's master electrical panel has provisions for using the NFT-Metro portable emergency-electric power plant if necessary.

The end result, as reported by Edward Tanski, vp-equipment and maintenance, is a practical bus garage melded into a modern, handsome structure.

Ten-bay garage on 16.4-acre site services 250 transit buses. Roof hatches and retractable exhaust ducts at each bus bay provide adequate ventilation. Roof structure is designed for ease of revisions or additions to garage's electrical, mechanical, or plumbing systems.

Tri-County Metropolitan Transportation Dist. of Oregon Satellite operating garage Portland, Ore. Architects: URS/Madigan-Praeger, and Koch, Sachs & Whittaker Engineers: Arthur M. James

High on the list of "musts" for the Powell satellite operating garage and shop of Tri-Met in Portland, Ore., was good relations with residents in neighboring homes. To that end, the facility incorporates a sound-reducing berm and fencing adjacent to residential areas, and a park for the use of neighbors.

Designed to add support for an outdated, crowded garage, and to slash deadhead miles, the strikingly handsome building in its park setting houses and services 250 42- to 51-passenger transit buses and several service vehicles.

To perform its award-winning maintenance, the shop has a separate air-conditioning-system overhaul room, separate steam cleaning and tire rooms, and separate fuel and washing islands. There are six hydraulic lifts and five pits, the latter with explosion-proof lighting. Over-

Sound-reducing berm and fence (left) minimize impact of garage on neighbors. Shop has six hydraulic lifts and five pits (below), the latter with explosion-proof lighting. Maintenance area has two-way drive-through bus access.

All operating areas of the site are paved with concrete; the employe parking lot is paved with asphalt. Shown below is a portion of the satellite garage's stores department.

head fluorescent fixtures light all shop areas.

With the latest and best in shop equipment, the facility operates with a personnel roster of 26 skilled mechanics, 30 utility men, and 5 supervisors.

The shop has a floor area of 24,875 sq. ft., and the support areas (the covered fuel and washing islands) an area of 6,750 sq. ft.

The entire 16.4-acre (718,681-sq.-ft.) site, with the exception of the asphalt-paved employe parking area and the landscaped area bordering the entrance driveways, is paved with concrete.

The "Rose City's" mild climate makes it practical to park the 250 buses outdoors for storage. That same climate also makes it possible to use heat pumps throughout the shop building. Space heaters supplement the heat pumps in the shop areas where buses are

serviced and repaired. Roof-mounted smoke hatches and retractable exhaust ducts at each bay provide adequate ventilation.

Electrical services include 220- and 480-V systems, backed-up by a stand-by generator that provides electricity in case of power outages.

The roof structure was specially designed to give maximum flexibility for revision or additions to the building's mechanical, plumbing, and electrical systems.

Architectural and engineering costs were $135,000, and construction costs was $2,900,000, for a total of $3,035,000 for the complete facility.

Balanced against operational dollar savings, reduced deadhead time, and an equitable pay-back ratio, the decision to build the new shop and garage is proving to be right and wise.

By Jack Lyndall, Senior Editor

From foundry to fleet shop

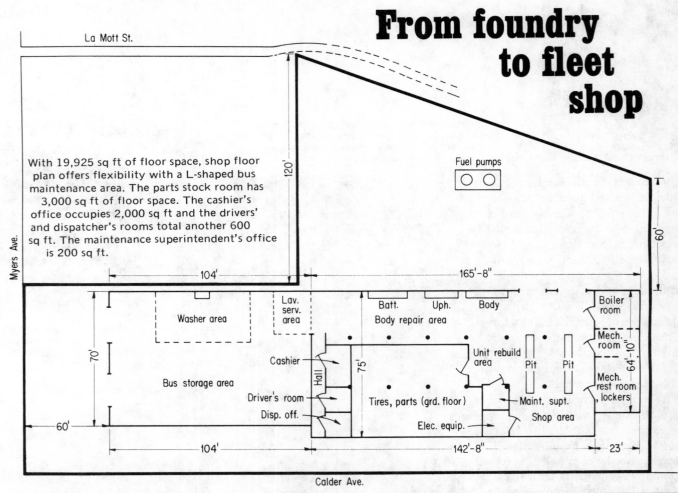

La Mott St.

With 19,925 sq ft of floor space, shop floor plan offers flexibility with a L-shaped bus maintenance area. The parts stock room has 3,000 sq ft of floor space. The cashier's office occupies 2,000 sq ft and the drivers' and dispatcher's rooms total another 600 sq ft. The maintenance superintendent's office is 200 sq ft.

Myers Ave.

120'

Fuel pumps

60'

104'

165'-8"

Washer area

Lav. serv. area

Batt.   Uph.   Body

Body repair area

Boiler room

70'

Cashier

Bus storage area

Hall

75'

Unit rebuild area

Pit   Pit

Mech. room

64'-10"

Driver's room

Tires, parts (grd. floor)

Maint. supt.

Mech. rest room, lockers

60'

Disp. off.

Elec. equip.

Shop area

104'

142'-8"

23'

Calder Ave.

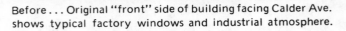

Before . . . Original "front" side of building facing Calder Ave. shows typical factory windows and industrial atmosphere.

After . . . Showing a modern facade, new executive and general office level set off with handsome entrance and front porch.

Long and arduous planning—backed by many years of bus maintenance experience—went into the project of converting a pre-World II manufacturing plant into a modern bus maintenance shop and company headquarters for Central N.Y. Coach Lines, Inc., Yorkville, N.Y.

"In search of a home" became a vital activity for Central N.Y. Coach Lines management in mid-1968. The city of Utica, N.Y., where the bus property was then based, formed a public transportation authority to take over and operate Utica Transit, the transit bus system that Central N.Y. Coach Lines had operated for some years. And the new authority also took over the company offices, bus overhaul shops, and operating garage in downtown Utica. This left

Central N.Y. Coach Lines without a home for its intercity and charter bus operations which were not involved in the authority take-over.

Neither funds or time were available to acquire land and build an all-new facility. And a convenient location seemed unavailable for such a building project, anyway.

But a search for other alternatives turned up an idle manufacturing facility in the Utica suburb of Yorkville. It seemed to offer possibilities for remodeling to the bus line management—the late Wallace S. Sweet, president at the time; Lee J. Oster, then a vice president, now president; and J. A. Murdie, superintendent of equipment and maintenance.

Originally built as a drop forge plant that produced castings for GE turbines, the former foundry was located only a block from a main artery and had a large, fenced yard area with access to two streets.

Because of its original purpose, the steel-framed building had ample height. In fact, the ceiling clearance was high enough to allow building a second floor level in one area for new company general offices. And the high ceiling gave ample clearnance for new dual-level coaches in the fleet. The property was for sale at a reasonable price.

Immediately after the bus line purchased the property in August, 1968, the re-modeling work was started by John E. Wilkinson and Sons, Inc., New Hartford, N.Y. We visited the building soon after work was started and again after completion for the full story of the project.

As shown by the floor plan and plot drawing, the old foundry is basically a long rectangular structure. The bus line management team redesigned the ground floor into an L-shaped bus overhaul, repair, and service area with access from two directions. A central core housing the parts and tire storage area, shop and operations offices, and driver's room was located along what became the "front" of the building.

Above this central core a second

floor level for corporate executive and general offices was built. A new front door and entrance lobby for these offices opens onto Calder Ave. which runs at the new office floor level.

From the office area's central hallway a convenient stairway gives quick access to the shop floor without going outside.

When essentially completed and occupied in November, 1968 the new shop and offices became the main control center and maintenance support base for three other bus properties owned and operated by Central

Before . . . Bus service pits take shape in new shop area after excavation is completed. Water drains and ventilation ducts were built in during construction.

Completed and equipped with compressed air lines for chassis lube pumps, new pits get steady use. A local ordinance bans electric outlets in pits for safety.

N.Y. Coach Lines: Syracuse and Eastern Transit Corp. which provides interurban bus service between Syracuse and Manlius, N.Y. It operates six coaches; Auburn Transit Corp. which operates city transit service in Auburn, N.Y. with 10 buses; and Onandaga Coach Corp. which provides interurban and charter service between Geneva and Syracuse, N.Y. with nine coaches.

The parent company operates 27 coaches in its intercity service in the up-state New York area, plus long distance charter service.

Designing the shop layout, Murdie drew on his near-half-century of transportation experience, 45 years of it in bus maintenance. Among his problems was the dozen steel roof support columns in the original building. He planned for minimum interference to shop operations from the columns and several of them were incorporated into the two-floor central service core's framing.

Across the end of the main shop area, two bus service pits were dug. The pits are 44 ft long and 56 in. deep. They measure 48 in. wide.

To provide drive-in access to the new pits, two doors were cut through the "back" wall of the building. The doors are power operated. To enter the doors, buses drive in through the large parking area at the rear of the shop.

Both pits are equipped with air line connections for impact wrenches, etc. The air lines also are connected to an air powered lube pump in each pit for chassis lubrication. There are no electric outlets in the pits because of a local ordinance forbidding them. A floor drain system for both pits drains into a common sump pump.

A suction ventilating system draws fumes from the two pits and exhausts them out doors. The exhaust removal pipe system for the other bus repair areas is slso tied into the same system with the pits. This somewhat novel set-up was designed and installed by Bowry Associates, Inc., Cambridge, Mass.

Alongside the pit area is a section of the shop set aside for unit rebuild. Murdie keeps at least one six cylinder engine and one V-8 on hand, rebuilt and ready for installation.

Bordering the "back" wall of the

Covered with fire-resistant wall panels, new central service and office core adjoins unit rebuild and pit area. Maintenance superintendent's office faces pit.

Jack A. Murdie, superintendent of maintenance, checks service specs from a manual in his well-kept library. Office has attractive wood panel walls and air cooling.

shop (the wall next to the parking area) an area is devoted to body repairs. Two fully equipped work benches along the wall are set up for the body shop work. One bench is for sheet metal work, with all the necessary tools. The second bench is for upholstery and body trim jobs which are all done here.

Another bench at the far end of the body repair area is for battery service and charging.

At the end of the body repair area starts a part of the building which was added to the original foundry building at a later date. This section of the building is five feet narrower than the original main section, as shown by the floor plan sketch. But it has the advantage of full span roof supports with no vertical columns to interfere with buses.

Along the "back" wall of this shop area, Murdie located the bus cleaning

Heavy duty peg board panels store tools and bus parts in stock room. Lights are between each row of parts bins.

Exhaust removal tube going into floor outlet connects to blower on wall above work bench which also vents pits.

facilities. Next to the body repair area is the bus lavatory servicing stand. Just ahead of the lavatory service area is the Ross and White automatic bus washer (which was moved from the former shop location).

To build the wash rack, a section of the original floor measuring 14 x 50 ft was removed. A new concrete floor with proper slope for water drainage was poured. The centrally located water drain has an oil trap.

To provide straight-line unimpeded access to the bus washer and lavatory cleaning stand, a new door was cut in the end of the building facing Myers Ave. Murdie notes that when the body repair area is unoccupied, a bus can drive through from there through the cleaning facilities. But if there are buses in the body shop area, buses needing lavatory servicing or washing are backed in through the new door and driven out after cleaning.

The remainder of the area adjacent to the bus washer setup is used for bus storage. Another door, the original one in that end of the building, serves the bus storage area.

Shop employee facilities are in a section of the building adjacent to the bus pit area.

There is a mechanic's wash room which also contains lockers for the entire shop force. Next to the wash room is another room used for lunch or during coffee breaks. The mechanic's rooms were part of the original building. But as we toured the building Murdie pointed out that new modern wash basins, toilet fixtures, towel dispensers, etc., were installed as the shop remodelling was done.

The shop force, in addition to Murdie, includes a shop foreman and six skilled mechanics. There are also two mechanic's helpers. Two cleaners, one a woman, keep the buses clean inside and outside.

A third room in the row houses the heating equipment. Although the foundry had originally had large boilers for its operations, Murdie commented that the old boilers were obsolete and were replaced with a modern new boiler during the shop reconstruction. Shop heating comes from overhead unit heaters supplied by the new boiler.

On the shop level, the heart of the new central service core is occupied by the parts and unit stock room. To reduce costs, the parts shelves were moved from the former shop. But new peg board racks were put up for storing many of the shop tools and some parts items.

Adjoining the parts room and overlooking the unit rebuild and pit area a modern office was built for Murdie. Tastefully wood panelled, the office has a drop ceiling with acoustic tile. Ceiling light fixtures are flush-mounted and the office is air conditioned in summer.

A small room next to Murdie's office houses electrical switches, circuit breakers, etc. Murdie reported that the building was completely rewired with all new electrical fixtures and outlets.

At the opposite side of the parts room, a hallway leads from the shop floor area to the operating department offices. As shown on the floor plan sketch, there is a driver's room plus separate offices for the superintendent of operations (dispatcher) and cashier.

Centrally located in the large rear parking area is a fuel pump island with a small shelter building for the fueling attendant. Both gasoline and diesel fuel pumps are on the island as the fleet operates some conventional school buses under contract with a nearby school district.

Constructed as a second floor above the parts room and shop and operations offices is the modern, attractive new executive and general office level. Because the building is on a slope, the new offices are on the street level of Calder Ave. which borders that side.

A front lobby entrance was cut through the building wall, together with window openings for the offices. The new front entrance was attractively faced and a metal porch, stairs, and wrought iron railings complete the connection to the street curb.

The office level, where five people are employed, has wood panelled walls and flush lighting.

Also included on the office level are new, modern rest rooms and a storeroom for office supplies, tickets, etc. plus a cloakroom.

An added advantage of the new bus company home is future expansion possibilities. The parking area is large enough to allow building an addition to the building without seriously reducing parking space for buses. An additional area just outside the Myers Ave. end of the building already provides car parking space for office personnel and visitors.

All told, the former foundry which once produced industrial products now helps greatly to produce top-level bus maintenance.

CONSOLIDATING MAINTENANCE

THE CASE OF COCA-COLA

Maintenance shop with a crew of ten mechanics and two body men services about 150 straight trucks, 120 tractors, and 140 trailers, plus specials.

Large door (in front of white car) is outside entrance.

Modern test equipment lined up along shop wall.

Housed within the highly modern distribution center it serves, a compact, efficient fleet maintenance shop has been built by the Coca-Cola Bottling Co. of Chicago/Wisconsin at Arlington Heights, Ill. The company bottles and distributes Coca-Cola and other beverages throughout the Chicago metropolitan area and parts of northern Indiana, northern Illinois, and Wisconsin.

The new facility relieved an overcrowding problem, consolidated maintenance operations from two older shops, and provided for more efficient product distribution routes.

Vehicles may enter the new layout, called the North Branch fleet shop, from inside the vast warehouse, where trucks pull in to load, or from the outside through one of six roll-up doors. The four doors from warehouse to shop also have fire-door protection (see drawing).

Trucks enter the shop from the warehouse after they have been unloaded, according to Arnold R. Foster, fleet maintenance superintendent.

Entrance to the body shop is only from inside the warehouse. Foster points out that vehicles going in for body repairs are usually there for an extended period, and there is less need for a "quick-in—quick-out" traffic flow and an outside door (see box for equipment list).

Much of the planning for the new shop was done by the late Walter Booth, fleet director for the company, who passed away suddenly in May 1980. The company engineer, Joseph Adams, also worked on the design, together with the architect, David B. Dearlove, Glen Ellyn, Ill. The general contractor was Terracom Development Group Inc., Des Plaines, Ill.

In a tour at the plant, Foster pointed out that there are

no firmly assigned bays in the main vehicle-service-bay area. Foster explained that the area on the north end, nearest his office and the parts room, is primarily used for maintenance and repair of heavy-duty trucks and trailers. The southern area, toward the drive-through lane, is mostly used for lighter-duty units and the fleet cars, plus fork lift trucks.

The truck wash room has a brush-type washer. Trucks enter the room through an outside, roll-up door, then enter the warehouse through an inner door.

Close to the outside door for the wash room, along the outside south wall of the building, is a large, covered fueling island. Drivers fuel their own trucks with card-controlled pumps that automatically charge the fuel to the driver and truck number.

A space has been allocated along the west side of the body shop for installation of a paint booth, using some equipment from the downtown Chicago shop, which was closed when the North Shop opened. The paint booth will be enlarged when it is re-erected to handle

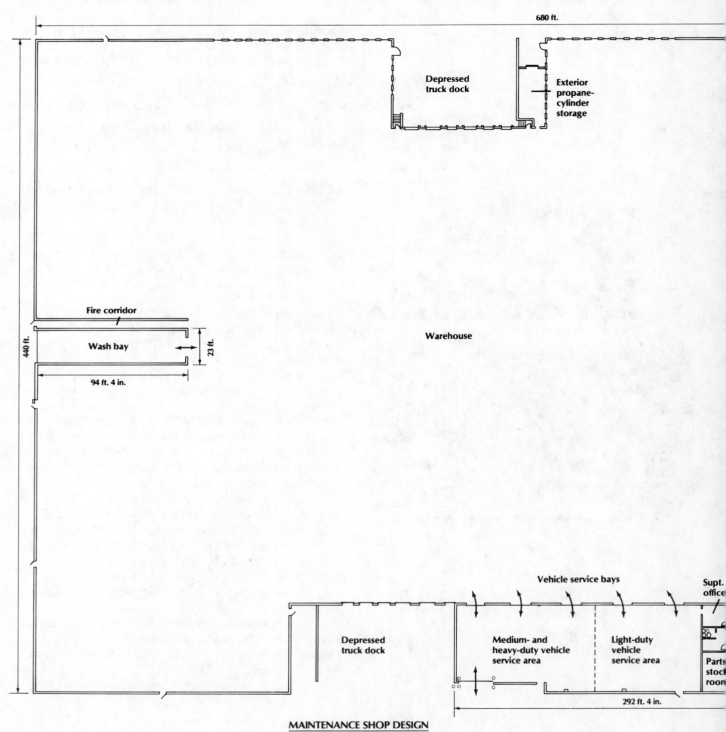

over-the-road trailers in addition to all other Coca-Cola vehicles.

The fleet at the new Arlington Heights distribution center includes approximately 150 straight trucks, 120 tractors, and 140 trailers. In addition, there are about 30 trucks used by service men who maintain and repair vending machines, customer coolers, and haul small beverage trailers used for special-events sales. The trailers are towed to sporting events, group picnics, and similar events and serve as mobile soda fountains. There are also about 30 fleet cars, plus 25 fork lifts used for loading and unloading trucks in the distribution center.

Foster says the fleet is not standardized. Most of the straight trucks with beverage bodies are Ford. Smaller service vehicles are divided between Ford and GMC. Tractors are Ford, GMC, and International, both medium-duty tractors pulling beverage-delivery trailers and heavy-duty over-the-road tractors.

The North Branch shop's 10 mechanics and two body men handle trailer repair for their own and other company locations. "We maintain about 80 trailers for the other shops," says Foster.

Each of the five fleet shops in the Coca-Cola of Chicago system is responsible for mechanical service and repairs on vehicles at its locations. There is another body man at the shop at Alsip, Ill., who does repairs on trailers based there and at the Gary, Ind.

Special-events area

Office area

220 ft. 8 in.

Area reserved for paint booth

40 ft.

60 ft.

ly shop

Storage

Body shop equipment

1 Wysong & Miles 6-ft. shear
1 Chicago 8-ft. sheet metal brake
1 Wayne 10-hp. air compressor
1 Miller Dualarc 250 AC-DC electric welder
1 Miller MIG welder
1 Cincinnati 250 motor-generator arc welder
2 Wallace adjustable portable gantry cranes
1 overhead crane (5-ton cap.)
1 floor drill press
6 Blackhawk 10-ton Porta-Power body repair ram sets
1 Blackhawk 4-ton Porta-Power body repair ram set
3 oxy-acetylene welding outfits
Electric drills, metal nibblers, sanders, and grinders.

Vehicle maintenance and repair shop

1 Sun portable console analyzer
3 Jenny steam cleaners (1 No.760 and two smaller units)
6 Walker 10-ton floor jacks
1 Blackhawk 5-ton floor jack
1 Walker dual-wheel dolly
1 Walker transmission jack (1,000-lb. cap.)
2 Blackhawk transmission jacks (2,000-lb. cap.)
1 Walker portable air jack
1 Blackhawk portable air jack
1 Silver Beauty 80-amp portable battery charger
1 Branick air-powered end lift (2,000-lb. cap.)
1 Sun 404 distributor tester
1 shop-built portable air compressor powered by a Buick V-6 gasoline engine driving the Porta-Air V-85 compressor made by General Supply and Leasing Co., Kansas City, Mo. The portable compressor unit is mounted on a sturdy wood pallet and can be moved by fork lift truck to any place in the plant area where needed.

PAT's New Main Shop Completes Rebuild Phase

By Jack Lyndall,
Senior Editor/Equipment

Capping a 10-year-long program to replace all of its bus operations and repair facilities that started with its formation in 1964, the Port Authority of Allegheny County (Pa.) recently opened its sparkling new combined central bus maintenance and rebuild shop and administrative headquarters.

Identified as the Manchester Main Shop and Administration Building, the ultramodern structure is situated on a four-acre site at the intersection of Beaver and Island Avenues near downtown Pittsburgh.

Built at a cost of approximately $9-million, the impressive structure has five stories. It incorporates slightly over 200,000 sq. ft. of floor space with approximately 70% of that area devoted to bus and service vehicle maintenance and related work, according to G. K. Hussong, manager of maintenance for the Port Authority (PAT).

The Manchester building employe roster totals 472 persons. Of these, 135 work on bus maintenance and repairs. The PAT administrative and maintenance offices are staffed by 310 employes and there are 27 members of the executive staff.

Much of the planning for the new Manchester shop was done by Joseph J. Naegelen, maintenance engineer, and Ralph Cornell, Hussong's predecessor who retired while the building was still under construction. Some final changes were suggested by

Hussong and Michael Manning, assistant manager of maintenance, as the building neared completion.

The architect was Carl G. Baker, with M. Baker Jr. as consultant. Coco Bros. Inc., Pittsburgh, Pa., was the general contractor.

General Description and Layout

The two lower levels of the building are basically a rectangle. Above them, near the front or east end of the building, rises a three-story office tower housing the administrative offices. The handsome facade is at the east end, facing Beaver Avenue, with beautifully landscaped lawn and shrubs.

The two lower levels extend westward along Island Avenue. As shown on the floor plan drawing included with this report, the first floor measures approximately 238 ft. wide and 556 ft. long. Because of the limited plot size, the building, which replaced an old trolley car barn, is built out to the property line on all sides.

Ground Floor Layout and Features

Starting our tour of the splendid new facility together with Hussong and Manning, we left the beautiful entrance foyer and reception lobby on the second floor level and moved on into the main shop area on the floor below.

View from north end of body shop, with one bus raised on hoist. Note portable work bench on casters, equipped with drill press and vise, alongside bus in foreground.

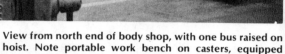

G. K. Hussong, PAT manager of maintenance, at his desk in his office.

Skilled workman in steam-cleaning room (left) degreases dirty parts. Storm-Vulcan cleaning cabinet in background cleans engine blocks, heads.

Under the lobby area is the large boiler and mechanical equipment room. The huge gas-fired boilers provide ample heat for the entire building even in Pittsburgh's rather cold winters.

The boiler room also houses the large compressor units for the office air-conditioning system, plus two unusual air compressors for the main shop supply. Those air compressors are Ingersoll-Rand Pac-Air Model PA-100 screw-type compressors. They operate very much on the principle of the familiar Roots-type scavenger blower used on Detroit Diesel engines instead of using the conventional piston design.

Another, smaller, Ingersoll Rand 1½-hp horizontal compressor with conventional two-cylinder, two-stage design is also in the boiler and equipment room. That compressor supplies air for the air-powered heating and cooling thermostats used throughout the entire building.

Two rooms adjacent to the boiler room house the telephone switching equipment and the main electrical service panels.

Ascending the steps from the boiler room (which actually constitutes a shallow basement room), we entered a wide corridor running across the front end of the building. It links with a center aisle running the length of the main shop and two more aisles nearer the north and south sides of the building.

Adjacent to that cross corridor and also accessible from the main center aisle is the main mechanic's locker and restroom. Hussong says the locker room has modern, individual steel lockers for 200 men and has five round-type wash fountains.

At the intersection of the two main aisles are two automatic elevators, one on each side, that connect to all five floors in the building.

Also adjacent to the cross corridor, at the opposite end from the men's locker room, is a similar women's locker and restroom. In addition to the main men's locker and restroom, Hussong notes that there are three more smaller lavatories strategically located so that there are men's restroom facilities in each quarter of the main shop. This reduces the time and distance for a man to reach a restroom, regardless of where he is working, and meets applicable OSHA requirements.

Next to the women's locker room and bordering the center aisle is an attractive, modern cafeteria. Hussong comments that the cafeteria is operated by a charitable organization serving the blind.

Continuing our tour, we entered a second cross shop aisle bordering the cafeteria and turned southward to another corridor running along the south side of the main shop area. Ranged along that corridor, toward the east or front end of the building, are two special storage rooms—one for volatile fluids and one for tool storage, with an additional tool security room alongside it. All of these rooms have their access doors opening into the large and heavy parts storage area that borders the entire south side of the main shop floor.

Hussong explains that the tool storage and security rooms are used partly for storage of mechanic's tool sets, boxes, and charts. He says that PAT supplies all hand tools to the mechanics.

Next to the two tool storage areas is the sign shop.

Here, signmaker Dominic Pranty produces destination signs for buses and helps in planning and working out the layouts for the colorful "mod bus" color schemes now being widely used on PAT buses (and trolley cars).

Following the long aisle, we next came to the brake drum turning room. Measuring 23 ft. 4 in. x 40 ft., it has two brake drum turning lathes. One, a new Bear machine, is equipped with a new Black and Decker vacuum cleaner attachment that collects the drum cuttings at the tool bit, keeping the machine

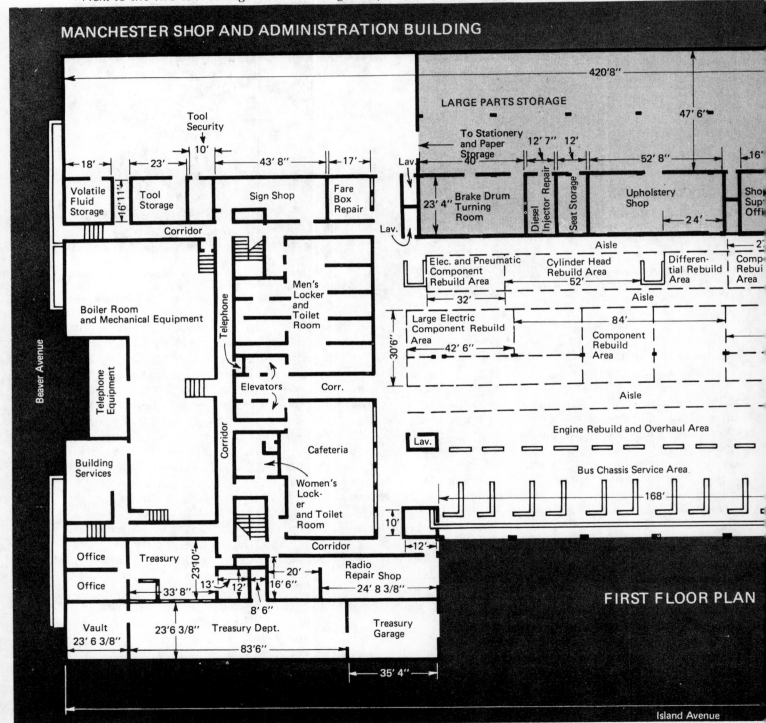

MANCHESTER SHOP AND ADMINISTRATION BUILDING

FIRST FLOOR PLAN

and floor area clean. Hussong explains that all brake drums are turned to a standard oversize to match lining purchased in those sizes. The reconditioned drums and relined shoes or lining sets are sent out to the various operating garages where all brake overhauls are done.

Next to the brake drum turning room is the diesel injector and pump service and overhaul room. Air conditioned, and kept hospital-clean, this room is equipped to rebuild and test all of the various makes and models of diesel injection equipment used in

the PAT fleet of 923 diesel buses. Among the modern equipment in this room is a Kent Moore Model J-7041 Injector Tester.

Alongside the injector room is a bus seat storage room which is located there because the upholstery repair shop adjoins it. Virtually the entire PAT fleet has upholstered, cushioned seats and the upholstery shop repairs and recovers the cushions and backrests.

Next to the upholstery shop are two lavatories; one opens into the aisle along the south side of the main shop while the other serves the large, heavy parts

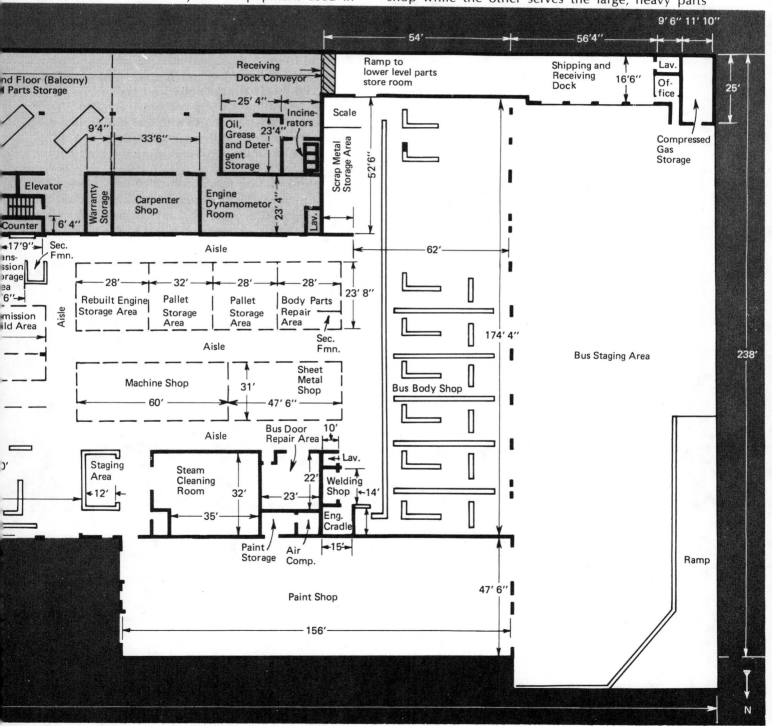

stockroom on the ground floor.

The shop superintendent's office is next to the two back-to-back lavatories, with the office of the storeroom manager adjoining. The stores office opens onto a counter service area bordering the south side shop aisle and another stores office door opens into the stockroom.

Behind the parts service counter is a stairway leading to the upstairs or balcony parts storage area. Alongside the stairway is a freight elevator for transporting any heavy objects between the ground floor shop and the upper level stockroom. A short corridor in front of the elevator and stairway links the south-side shop aisle and the heavy parts storeroom, allowing forklift truck movement of heavy items.

Bordering that short corridor is a room used for storage of items being held for pending warranty or adjustment claims. It has doors opening into both the heavy-parts stockroom and the south-side shop aisle.

Alongside the warranty storage room is the carpenter or woodworking shop. It is equipped with the most modern of tools and equipment to handle the making or repair of almost any wood part.

Adjoining the carpenter shop is the engine dynamometer room with another of the conveniently located shop lavatories in one corner of that area.

Abutting the dynamometer room, on the side toward the heavy-parts storage area is a room for storage of oils, greases, and detergents. And next to that room is the incinerator that burns all of the building refuse.

Moving over to the next aisle, we entered an area roughly centered in the main shop floor devoted to various categories of component rebuilding.

Starting at the east end of that aisle, where a section foreman's office is located, we passed the area where small electric and pneumatic components, such as heater motors, door-closing motors, etc., are

rebuilt.

Next in the row of component rebuild "departments" is the cylinder-head rebuild area. In that area, Hussong pointed out a new Sweco Vibro-Energy Mill, manufactured by Sweco Inc., Los Angeles, Calif. The machine had a circular hopper approximately 4 ft. in diameter, filled with short, cylindrical-shaped ceramic pellets that are coated with a detergent solution.

Hussong explained that dirty, carbonized parts such as rocker arms, valves, valve springs, and other small parts are placed in the hopper and the machine turned on. The hopper vibrates at a high rate of speed, tumbling the dirty parts among the ceramic pellets that remove all the contamination, carbon, oil, and other foreign matter from the parts, which were formerly hand-washed in solvent or soaked in a small chemical bath cleaner.

After the dirty parts have been agitated in the Sweco machine for one to one and half hours, they are removed looking like new. Hussong comments, "We have never thrown a part away since we got this machine."

Another section foremen's office is located at the end of the cylinder head rebuild area, between it and the differential overhaul and storage area next in line. Beyond that is an area for storage of rebuilt transmissions, with another section foreman's office at the end.

Along the north side of that same aisle, starting from the east end, is a series of other component rebuild departments measuring 30½-ft. wide. The first, measuring 42½-ft. long, is the major electric component rebuild area where such items as starters and alternators are rebuilt and tested.

Another area, measuring 84 ft. long, is used for overhaul of a number of items including engine blocks. This area has a Pangborn sand blaster in addition to other modern equipment.

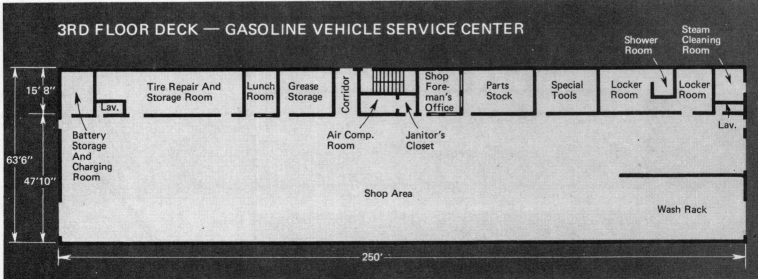

The final area in this row, measuring 56 ft. long, is devoted to transmission rebuilding. When completed, the transmissions are moved across the aisle and placed in the transmission storage area.

Engine Overhaul and Rebuild Area

Another aisle separates the major component rebuild areas described above from the engine rebuild area. This area has 10 engine rebuild stands, each manned by a skilled engine rebuild mechanic. Hussong states, "We still follow the time-proven policy of rebuilding the complete engine in one location. The subsidiary component rebuild areas surround the engine rebuild area and feed into it." At the east end of the engine rebuild area is another of the subsidiary lavatories.

Located throughout the entire component rebuild areas are a number of jib cranes. These eliminate manual effort to lift any of the heavy components during the various repair or rebuilding operations.

At the end of the component rebuild area, there is another cross shop aisle. On the west side of that aisle are two storage areas that are closely related to the component rebuild operations.

One of the storage areas is equipped with pallet storage racks. In that area, worn, broken, or damaged components received from the operating garages are stored on pallets until they can be steam-cleaned. Then the components are routed to the proper rebuild area.

Next to the cross shop aisle is an area reserved for storage of completed rebuilt engines. When an engine has been fully rebuilt, tested, and painted, it is placed on a storage pallet in that area, ready for shipment to an operating garage or use in the Manchester shop's bus chassis repair area.

View from east end of bus chassis overhaul area (above) which has twin post hoists for each bay and overhead service reels every second bay. Modern shop contrasts with ancient car barn (left).

Component rebuild areas such as the transmission and V-Drive department shown have jib cranes for lifting and moving heavy parts.

Gasoline vehicle shop has angled service bays. Mercury vapor lamps in all shop areas give 100 ft. candles of light at workbench height.

Bus Chassis Repair Area

Ranged along the north side of the main shop, separated by a wide aisle from the engine overhaul area, is the bus chassis repair area.

This area, measuring approximately 160 ft. long, is equipped with 12 twin-post lifts, with drive-in access from a concrete paved area abutting Island Avenue. There are six large powered rollup doors, each serving two lifts.

Buses are backed onto the lifts, Hussong notes, so that the wide aisle at the rear of the area provides convenient working access for engine removal and other major power train work. The bus chassis repair area is also equipped with a Carmont in-floor exhaust-removal system.

Steam-Cleaning Department

Near the bus chassis repair area, toward the west end of the shop, is the large steam-cleaning room measuring 32 ft. x 35 ft. A concrete block-walled area near the front entrance of the steam-cleaning room serves as a staging area for parts being disassembled for cleaning. As we paused a moment in our tour, two mechanics were tearing down an engine prior to cleaning and inspection.

The large steam-cleaning room, with a highly efficient ventilation system to remove steam vapor and cleaning solvent fumes, is equipped with high-pressure steam-cleaning equipment plus a Magnus Aja-Lif parts degreasing tank.

In addition, the steam-cleaning room has a new Storm-Vulcan parts cleaning cabinet. Hussong explains that dirty, badly carbonized parts as large as a V-8 engine block are placed on a power-driven turntable inside the cabinet-type cleaner. As the part slowly revolves, heated cleaning chemicals are blasted against the part from two rows of vertically mounted nozzles. The doors on the cabinet prevent loss of the cleaning solution and reduce fumes and mist. Hussong reports the new machine can clean an engine block like new, no matter how dirty, in three hours. Formerly, he says, such engine blocks sometimes required soaking up to three weeks in a cleaning solution tank.

Paint Shop

Abutting the steam-cleaning room on the north side of the building is the large paint shop. Measuring 47½ ft. x 156 ft., it is equipped with a De Vilbiss traveling paint-spray booth. It runs on tracks in the floor, with an overhead ventilation and fume removal duct system. The traveling spray booth has a builtin "waterfall" system for trapping paint overspray.

The remaining area in the paint shop provides a staging area for sanding, masking, and other pre-painting operations, or for small touchup paint jobs.

Body Shop

The body shop and its subsidiary departments actually start with the bus-door repair room next to the steam-cleaning room.

Next to the bus-door repair room is the fully equipped welding shop, able to perform electric and oxy-acetylene or inert gas welding on any metals used in PAT buses.

Ranged along the west end of the building are 10 bays for bus-body repairs. Eight of the drivein bays have twin-post lifts, and all 10 bays have individual rollup doors opening onto a staging area next to the body shop area. The body shop area is 9,468 sq. ft.

Among the shop equipment items in the fully equipped body shop are a Model SAE 300 Lincoln electric arc welder and several Powermatic vertical floor-stand-type drill presses manufactured by Powermatic Houdaille Inc., McMinnville, Tenn.

Among other body shop equipment items are a Keller power-driven hack saw, a Rockwell-Delta band saw, and a Kansas Jack Power Post floor pull system for straightening major bus structural members.

The eight twin-post hydraulic lifts in the body shop permit work to be done on the upper or lower area of a bus, at any desired height. The two bays not equipped with lifts are used for body repairs or interior trim work where it is not necessary to lift the bus.

Across the wide cross aisle bordering the body shop area, located about midway and adjacent to the body shop section foreman's office, is an area measuring approximately 24 ft. x 28 ft. This is used for repairs to small body panels or components which can be better done on a bench than on the bus body.

Adjoining the south end of the body shop area, across the bordering aisle, is a material storage area for scrap metal and body parts damaged beyond repair. These are held until sent to a scrap metal yard for disposal. At the far southern end of that area is a floor scale, which can weigh outgoing shipments of scrap or incoming parts or materials orders.

Shipping and Receiving Dock

At the extreme southwestern corner of the main shop floor level is the shipping and receiving dock. It has space for three trucks at a time, with adjustable dock boards. Trucks reach the dock through the body-shop staging area which has a ramp connecting to Island Avenue.

At the outer end of the dock is an office for the shipping and receiving clerk plus an adjoining lavatory. At the outermost end of the shipping dock "wing" is a room for storage of compressed gas containers such as oxygen, acetylene, refrigerant gases, etc., which fully complies with OSHA regulations.

From the receiving dock, a long sloping ramp leads downward to the lower level parts storage room, where heavy, bulky parts are stored. The ramp is wide enough for forklift traffic with a side access door leading to the scale.

The wide ramp area also provides room for a conveyor belt system to transport parts and other items from the receiving dock to the upper level parts room (indicated by the shaded area on the floor plan drawing). Any heavy items or cartons too bulky to move to the upper level parts stockroom via the conveyor can be readily transported by forklift truck and the freight elevator.

Balcony Parts Storage Room

The balcony, or main stockroom, covers 46,368 sq. ft. It is equipped with steel bin and drawer sections with sloping tops.

Near the center area of the balcony parts room is a Kohler Model 85R78 standby electrical generator. Rated at 75 kw, it is fueled by natural gas and is powered by an International industrial V-8 engine. Manning explained that the standby generator handles vital emergency lighting, heating, and other services in case of a general power failure.

Close to the elevator and stairwell leading to the lower, main shop floor level, there is a screened-in, locked area for storing "take home" items. Manning pointed out that the screened area stores such items as cleaners or other items in aerosol cans, and other things that have a regrettable tendency to disappear when not kept locked up.

Gasoline-Vehicle Shop

The roof of the second-floor parts room is reinforced and is actually the third-floor level of the building. The front part of the third-floor area is occupied by the base of the office "tower." Behind the office area is a special shop exclusively used for repairs and service for all PAT gasoline-powered vehicles plus a blacktop-paved parking area for approximately 200 cars.

The gasoline-vehicle service shop is built along the south side of the third floor level. Access to that shop and the roof level parking is by a long ramp leading to Beaver Avenue. It serves the 86 trucks and 49 cars in the PAT fleet.

The gasoline-vehicle shop measures 63½ ft. x 250 ft. It can service up to 12 gasoline service trucks or cars at a time. It is equipped with two twin-post hydraulic lifts for truck service and two single-post lifts for fleet cars.

At the western end of the gasoline-vehicle shop is a drive-through wash bay. The shop itself also has doors at each end so it too has drive-through access.

Ranged along the southern side of the gasoline-ve-

hicle service shop are 12 unit overhaul rooms, parts stockroom, locker and restroom for the mechanics assigned to the gasoline-vehicle shop, foremen's office, supply storage closets, etc.

The gasoline-vehicle shop also has four sets of overhead reels for PM and lubrication service. These are located near the vehicle lifts. Each reel set contains six reels for an electrical drop light and hoses for water, motor oil, gear oil, automatic transmission fluid, and compressed air. A Carmont in-floor exhaust system serves each of the 12 vehicle service bays.

Othe shop equipment items in the gasoline-vehicle shop include a Model 931-A Bishman truck-and car-tire changer plus an older NAPA tire changer used only for car tires. There are also two wheel balancers—a Model 4-3540 Balkamp wheel balancer and a Model 7064S Alemite Electronic wheel balancer. There is also a Sioux Model 7 heavy-duty bench grinder.

Located near the wash rack corner of the gasoline-vehicle shop in the rooftop parking area is a Maxon snow-melting unit. The snow melter has a large sunken pit covered by two heavy hinged steel doors and a heating unit resembling a jet aircraft engine.

Explaining the operation of the snow melter, Manning says that in the Pittsburgh area, snowfalls can be frequent and deep. The PAT plow can plow snow off the roof-top parking area, of course. But, if the snow had to be pushed against the borders of the area or into big piles, successive snowfalls before a general thaw could result in a substantial reduction in the roof parking area due to the accumulated snow. With the snow melter, as the plow clears the snow, it pushes the snow into the sunken pit after the doors are opened. Hot air from the jet-like heater and blower melts the snow in the pit and it drains off into the storm sewer system.

Administrative Offices

Offices for Hussong, Manning, and the other administrative staff of the PAT headquarters are located in the three upper floors of the Manchester building, comprising the "office tower." The third-floor level opens onto the roof-top parking area.

Summing up, Hussong emphasized that PAT today is a vastly improved operation over the one that a decade ago inherited 31 bus companies and a fleet of 19 different makes and 92 different models of buses with 18 different engine makes, all housed in some 40 garages (some with dirt floors). With the completion of the Manchester shop, plus five operating garages completed since 1966, all of the outmoded facilities and most of the outdated vehicles are gone. Hussong comments, "From all indications, the next 10 years will be equally impressive."

273'-2"

Cold storage

Warm room

Storage

Wash room

A shop-terminal that serves more than fleet vehicles

by Jack Lyndall

In less than a year of its existence, the Carrano Express Inc. distribution center at Northford, Conn. has proved a resounding success on a number of levels.

Not only is the operation a complete freight handling and delivery system; it is a warehouse distribution setup that does break-bulk and delivery for manufacturers, and is a model of efficient, high-security, sophisticated management and planning.

The newest specialized facility, which differs in many respects from a conventional truck terminal, caps a period of rapid growth for Carrano Express, an intra-state carrier serving the entire state of Connecticut. Headed by Neil F. Carrano, president, the company was founded with three trucks in 1955 by Carrano's father, who passed away several years later. Then still in his teens, Carrano took over the company and began a history of growth that has averaged 30% per year for the past three or four years.

The Carrano Express fleet now includes 40 Mack diesel tractors, approximately 70 trailers, and 10 straight trucks. There are also four service vehicles—a fleet fueling truck, a large dump truck with snow plow, an International Scout also fitted with plow blade, and a pickup truck for shop errands. Five company owned fleet cars are also maintained by the

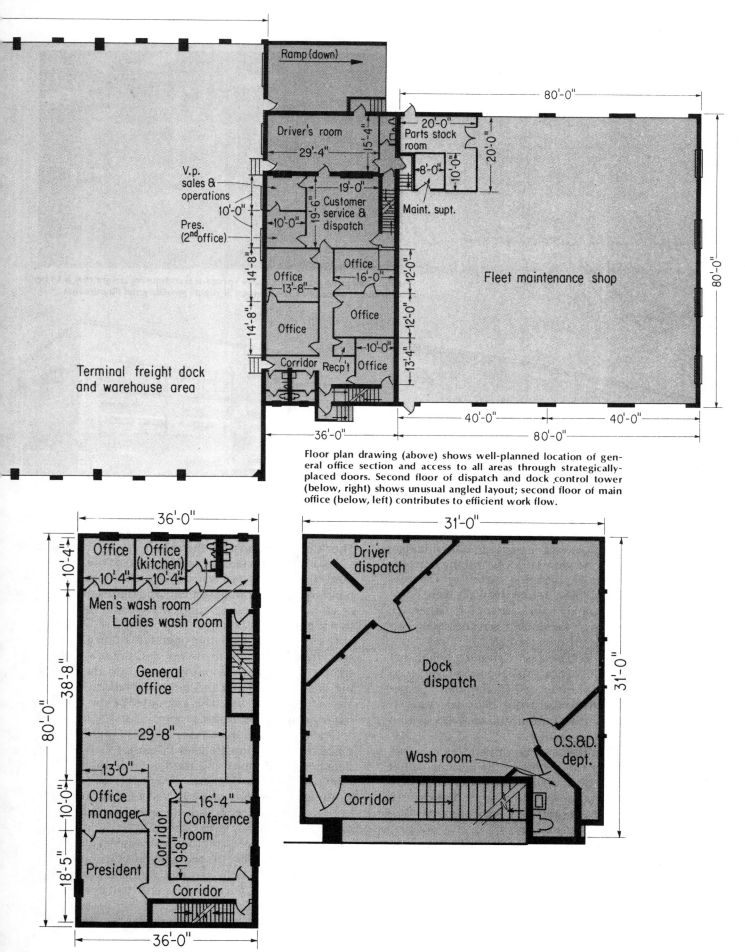

Ramp (down)

Driver's room

Parts stock room

V.p. sales & operations

Pres. (2nd office)

29'-4"
15'-4"
20'-0"
8'-0"
10'-0"
20'-0"
80'-0"
80'-0"

10'-0"
19'-0"
9'-6"
10'-0"
Customer service & dispatch
Maint. supt.

14'-8"
Office
13'-8"
Office
16'-0"
12'-0"
Office
Office
12'-0"

Fleet maintenance shop

14'-8"
10'-0"
13'-4"

Corridor
Rec'pt
Office

Terminal freight dock and warehouse area

36'-0"
40'-0"
40'-0"
80'-0"

Floor plan drawing (above) shows well-planned location of general office section and access to all areas through strategically-placed doors. Second floor of dispatch and dock control tower (below, right) shows unusual angled layout; second floor of main office (below, left) contributes to efficient work flow.

36'-0"

Office
Office (kitchen)
10'-4"
10'-4"
10'-4"

Men's wash room
Ladies wash room

General office

38'-8"
80'-0"

29'-8"

13'-0"
Office manager

16'-4"
Corridor
Conference room
19'-8"

10'-0"
18'-5"

President

Corridor

36'-0"

31'-0"

Driver dispatch

Dock dispatch

31'-0"

Wash room

O.S.&D. dept.

Corridor

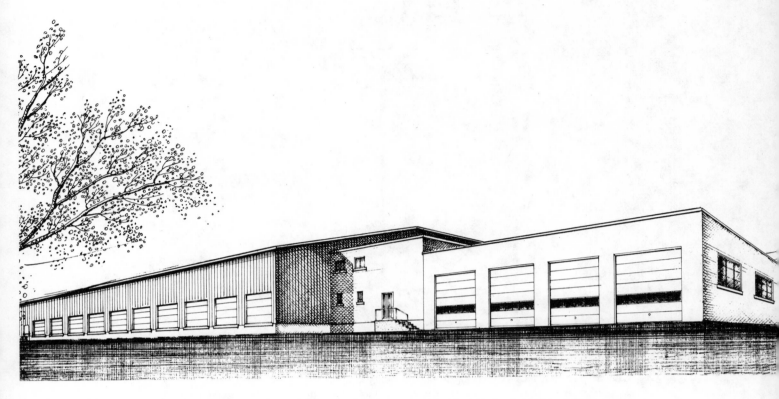

modern fleet shop, which is part of the new distribution center.

After a succession of ever-larger terminal buildings, including the last one with 41 doors and the conventional 60 ft. wide dock, planning started for the new distribution center. "Even before the walls were completed on that terminal," says Lawrence E. Fisher, vp, operations and sales, "we knew it was too small, and started planning for the new facility."

That planning was based on Carrano's belief that the major opportunity for a smaller carrier lay in consolidation and distribution of LTL shipments, especially for private fleets or major national corporations, and also in distribution and delivery within Connecticut for major carriers.

With that specialized service uppermost in mind, the detailed plans for the new distribution center were worked out by Carrano and Fisher with help from Frank J. Carrano, executive vice president, a younger brother of the president. Fisher reports, "We spent 1½ years on the planning."

That planning created the novel warehouse-distribution-fleet administration-maintenance shop layout that is a model of secure, efficient, and successful operation. The facility was built in the Almar Industrial Park on Conn. Rt. 17 approximately five miles NE of New Haven, by Franklin Construction Co., Inc., New Haven, Conn. Carrano reports the completed cost was approximately $1-million.

The "Command post" at the center

Because the successful performance of the Carrano pool distribution and fast delivery of shipments depends on efficient management and tight supervision of all facets in the operation, the general office section is centrally located.

The nerve center is the operations office. In that area, freight bills are made up, and driver's runs assigned. Sliding glass windows open into the adjoining driver's room and the freight bill manifests, etc. are handed to drivers over a counter below the sliding windows in the driver's room.

Opening off the operations office is Fisher's private office, enabling him to keep in close touch with all details of operations and the freight floor, and customer service housed there.

Alongside Fisher's office is Neil Carrano's second, or "working" office, where he spends much of the day, working closely with Fisher.

Next, we entered another stairway leading from the operations office to the general office above on the second floor. Fully carpeted and also wood paneled, the general office space is only half occupied at present.

Upstairs adjoining the office manager's office, with a connecting doorway, is Neil Carrano's large, beau-

Roll-up doors on freight dock have tracks located vertically on the wall, eliminating the conventional curved tracks and giving unlimited overhead space above the door. Note close fit of dock seal at sides.

Driver dispatcher maintains close radio contact with all trucks from his triangular-shaped offset office in control tower above the area.

tifully furnished and decorated office. Carrano uses that office for receiving visitors, for meetings with staff members, and when working on extensive projects.

Offering a unique shipper service

The immediate impression as one steps onto the dock, is one of spaciousness and cleanliness. A Tennant motor-driven sweeper cleans it every morning. The dock has 24-ft. ceilings. The high overhead room is used for storage.

Working aisles extend across the 120 ft. wide dock from door to door, with a wide aisle along each side of the dock next to the truck doors.

The remaining space is filled with adjustable, multi-tier pallet racks for storage of products pending delivery.

Fisher pointed out a typical example of the type of service Carrano Express specializes in, calling attention to a number of pallets filled with a well known brand of anti-freeze in gallon jugs. The anti-freeze manufacturer had made a large bulk shipment direct to Carrano Express, together with a list of all the various customers in Connecticut who were to receive some of the anti-freeze and the quantity to be delivered to each.

Working from that list and a schedule sheet, Carrano Express then makes up the orders as directed,

adjusting the inventory records for the anti-freeze manufacturer as each order is withdrawn from the large shipment. Carrano Express then originates a bill of lading for each order and delivers it at the time specified. A similar large shipment of lawn mowers and snow blowers of a well-known make was being handled in the same way.

Thus, Fisher explains, the Carrano service includes warehousing, order filling, inventory records, and delivery and the high-ceilinged dock was designed accordingly.

But the Carrano Express trucks also pick up and deliver freight, from a single package to full trailer loads, in the conventional way. The wide aisles on the dock allow cross docking the freight efficiently as trucks are spotted at the dock as near the freight it is to haul as possible.

Located on the dock next to the north, or front, wall is an elevated office or "control tower." From the glass enclosed office, the dock supervisor sets up and controls the freight movements on the dock and the separation of bulk shipments into deliveries or for storage on the high racks.

The inner room of the elevated office is angled, relative to the exterior walls, creating small triangular areas at each of the office's outer corners over the dock.

In one of those areas, the radio dispatcher, Bernard

All dock doors have adjustable levelers plus dock seals which retain warm air in winter and discourage freight theft. Idle trailers are angle-parked in the paved yard for easier parking and space saving.

Claflin, keeps in minute-to-minute touch with drivers.

Fisher notes that all Carrano Express trucks are radio equipped; "We have found it to be a tremendous benefit, well worth the investment." In addition to their value in supervising drivers and scheduling deliveries or pickups, the radios also provide added security for high value loads or shipments.

During the tour of the dock, Fisher noted that each dock door was equipped with flexible dock seals and adjustable dock board. They assure a tight fit as a trailer backs in, preventing heat loss in winter, and added security against pilferage.

Because of the high ceiling, the tracks for the roll up dock doors extend straight up on the upper outside dock walls. That design, eliminating the conven-

Below the elevated dock office are temperature-controlled rooms for storage of perishable or very high value shipments.

tional track curves and horizontal overhead section, gives unrestricted overhead room all along the dock door aisle for fork lift movements.

Heat for the dock in winter comes from only two large overhead gas-fired unit heaters, located next to the "control tower." With fully insulated walls and ceilings, Fisher says the dock was easily kept at comfortable working temperature last winter in its first year of operation. Although not air conditioned, the

insulation also keeps the dock temperature comfortable in summer.

At the west end of the distribution center is a modern fleet shop. Measuring 80 x 80 ft., it has three drive-through work bays and one single bay. All bays have roll up doors.

In the northeast corner of the shop area is the shop service center. It includes a small but neat office for John Maselli, superintendent of maintenance. Like the other offices, it too is wood paneled, and also has a large picture window overlooking the shop floor.

Behind Maselli's office is the parts room and shop rest room. Maselli explains that the stock room's modest size is largely due to the fleet's standardization on Mack tractors and that a well-stocked Mack distributor is close by, making a large parts stock unnecessary. Fast moving items are kept on steel shelving in the parts room.

Carrano pays tribute to Maselli and his crew of two skilled mechanics. "Except for very specialized work, the shop can do almost any work, including building up glider kits and truck body kits."

As part of the emphasis on fast, unfailing deliveries on schedule, Fisher says the small but highly skilled fleet shop force is not burdened with tire repairs, especially flats. An outside contract tire service sends a service truck to the Carrano Express facility at 5:00 a.m. daily to check the tires on all vehicles as all Carrano Express trucks return there every night. (There are no branch locations.) The tire service crew changes any flats, and maintains a bank of mounted spares.

To save driver time and fuel, all trucks are fueled in the yard during the night by the fueling truck. A converted fuel oil delivery truck moves down the rows of parked vehicles—filling fuel tanks, checking oil and coolant, and adding as needed.

Underground tanks at the site store 20,000 gal. of diesel fuel and 500 gal. of waste oil. Motor oil is purchased in 55-gal. drums.

Delays in starting trucks on cold mornings is avoided by storing up to 22 tractors inside the heated fleet shop at night. Tractors can also be stored on the freight dock by driving up a ramp from near the back wall of the shop. In case inside storage is not available for all vehicles, a row of 22 electric outlets on the fence at the rear of the property provides plug-in points for engine heaters. Additional outlets along the edge of the dock are used for plugging in engine heaters on the straight trucks backed against the dock.

Security—so far, 100%

A measure of the success of the carefully planned security system is shown by Fisher's comment, "We have not lost a single package since moving into the new facility." He pointed out the many security features as we made our walking tour.

Every door in the distribution center except the front doors is locked at all times with spring loaded locks. Doors were located to separate working areas and to exclude unauthorized outsiders. Employees are given keys that only open doors to areas they are authorized to enter. Master keys that will open any door in the facility are restricted to the four top executives.

Fisher also points out that the tight-fitting dock seals and adjustable dock boards make it virtually impossible for anyone on the dock or in a trailer to pass a package to a confederate outside.

Outside drivers coming to the distribution center to make deliveries or pick up must enter one of the two front doors which is in the center of the lock, directly below the "control tower." The vestibule inside that door was deliberately made small to discourage loitering; it is only large enough to allow the door to swing open and for a wall mounted telephone used by outside drivers to call their terminals.

A stairway from that vestibule leads directly to the "control tower" which has a sliding glass window and counter for service to outside drivers who can not enter the control tower except through a locked door.

All emergency exits have alarm bells that are set off if a door is opened.

Ten closed circuit television cameras monitor the dock, yard, main entrance gate, and other points.

All vehicle drivers wanting to pass through the gate, inbound or outbound, must identify themselves to the man on duty in the operations office, who controls the gate and uses the television and an intercom to communicate with the gate.

High ceilings on freight dock give space for warehousing freight that is to be distributed on orders from shipper. Skylights provide good illumination.

For weekend or holiday security, when the building is unattended, there is a sound level warning system. Fisher explains, "If a sound occurs in the building above a certain decibel level, it lights a warning lamp in the control office of the protection service in New Haven. An attendant there immediately plugs in a tape recorder which is linked to the microphones at strategic locations in our building. The tape is monitored as it is running and if any suspicious sounds are heard, the attendant immediately notifies the police. The system has been activated twice since we moved in, once by a falling pallet on the dock and once by a bird trapped inside. It has proved to be very effective."

Fire protection is by a sprinkler system throughout the entire facility, tied to a 75,000 gal. underground water storage tank and a high capacity pump.

And to insure that the fire pump and other essential services are not crippled by a blackout, the facility has a stand-by diesel generating set. It is rated at 35 kw and powered by a six-cylinder Waukesha diesel engine. Neil Carrano recounted the crippling effects of a hurricane early last year, before the stand-by generator had been installed. "We lost power from approximately 2:00 p.m. one day to 3:00 a.m. the next—about 13 hours. We can't afford not to have the stand-by generator."

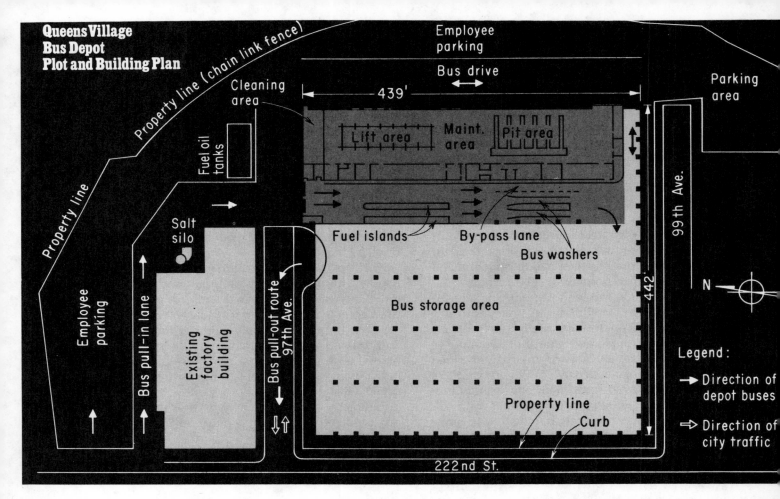

Queens Village Bus Depot Plot and Building Plan

Property line (chain link fence)

Employee parking

Bus drive

Parking area

Cleaning area

439'

Fuel oil tanks

Property line

Salt silo

Bus pull-in lane

Existing factory building

Bus pull-out route 97th Ave.

Lift area

Maint. area

Pit area

Fuel islands

By-pass lane

Bus washers

99th Ave.

442'

N

Bus storage area

Employee parking

Property line

Curb

Legend:
→ Direction of depot buses
⇒ Direction of city traffic

222nd St.

BUS GARAGE COMBINES BEAUTY WITH PRACTICALITY

By Jack Lyndall,
Senior Editor/Equipment

Combining excellent utility and efficiency with a highly esthetic design specially planned for its residential area location, the new Queens Village Bus Depot of the New York City Transit Authority functions as an operating garage and maintenance center for all but major component rebuild and replacement for its 246 buses.

Original Planning—and Obstacles

The need for the Queens Village bus depot became steadily more apparent as the other two NYCTA bus facilities in the area—the Flushing and Jamaica garages—became steadily more overcrowded, notes Marcus G. Gibson, acting senior general superintendent of the NYCTA surface division. (At this writing, Gibson is slated to succeed Jack D. Belsky, senior general superintendent, surface, operation and planning, upon Belsky's imminent retirement after a

long and distinguished career.)

Gibson reported that the location deemed best for the proposed new Queens Village Bus Depot was at 99th Avenue and 222nd Street, in an area partially industrialized but bordered by a residential area. The actual site was occupied by a large bakery plant, which had gone out of business, plus two smaller tracts occupied by a candle maker and a candy plant. The total site was condemned by the City of New York and acquired at a cost of approximately $3,500,000.

However, before construction of the new bus garage could proceed, vigorous opposition from some segments of the nearby residents had to be overcome. These homes bordered the garage site on the south and west sides, along 99th Avenue and 222nd Street. Accordingly, Gibson noted, the building lines have been set back 20 ft. beyond that permissible by the building code, thus creating a wide, attractive sidewalk on those two sides. Also, no windows or bus doors are located on those two sides of the building to eliminate light and noise effects on the residential area.

In addition, attractive thornless honey locust tree plantings in the broad sidewalks and special design street lamps with large circular globes enhance the appearance of the sides facing the residential area.

These measures largely alleviated the neighborhood objections. But Gibson pointed out that while

'Front' wall of building facing 222d Ave. has spacious, wide sidewalk with ornamental tree plantings and large globe streetlamps. Exterior of building is faced with light brown brick.

John Sweeney, location chief of maintenance (right) discusses a repair job in progress on one of the snow plow trucks with a foreman. Buses in background are in the hydraulic lift area.

Exit doors from bus parking area lead into 97th Ave. Large round globe lamps on building between each two doors harmonize with similar globe-type street lamps installed along garage sidewalls.

nearly everyone wants more and better transportation, no one wants a large bus garage in his neighborhood. Though a few problems of community adjustment remain, the active areas of protest now are mainly concerned with the run-on and run-off bus traffic to and from the new garage through unaccustomed areas. Efforts to end these problems are still under way, with buses sometimes routed several blocks off the most direct route to minimize the traffic flow impact on the area.

General Description and Layout

Including driveways and staging areas, the entire Queens Village garage complex covers 319,000 sq. ft. The nearly square garage building itself, measuring 441 x 439 ft., has 193,599 sq. ft. of ground floor area. An additional 12,372 sq. ft. is included in a second floor area devoted to transportation department facilities.

Built at a total cost of approximately $12-million, the functional yet handsome building was designed by Edwards and Kelcey, New York, N.Y., with Kuhn + Drake +·Hessberger as associate architects. There was no single general contractor due to a New York City law covering public building projects of this size. Several different contractors each built specific parts of the project.

The Queens Village garage operates 225 buses. They are assigned to 10 regular routes and three express routes. The additional 31 buses represented by the total capacity of 246 are maintenance spares and extra units for heavy service periods, etc.

Personnel at the new garage totals 475. Of these, 381 are transportation personnel while 94 staff the bus maintenance department. Gibson supplied a breakdown of the personnel as follows:

- Maintenance department:

Supervisor (John Sweeney, location chief of maintenance.)	1
Assistant supervisor	1
Foremen	7
Administrative-clerical	1
Bus Maintainer "A" (body mechanic)	4

View down wide aisle behind bus lift area, with four buses raised on twin-post hoists. Infrared overhead unit heaters flank door openings; lighting is by mercury vapor fixtures above.

Twin wash racks are equipped with wraparound-type washers that clean the front and rear of a bus as well as the sides. Bypass lane at left is for buses not scheduled for washing.

Foreground area of service lanes and bypass lane has been treated with a grainy texture epoxy-like coating to reduce slippery conditions experienced with smooth trowelled concrete when wet.

Bus Maintainer "B" (chassis mechanic)	45
Vehicle cleaners	12
Turnstile maintainer	1
Maintainer's helpers	11
Railroad caretaker	8
Railroad stockman	1

- Transportation department:

Chief surface line dispatcher	1
Senior surface line dispatcher	3
Surface line dispatcher	26
Bus operators	351

As shown by the plot and floor plan drawing included with this report, approximately two-thirds of the garage's ground floor area is devoted to bus storage. The remaining area is divided about 40% into bus pull-in lanes, fueling and washing lanes, and about 60% devoted to the bus maintenance area.

On a bright, crisp day in late December, I inspected the new Queens Village garage with two veteran Transit Authority supervisors. My hosts were Charles Milau, assistant superintendent division chief (whose jurisdiction over six garages includes Queens Village) and Segundo V. (Sig) Ortega, assistant superintendent, fleet engineering.

Mechanic pumps new oil into bus engine with overhead reel system hose and nozzle. Note exhaust vent hose leading to exhaust removal system outlet in floor. Hose retracts when not in use.

Following the path of incoming buses, we walked along the driveway from 222nd Street into the pull-in lane area. This drive borders a sort of 'island' in the garage tract, a small factory that was not condemned for the bus garage in order to allow the business to continue and preserve the jobs of its employes in that area.

From the pull-in drive, buses have a straight-in entry to the service lane area. Measuring 81 ft. 9 in. wide and 439 ft. long, the service lane area has two service islands on the right side with a bypass lane on the left.

The service islands are each equipped with fuel, motor oil, and water dispensing systems. Each service island also has a new Keene vacuum money collection system which sucks the money from bus coin boxes in seconds, sorts it, counts it, and places it in vaults for delivery to the bank. The NYCTA first installed and tested the Keene money collection system at its main East New York shop and garage

Two new wrap-around bus washers are installed in line with the service islands. As bus servicing is completed, the buses move on into the washers. From there the buses can turn right into the huge parking area or turn left through a ramp leading to the mechanical and repair area if there is a driver trouble report or a bus is due for scheduled maintenance.

As we walked through the wide service lane bay, Ortega pointed out that there were no internal col-

Floor Plan-Bus Maintenance Area

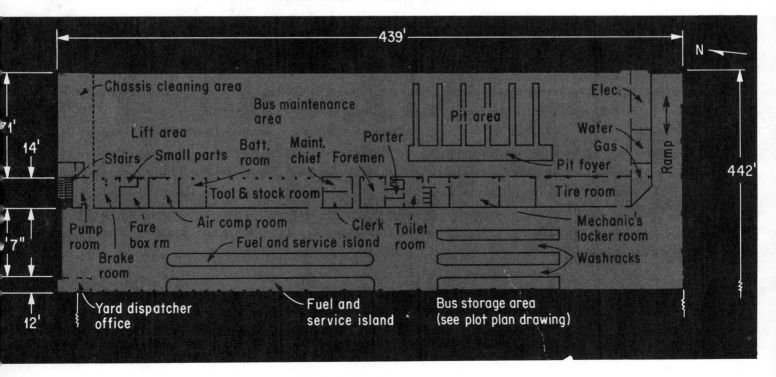

Buses parked in storage area after fueling, servicing, interior cleaning, and washing are ready for dispatch on their routes.

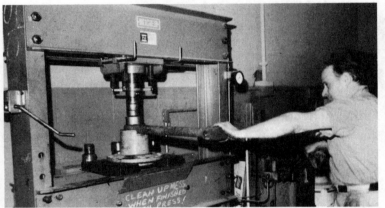

Mechanic uses large Nugier air-hydraulic arbor press to replace a torque arm bushing. Shop has much new, modern equipment.

umns. The roof support beams are made of pre-stressed concrete. The building itself is constructed of concrete blocks with an attractive buff brick facing.

Also, Ortega noted an area of the service lane floor which had been coated with a grainy surface epoxy material as a test project. The original floor is steel-trowelled concrete which, while attractive and easy to clean, tends to be somewhat slippery in the areas where water or oil drippings get on the floor. If the test section proves durable and effective, Ortega said that the entire service lane floor area may be similarly coated.

Through a door in the wall between the service lane bay and the maintenance area, we next visited the modern shop. Commenting on the level of maintenance performed at the Queens Village shop, Milau says, "We change every component on a bus here except the complete engine. We will change cylinder heads or perhaps do an in-frame overhaul, and change all engine accessories.

"When a bus reaches 200,000 to 300,000 miles and the engine needs a major overhaul, many other items

on the bus are likely to be in need of attention, too, so the bus is sent to the main East New York shop for that major work. But otherwise, nearly all other repairs and all regular maintenance is done here."

He also said that the Queens Village shop can handle most routine body work but does not attempt to rebuild a major wreck job. "We change window panes, install new body side panels, and make minor accident repairs."

The maintenance section has nine twin-post hydraulic lifts plus a bank of six below-floor pits. There are also eight work stalls which do not have pits or lifts. Ortega said that one of the lifts is used for bus chassis cleaning while the others are used for all types of chassis repairs.

The six pits open off a large below-floor foyer area which has protective railings and safety-designed steps to meet OSHA requirements. The pits have explosion-proof lights in the pit walls and in the foyer area also for good visibility. At each end of the pit foyer, there is a large sump pump with oil separator to handle underground water seepage or spills.

Milau also pointed out that large oil separators are installed at several locations along the length of the main maintenance shop area.

Because of the space required for the pit foyer, those service bays and the two floor pits adjoining on the south end measure 150 ft. 9 in. long. But the other

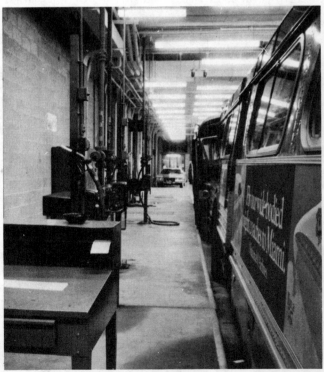

View along service lane island shows diesel fuel and motor oil dispensers from shop's centralized system. Desk in foreground is used by service lane supervisors as buses come through.

Wide 'foyer' area serves as entrance to pits used for PM inspections and service. A stairway at the rear of each pit provides entry or exit from that end also. Note lights in 'foyer' wall.

View in lift area, with one lift raised for cleaning, shows spacious dimensions and excellent lighting. Service 'core' rooms are in background, behind the dividing wall of steel screens shown.

11 bays, including the nine equipped with lifts, measure 184 ft. 8 in. long. All of the bays measure 16 ft. 9 in. wide and each is equipped with a power-operated, roll-up door so that any bus can be moved in or out of the shop without disturbing any other. The long bay dimensions allow ample working room at the front and rear of a bus except for those over the pits which are usually nosed up to the protective forward rail.

A wide aisle area runs along the front end of the entire service bay area.

Each of the service bays is equipped with an outlet for the in-floor exhaust removal system. When not in use, the flexible exhaust duct tubing retracts into the floor receptacles and a hinged, cast aluminum cover snaps shut to close the opening.

Foremen's desks are located strategically along the wide aisle, permitting easy supervision of the area assigned each foreman. Milau pointed out a feature he installed to assist the foreman at the center or main desk. Two large convex mirrors mounted overhead near the rear of the two center service bays give the foreman a view of the work area behind the buses.

Service Department Core Rooms

Bordering the maintenance area aisle, next to the dividing wall between the maintenance area and service lanes, is a row of specialized support department rooms and offices.

At the extreme north end of the row is a pump room housing pumps for the lube and fuel-oil pumping systems. The fuel system has eight underground fuel tanks, each with 5,000-gal. capacity, located outside the building. These supply the four diesel-fuel pumps on the service islands. These four pumps, filter separator, and air release are augmented by a vacuum priming pump used to prime the fuel lines initially and to maintain prime when necessary. A special leak detector, required by New York City Fire Department code, is installed at the fuel dispensing pumps.

The centralized lube oil system, with a 2,000-gal. underground tank, supplies the service lines and the maintenance area bays through either of two motor driven pumps.

The inhibited water system of 1,000-gal. capacity

Trailer delivers a load of salt to the silo which stores it for use by the salt spreader trucks. A high-capacity conveyor rapid-transfers the salt from the trailer to the glass-lined silo.

Mechanic in battery room adjusts charger for proper charging rate for batteries on racks. Overhead vent ducts remove all battery charging fumes. The NYCTA owns all of its batteries.

Specially trained mechanic conducts complete analysis of used motor oil samples taken from each bus periodically. If the analysis shows any problem, the bus is promptly called in.

used for engine coolant is powered by the shop's air system.

Next to the pump room is the brake room. In this room, brake lining blocks are stocked and installed on brake shoes. A new Van Norman brake drum lathe turns brake drums to correct oversize.

Adjoining the brake room, which also houses the oil analysis department, is a room where fare boxes are repaired and tested. A small parts stockroom is part of that area.

Next is the air compressor room housing two 50 hp compressors supplying the entire facility. The battery room comes next, with its facilities for cleaning and testing batteries under load and racks for batteries on charge. A special overhead vent system removes the dangerous fumes from charging batteries.

Then we entered the tool and stockroom, 100 ft. long, along the wide shop aisle. It stocks parts regularly used; a neat tool board at one end holds all shop-owned power or special tools.

Ortega described the well-planned stocking system which is used at all NYCTA shops including the new Queens Village depot. A Transit Authority part number is assigned to each part in addition to the OEM part number. The TA part number comprises three segments: The first segment identifies the class or type of part; the second segment identifies the bus make and/or model it is for; and the third segment is the individual part item of its class by sequence. Parts are arranged in the various TA parts rooms by the TA number system, with parts on shelves in accordance with the third stage sequence number. This greatly simplifies the job of stocking parts and locating needed items on the shelves or in bins.

Each part number stocked is also assigned a maximum and minimum inventory figure. Using a perpetual inventory system, with daily parts withdrawals deducted from the previous quantity on hand, a TA parts room clerk or stockman can quickly tell when the minimum inventory for any part has been reached or is imminent. He then re-orders enough stock to restore the maximum inventory quantity.

Ortega also noted that the parts usage and ordering from each stockroom is continually monitored. If minimum inventory quantities of some items are reached too often or a part item usage is seemingly too high in comparison to that part's usage by other TA shops, an investigation determines the reason. If the high usage is for good cause, such as a shop assigned a large number of old coaches of one make and model, the maximum quantity number is increased to reduce the frequent reordering of small parts quantities.

But for parts with slow usage, inventory quantities may be reduced. And when the TA plans to phase out a particular bus model, parts inventories are reduced accordingly to avoid having a large supply of obsolete parts when the buses are disposed of.

Next to the parts stock room there are two offices. The outer one, next to the shop aisle, is for the location chief of maintenance while the inner office behind the chief's office is for his shop clerk.

Alongside the maintenance chief's office is a passageway leading to the service lane area. Next to that passageway on the south side is a shop foreman's office, with a restroom next in line. Behind the rest room is the porter's closet and supply cabinets for shop housekeeping supplies.

The shop mechanic's toilet and locker rooms are next in line in the service core, with a lunch room adjoining the locker room. It has a connecting doorway to the locker room. Last in the row of service core rooms is the tire storage and service room.

Across the south end of the maintenance area are small rooms for natural gas, water, and electric controls and meters.

While the lathe turns a brake drum, mechanic in brake room relines brake shoes. Lining is stocked in standard size and regular oversizes; brake drums are turned to the size of the lining to be used. Drums worn beyond a safe oversize and damaged shoes are discarded.

Transportation Department

The entire second floor area, located above the service lane area, is devoted to the transportation department which is responsible for the operation of the buses. The second floor contains offices for the location chief, general dispatcher, and crew dispatchers. There are also rooms for records storage, radio equipment, and a safety room.

Modern, sanitary locker rooms are provided for dispatchers and drivers. Toilet and shower rooms serve both locker rooms.

In the central area of the second floor is the large crew room where drivers wait for assignment to runs.

In addition to the second floor area, the transportation department occupies a small office at the right side of the service lane entrance. The yard dispatcher is located there.

Heating and Ventilation

Because of the problems caused by large scale bus movements during short time periods such as rush hour schedules, the Queen Village facility has a highly efficient ventilation system. Ortega reports the system's capacity for several areas:

- Bus storage area—one cfm per sq. ft.
- Mechanical shop work areas—four air changes per hour
- Exhaust removal system—450 cfm per tail pipe

Building heating combines two types of gas-fired heaters. At strategic locations throughout the entire ground floor work and storage areas, there are Reznor overhead unit heaters which deliver fan-forced hot air.

In addition, Reznor gas fired infrared heaters are mounted overhead along each side of all the maintenance area rollup doors. The heating system is capable of providing the following interior temperature levels with outside temperature at 0 deg. F.

- Bus storage area—60 deg. F.
- Fuel service island and wash area—65 deg. F.
- Maintenance shop work areas—70 deg. F.
- Office areas—75 deg. F.

Special Features

Among the interesting special features of the Queens Village facility is a large, tall salt silo. Located just north of the pull-in line area, alongside the inbound drive, the silo stores 150 tons of salt for winter snow melting on the depot yard and drives plus certain streets. The steel silo is lined with fused glass to prevent internal corrosion and has a conveyor that handles 80 tons of salt per hour in continuous operation.

Two snowplow-equipped trucks with salt-spreader attachments are operated by the Queens Village de-

pot, Ortega said. He pointed out that the New York City Department of Sanitation is responsible for snow cleaning on city streets and usually cleans main streets promptly after a heavy snow. The Queens Village shop units supplement the city units in particularly troublesome areas on some side roads or streets which city units might not be able to reach promptly enough to assure dependable bus service.

In addition to the large dump trucks equipped with the plow blades and salt spreaders, the Queens Village shop has a small Clark industrial truck used primarily for pushing stalled or inoperative buses in or around the shop. A small snow-plow blade is quickly attached to the little "shop mule" during a snow storm and it clears the depot drives, staging area, and employe parking area.

Communications

All of the buses based at the new Queens Village depot are equipped with two-way radio. Ortega said that the Transit Authority operates the world's largest two-way bus communication system; the completely solid-state system encompasses 4,401 buses, 104 patrol cars and emergency vehicles, and 252 portable radios used by street dispatchers.

In addition to the radio system, the Transit Authority maintains contact with all 19 depots in the system (including Queens Village) by teletype plus a new system called Electro-writer. This latter system transmits hand-written messages to and from Transit Authority Control to all depots. In addition, telephones are used.

Future Expansion

Though the Queens Village depot size and bus fleet is adequate for present and immediate future needs, Ortega notes that future expansion is still possible. The existing small factory building between the depot building and pull-in drive can be acquired in case the factory should relocate or go out of business. If expansion demands were severe enough to justify it, the city could, of course, condemn and acquire the factory.

Final Evaluation

Speaking for the surface division of the Transit Authority, Gibson commented on the Queens Village facility after completion in September, 1974, and several months of operation: "Considering financial limitations, community constraints, and irregularity of the land parcel, surface is satisfied that the best use has been made of all material and economic resources. The changes in design have been minor and complaints from operating supervision and personnel have been minimal."

TOMORROW'S SHOP TODAY

By Jack Lyndall, Senior Editor

Cooper-Jarrett's new terminal and shop at Sharon, Pa., a stone's throw from the promising 1-80 Keystone Shortway, has expansion already built in for the 1980's

Here is a truck terminal and major maintenance facility that just opened—but it's not just for today. It's for 1980 and beyond!

Differing from most new shops of recent years, where future growth is planned by building additions at some future time, the new shop built by Cooper-Jarrett, Inc., at Sharon, Pa., has that expansion already built in. But the expansion space is not waste space until some future day—it is put to productive use right now, with quick conversion designed in when needed.

A new hub location.

The completion, at long last, of the Keystone Shortway (I-80) across Pennsylvania offered a new crossroads of major Cooper-Jarrett routes. Top management of Cooper-Jarrett, Inc., Orange, N.J., could see potential, large economies and opportunities for improved customer service with a major new relay terminal and central fleet maintenance base at or near the crossroads in western Pennsylvania.

The actual site is near Sharon, Pa., only a bit over a stone's throw from the intersection of I-80 and Pa.

Rt. 18. The location is just a score or so miles east of the intersection of I-80 and the Ohio Turnpike. And some 15 miles east of the new C-J facility, newly completed I-79 crosses I-80 linking up to the New York Thruway and the Pennsylvania Turnpike.

Planned for the new location were a freight relay terminal where loads could be consolidated for C-J terminals in such major cities as Boston, Bound Brook, N.J. (New York City), Chicago and others.

The new operations set up would bring all line haul equipment regularly through the Sharon terminal, making it possible to center all major maintenance, rebuilding, and PM inspections there.

Other buildings plnned for the complex included an administration and central dispatch building and a vehicle wash building.

Overlooking an old canal basin for a former offshoot of the Erie Canal system, the Cooper-Jarrett facility is on a 27-acre plot. Because of its importance, it is under the direction of Roy Shaver, a vice president of Cooper-Jarrett.

The huge new shop is the nerve center for all Cooper-Jarrett fleet

maintenance, and is headquarters for Paul V. Pancotto, director of maintenance.

Operating 24 hours a day, 7 days a week, the Sharon complex when fully operational will employ 300-325 people with an estimated annual payroll of $3.5 million. Approximately 177 road drivers are domiciled there. Of the total roster about 50 employees are in the humming new 44 door relay terminal and its offices.

Builder of the new complex was Dues Building Systems, Inc., Dayton, O. The architect was Lewis D. Klein with John M. Schweiger and Associates as mechanical engineers, both also in Dayton.

The shop for today and tomorrow.

Built in a basic T-shape, the shop contains approximately 71,220 sq ft of ground floor space. In addition, there is a second floor level over the central service area of the building which contains some 19,800 sq ft. The shop is a "Star" pre-engineered building.

Taking a walking tour of the entire shop with Pancotto, good ideas and possibly some innovations were everywhere.

As shown on the floor plan drawing, the tractor shop occupies the upper half of the T-cross bar. Measuring 90x220 ft, it has six roll-up doors in the side wall plus doors at each end opening to an aisle the full length of the tractor shop.

The brightly lighted tractor shop has a different atmosphere from any other fleet shop I've visited. This one has a Musac system and pleasant music comes from speakers all over the building.

Five of the doors in the tractor shop's North wall give access to service pits. Pancotto explained that the pits are for PM service on line haul tractors while trailers are at the terminal.

Measuring 42-in. wide, the pits are equipped with air and water lines, gear lube and chassis grease dispensing hoses, plus swivel-mounted funnels for draining waste oil. A 6,000 gal capacity waste oil tank is buried outside the doors, under the concrete apron.

One of the tractor shop pits embodies a highly unusual feature—a narrow extension of the pit for servicing fork trucks.

Pancotto noted that the new Sharon shop will service all fork trucks from all Cooper-Jarrett terminals. They will be shipped back and forth on trailers with room for them. With the concentration of fork truck work, the special pit will save time in changing oil and lubricating fork trucks. And make it a safer job, too.

The rest of the tractor shop contains service bays. Tractors reach them from the center aisle. Pancotto reports that the tractor shop can handle 25 units, but up to 36 can be squeezed in if necessary.

Overhead lines in the tractor shop carry compressed air, chassis lube, and pre-mixed anti-freeze. These lines have drop off hoses at every second service stall. But typical of the far sighted planning, pipe tees with the side outlet plugged are already installed so drop lines can be provided for each stall when work volume demands. The pipe plugs can be removed and hoses threaded in very quickly.

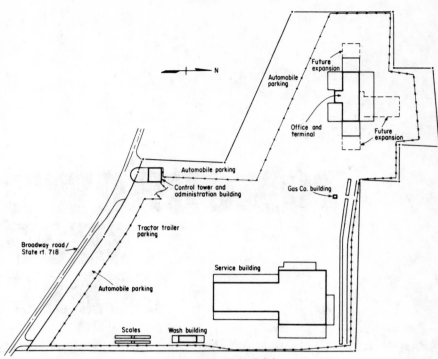

PLOT PLAN

There is ample light in the tractor shop, day or night. Skylights of translucent fiberglass panels are in the shop roof. And a continuous band of the same material extends all around the three exterior walls, just below the roof line. (This set-up is used throughout the entire building, in fact.) For night or dark, cloudy days, mercury vapor lamps overhead give ample light.

Overhead gas fired unit heaters keep the tractor shop warm in winter.

Also mounted overhead are the exhaust removal lines, connected to suction blowers. There is a drop tube for each service bay and pit. For tractors with dual vertical exhaust stacks, individual hoses for each exhaust stack go into a Y-fitting to feed the exhaust into the main suction tube.

Tie down rings built into the floor of one service bay are for body or frame straightening jobs.

The service core.
In the other half of the T-crossbar is the centrally located complex of "service" departments for the entire shop building. As shown in the floor plan drawing, this area houses the

parts stock room, paint spray room, engine and chassis dynamometer rooms, diesel fuel injection room, component rebuild area and machine shop, electrical component rebuild room, tire repair and storage room, steam cleaning room, and a general utility room. A men's rest room is also in that area.

Two wide corridors through the central service area gives easy passage from the tractor shop to the trailer shop and check lanes in the leg of the T.

In the corridor bordering the parts room are two large counters where mechanics from either area of the shop come for parts. Directly opposite, across the corridor, large windows are built into the unit rebuild room wall.

The paint room and engine and chassis dynamometer rooms are still incomplete. But the rest of the ground floor service core is in full or partial use.

The huge component rebuild and machine shop area appears half empty. But that is because it, too, was built with floor space for years ahead.

An extensive overhead monorail

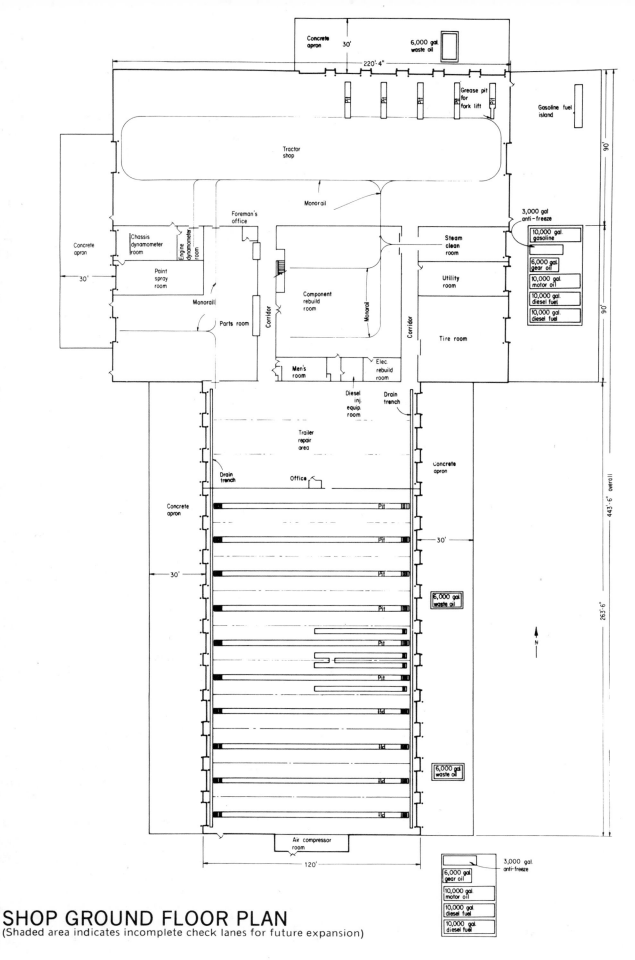

Concrete apron 30'

6,000 gal. waste oil

220'-4"

Pit Pit Pit Pit

Grease pit for fork lift

Gasoline fuel island

Tractor shop

Monorail

90'

Foreman's office

Chassis dynamometer room

Engine dynamometer room

Paint spray room

Concrete apron

30'

Parts room

Monorail

Corridor

Component rebuild room

Monorail

Corridor

Steam clean room

3,000 gal. anti-freeze

10,000 gal. gasoline

6,000 gal. gear oil

Utility room

10,000 gal. motor oil

10,000 gal. diesel fuel

10,000 gal. diesel fuel

90'

Tire room

Men's room

Elec. rebuild room

Diesel inj. equip. room

Drain trench

Trailer repair area

Concrete apron

Drain trench

Office

443'-6" overall

Concrete apron

30'

Pit

Pit

Pit

30'

Pit

Pit

6,000 gal. waste oil

263'-6"

Pit

N

6,000 gal. waste oil

Air compressor room

120'

3,000 gal. anti-freeze

6,000 gal. gear oil

10,000 gal. motor oil

10,000 gal. diesel fuel

10,000 gal. diesel fuel

SHOP GROUND FLOOR PLAN
(Shaded area indicates incomplete check lanes for future expansion)

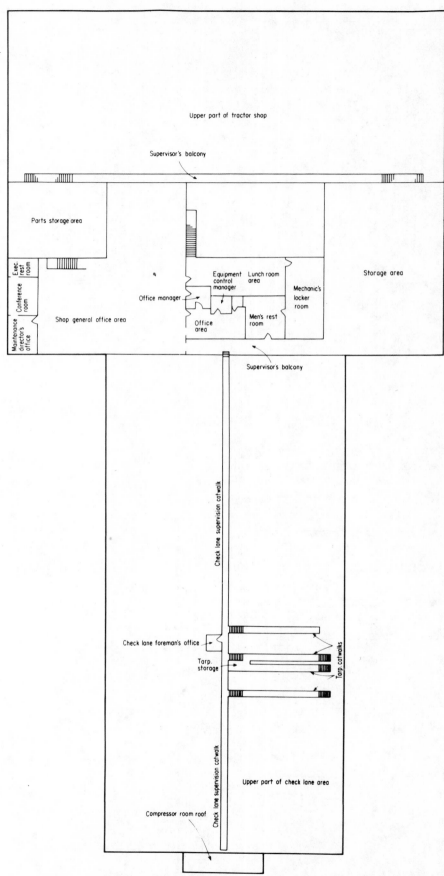

Upper part of tractor shop

Supervisor's balcony

Parts storage area

Exec. rest room

Conference room

Maintenance director's office

Shop general office area

Office manager

Equipment control manager

Lunch room area

Mechanic's locker room

Office area

Men's rest room

Storage area

Supervisors balcony

Check lane supervision catwalk

Check lane foreman's office

Tarp. storage

Tarp. catwalks

Check lane supervision catwalk

Upper part of check lane area

Compressor room roof

SHOP SECOND FLOOR LEVEL PLAN

system serves the component rebuild room, parts room, and the two rows of service bays in the tractor shop. With a capacity of one ton, the monorail crane can handle engines or any other heavy component.

Along the south wall of the component rebuild room are the diesel fuel injection room and the electrical component room.

Air conditioned and built to be dust proof, the diesel fuel injection room handles any repair, rebuilding, and calibration of diesel fuel injection pumps and nozzles.

In the electrical rebuild room, solenoids and other major electrical components will be repaired or rebuilt.

The tire room is equipped to mount, dismount, and repair any type or size of tire used on C-J vehicles. Spare tires are stored there, too. The shop does not have a recapping set up.

Next to the tire room is the utility room housing air powered pumps for the centrally supplied oil, grease, gear oil, fuel, and anti-freeze.

There is a bank of six of the air pumps, two each for motor oil, gear lube, and anti-freeze. Along with the two pumps for each product is valving and piping that allows either pump to take over if the other fails.

Another plumbing hook up allows these utility room pumps to supply the check lanes if a similar set of pumps in the check lanes should fail.

As a point of interest, Pancotto explained that the proper amounts of permanent type anti-freeze and water are put into the underground storage tank. The Balcrank air powered pump then agitates the mixture before it is pumped to the various dispensing hoses.

Just outside the utility room are underground tanks with the following capacities:
Diesel fuel—20,000 gal (2 10,000 gal tanks)
Motor oil—10,000 gal
Gear oil—6,000 gal
Anti-freeze—3,000 gal

Gasoline—10,000 gal

The steam clean room next to the utility room has complete high pressure steam cleaning equipment plus degreasing tanks for engine blocks, etc. A roll up door allows tractors to be driven in for steam cleaning of engines, chassis, and fifth wheels.

The tire room, utility, and steam rooms border on the second corridor running between the tractor shop and the trailer repair area giving easy access to mechanics working in either shop.

In addition to the large counter windows bordering the corridor, the parts room has door openings into both the tractor and trailer shops. The latter is a roll-up type, large enough to permit rolling heavy components out on a hand truck or movement by fork truck.

Another roll-up door in the outside parts room wall permits delivery of incoming parts direct from a truck or trailer.

Lighting throughout the service core is by modern fluorescent fixtures. Heat is ducted from the roof mounted hot air unit in the check lane area.

The trailer shop.
Bordering the south side of the central service core is the trailer shop. This area has three drive-through bays, since both sides of this shop section has roll-up doors the full length of each side.

The trailer repair bays are each 20 ft wide and 120 ft long. At present, half of one bay is used for storage of steel used in vehicle repairs.

An overhead traveling crane with 2-ton capacity spans all three bays. Pancotto reports that it can be invaluable for lifting a complete trailer roof off for repairs or replacement. It also unloads and stacks steel in the storage area.

The two full length trailer repair bays are each equipped with powerful Weaver hydraulic hoists that can lift an entire trailer, fully loaded. They are adjustable for different trailer lengths.

The fully equipped trailer repair

Check lanes (above) are 120 ft long to accommodate two tractor-trailer combinations at a time. Separate batteries of servicing hoses are at each tractor location to save time. Mechanic (below) cleans tractor cab with vacuum cleaner wand. Other hoses are for fuel, motor oil and gear oil, anti-freeze and air.

Trailer in check lane with tarpaulin-service catwalks. Stairs in background lead to catwalk spanning all six check lanes and used for supervisory purposes.

Check lanes at 20 ft. wide give ample working space on each side of trailer. Portable bridge (above) over pit permits safe crossing without jumping. Future expansion area on second floor (below) is for maintenance director's office.

department handles 6 to 10 trailers a day.

Check lanes.

Separated from the trailer shop by a low wall, there are six fully equipped safety check lanes. These also measure 20 ft wide and 120 ft long, ample to handle two tractor and trailer combinations at a time. Each check lane has a full length pit. Like the pits in the tractor shop they are fully equipped with chassis lube, air lines, waste oil lines, and water. The pits widen below the floor level and have explosion proof lights. Ventilation fans keep the pits free of fumes.

At the entrance to each check lane is a Black and Decker central vacuum cleaner system for cleaning tractor cab interiors. The dirt hoppers alongside the entrance doors are easily emptied as needed.

At two locations along each check lane is a battery of vehicle servicing hoses. Connected to color-coded supply pipes running overhead through the entire shop, they speed check lane servicing. Diesel fuel pipes are green; motor oil pipes are dark blue; pre-mixed anti-freeze pipes are light blue; water pipes are white and compressed air lines are painted light green.

In addition to these service lines, drop hoses from the vacuum cleaner system are included at each vehicle service point.

Another time saver is a dual pipe arrangement for dispensing diesel fuel. This allows fueling tanks on both sides of a tractor simultaneously with all fuel dispensed recorded on a single meter.

With the pit set up, Pancotto says, "we can do a PM on a tractor as it is bmoving over the pit."

Another 6,000 gal waste oil tank buried under the check lane apron handles drained oil from the pits.

Two of the check lanes are equipped with overhead catwalks for installation or servicing of tarpaulins used on open top trailers. These catwalks are constructed of strong steel grating.

Another catwalk, the first of its type I had seen in a fleet shop, runs overhead the full length of the check lane area.

Steel grating steps lead down from this catwalk to the lower level catwalks for tarp service.

The overhead catwalk starts at the second floor level above the parts room.

As in the tractor shop, mercury vapor lamps provide brilliant lighting in the entire check lane area.

Beyond the six fully equipped check lanes is another example of planning and building for the future. Four more check lanes with fully built pits are all completed. They lack only the necessary plumbing, wiring and other service connections to make them operational when future Cooper-Jarrett growth requires.

But in the meantime, this is not just waste space. Pancotto pointed out that these future check lanes provided indoor, heated parking space for tractors during the past winter, saving the usual cold starting problems for tractors stored outdoors.

In addition, space in this future check lane area is earmarked for spare tandem assembly storage and a lane for performing Pennsylvania inspections.

At the far end of the check lane wing of the building is an annex housing two high capacity air compressors and an air drier.

The air compressors are Ingersoll-Rand Model H-50BK two stage units and the moisture removal unit is an Ingersoll-Rand "Thermal Mass" Model 11.

Ventilating louvres in the air compressor room wall are progressive type, controlled by a sensitive thermostat. The louvres maintain an even temperature in the compressor room and the separate annex room keeps the compressors completely out of the shop area.

Good housekeeping ideas show everywhere in the shop areas. Drain trenches with removable steel gratings run the full length of the check lane wing on each side, just inside the door openings. The trenches have oil traps.

Tractors in tractor shop (above) for major work, Overhead lines supply lube oil, chassis grease, compressed air and pre-mixed anti-freeze. Exhaust removal system shown below has tubes for dual stacks feeding into a Y fitting and single hose.

Special pit in tractor shop (left) has narrow 6 ft extension for PM service on fork lift trucks. Hydraulic hoists (above) in trailer shop can pick up a fully loaded trailer. Holes in hoist top plates are for trailer king pins

Pancotto commented that the check lane floor has a slope from the center point toward each side of the building. This prevents water puddles on the floor from rain or melting snow dripping off vehicles-moving through the check lanes.

Because of the frequent door openings in the check lanes, the heating system differs from the tractor shop. There are two Panelbloc gas-fired infra-red type overhead unit heaters for each check lane, one mounted at each end of the lane. Four more of the overhead units are in the future check lane area.

In addition another large ceiling mounted heating unit warms incoming air drawn in by the ventilating system to 65°-70°. Large ducts distribute this supplemental heated air throughout the shop to strategic areas and to the service core area.

Air in the shop is also re-circulated through the auxiliary heating unit for re-heating. This reduces overall heating costs while still maintaining an adequate level of fresh, incoming heated air.

In summer, the same system will function as a ventilating system.

Supervision.

In every area of this shop it is easy for supervisors to see what is going on. This is true now and future expansion changes will retain this feature.

As shown in the floor plan drawing, a shop foreman's office with all glass walls is in the corner of the parts room bordering the tractor shop and corridor to the trailer shop. At present, Pancotto makes his headquarters in that office. From it he can see the length of the tractor shop, the north end of the parts room and parts dispensing counter and across the corridor to the component rebuild room.

Another foreman's office was built in the wall between the trailer shop and check lanes. From this glassed-in office, Don Brant, shop superintendent, keeps an eye on the six vital check out lanes and the trailer shop.

Check lane supervisors are stationed at the end of the lanes. Later,

when the four additional check lanes are equipped and put into use, a check lane supervisor's office will be located alongside the catwalk the length of the check lanes.

Showing again the forethought that went into this facility, the steel framework to support that supervisor's office is already installed in the check lane roof framing. When the office is needed it can be quickly completed by building walls, ceiling, and floor.

The office now used by Brant will then become the office for the full time trailer shop superintendent who will be needed by that time.

Also planned for "Phase II" is a new office for the director of maintenance, located on the second floor level above the parts room. The already designed office location will give a vantage point overlooking the trailer shop and check lanes plus a view of the vast paved area in front of the shop and the vehicle ready line. By the time that growth calls for Pancotto's move to the new second level office, a new full-time tractor shop foreman will take over in the existing office.

Other future growth ideas.

In addition to the new maintenance director's office planned for the second floor level, this area will also house shop general offices with additional men's and women's rest rooms, a conference room, an office for the equipment control manager and a large drivers training room.

Additional space on the upper level will store large, bulky, or slower moving parts.

Already completed on the second level is the shop mechanic's locker room and shower room.

Another idea for the future is a gasoline fueling island near the northeastern corner of the tractor shop. Pancotto commented that the gas pump island is not needed now as Cooper-Jarrett has no local PU&D trucks at the Sharon facility. But because there is a possibility that Cooper-Jarrett may acquire local PU&D authority in the nearby Pittsburgh area, the gas pump island and gasoline storage tanks

were installed to handle the gas powered trucks that would be used.

Personnel.

Because of its many efficiencies, Pancotto reports that he expects the new shop labor force to stabilize at 75-80 men. At present, 10 mechanics work in the check lanes on each shift. There are four trailer repairmen on each shift. The balance of the force are tractor shop mechanics, component rebuild room mechanics, parts clerks and a utility man.

Since the shop must operate seven days per week, Pancotto says that there are 10 to 11 men per shift on Saturdays and Sundays.

With the completion of the new Sharon complex, Cooper-Jarrett closed its former shop at Irwin, Pa. Despite the nearly 90 miles from Irwin to Sharon, Pancotto commented that 13 terminal dockmen, 49 mechanics, and 8 office workers relocated. "I think Cooper-Jarrett was very fortunate to retain the number of experienced people that we did."

Additional employees needed were recruited locally, most with no previous trucking industry experience. Pancotto reports that the nucleus of experienced employees have helped greatly in training the new employees.

Wash room and scales.

Conveniently located along the east side of the terminal plot is a wash building housing modern new automatic washing equipment. Vehicles leaving the check lanes can swing into the wash building.

Two scales just beyond the wash building check vehicle weights. From the scales, vehicles go out on runs or to the ready line for dispatch.

Economic benefits.

Despite the manifold problems of moving into an incomplete building, still swarming with contractor's workmen, Pancotto reports, "We handled 19,700,000 lb of transfer break bulk freight here in October (1970), our first full month here." He sets truck movements as an average of 180 units in and out each 24 hours.

As planned, the new Sharon facility has allowed the closing of at least one other Cooper-Jarrett shop. Operations at the Chicago shop, the former major overhaul location, have been reduced. Other shops have been cut back too, with the transfer of all major maintenance to the Sharon shop.

Overall, Pancotto reports the new shop resulted in a reduction in the maintenance force of 16 men. He also notes that the maintenance work load is expected to lessen with the recent adoption of a three year replacement policy for line haul tractors.

With the forward thinking that went into the new shop and terminal, also planned for growth, Pancotto expects the economies to continue and perhaps even improve as "Construction Phase II" is completed. He says with considerable justifiable pride, "We built for 10 years ahead."

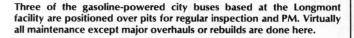

Three of the gasoline-powered city buses based at the Longmont facility are positioned over pits for regular inspection and PM. Virtually all maintenance except major overhauls or rebuilds are done here.

Regional Transportation District, Metro Div. terminal, office and shop, Longmont, Colo.
Architects: Community Architects Inc.
Gen. contractor: Poole Construction Ltd.

Combining an intercity passenger-bus terminal, a local transit-bus stop, and bus-maintenance and service shops, the Longmont bus facility blends well with its eastern Colorado environment.

Built on 3½ acres in the Denver metropolitan area, bus-terminal facilities occupy about one-third of the site, with bus shops and a service/storage area taking up the rest. That amounts to 4,000 sq. ft. for the terminal area and 20,600 sq. ft. for the shop and bus-servicing areas. Staffed with three mechanics, those latter departments service, clean, inspect, and do running repairs, including component changeout, for the nine gasoline-powered and two diesel buses based there.

The intercity-bus passenger terminal area includes an inside waiting room, package-express and ticket counter, freight storage room, and an outside bus-loading station with canopy cover.

Offering a pleasing appearance, the raked precast-concrete interior combines with brick and etched-

Exterior of building shows clean lines and low, Western-oriented theme. Entrance doors were designed for easy, unimpeded vehicle movement with smooth traffic flow. Large expanse of glass in passenger-terminal wing (below) gives airy and inviting atmosphere. Intercity-bus loading area is adjacent to passenger waiting room.

Passenger waiting room serving intercity-bus passengers includes ticket counter. The smooth molded seating, tile floor, and brick walls were designed for long-lasting appearance and low maintenance. Waiting room and passenger area can be expanded in the future if needed.

concrete feature elements. Brick and quarry tile are also used extensively in the interior.

The waiting room is lit by mercury-vapor cylinders; the remaining indoor areas by fluorescent lights. Mercury-vapor lamps provide outdoor lighting.

Although the site is convenient to the central business district, it taxed the ingenuity of its designers. The proximity of existing and future residential areas on the east required special environmental protective measures—berms, sound walls, non-glare lighting, and landscaping. Also, separation of bus drivers and mechanics from public patrons of the terminal posed a problem.

Bus traffic flow is basically counterclockwise. Intercity buses loop the site; local and intercity buses can pull into the storage bays; buses can circulate through service and repair bays and back to the parking area and buses can leave without delay and proceed to routes.

The shop area, which includes five bus-storage bays, one service bay, and one repair bay, is heated by

pressurized make-up units with direct-fired gas furnaces. A mechanized exhaust-removal system serves the floor pits and the buses in the repair area, and zone air conditioning is adjusted to seasonal variations and to the needs of various areas within the facility.

Security features include a fire-sprinkler system throughout, a fire-detection system (thermal and smoke), a burglar alarm linked to the police department, a fenced yard, and master and systematic keying.

Land cost was $317,375; architectural fees came to $177,300; and construction (including land preparation) amounted to $1,441,300—for a total cost for the completed facility of $1,935,975.

With the future in mind, the facility has been arranged so the driver and operations area can be expanded to the west, passenger and package-express areas to the east, and administrative areas to the south. The service lane is suitable for bus washing (with water reclamation) and indoor fueling in the future.

Modern hydraulic lifts give mechanics easy access to bus chassis and underbody areas for inspection and repairs. Overhead reels and hoses dispense oil, grease, air, water, etc., from bulk tanks.

**Ottawa-Carleton Regional Transit Comm.
Merivale Transit Center,
Ottawa, Ontario, Canada.
Architects: J.L. Richard & Assoc.
Contractors: R.J. Nicol
Constructions (1975) Ltd.**

Built with a design patterned on OCRTC's three-year-old Pinecrest Transit Center (FO—6/78, p. 144; and 7/78, p. 102) and on experience from its operation, the Merivale Transit Center is the fifth OCRTC operating garage serving the growing Ottawa metropolitan area. Providing indoor storage for 200 buses, it handles normal running repairs and body work component exchange, and daily servicing.

Design goals included reduced construction costs and reduced energy consumption—especially for building heating, which is vital in Ottawa's frigid winters. Construction costs were kept in line by making the precast, insulated concrete wall panels as single pieces from foundation to roof, and by eliminating drainage troughs in storage-bay floors in favor of greater floor slopes toward catch-basins. The latter design also reduced cleaning costs.

The carefully planned heating system includes heat exchangers that permit recovery of up to 71% of heat

Exterior views show large, paved employe parking area and grassed, landscaped grounds (left). Special large areas were provided at driveway intersections for piling snow, which is later hauled away. Wide driveways give good turning room for buses and expedite peak-hour movement of buses.

Special panel of switches on foreman's office wall controls heating units throughout the shop and bus storage bays, with lights on adjoining panel indicating whether units are "on" or "off." A similar panel controls all shop lights to save energy.

that would otherwise be lost in exhaust air. As a result, natural-gas consumption at Merivale is 15% lower than at Pinecrest, even though Merivale is 18% larger.

Also contributing to heat conservation, and to working efficiency, as well, is the internal turning area at the front and rear of the building. "It permits us to drive buses from storage, through service lanes, and back to storage without going outside. Reduction in heat loss is significant," says P.J. Newgard, OCRTC equipment and plant engineer, who helped design the building.

Located on a 12½-acre site in an industrial park that is ideally situated to reduce deadhead mileage, the Merivale center has 167,000 sq. ft. of floor space.

Facilities for training drivers and mechanics were incorporated into the second floor of the front office, which has a smooth, white-concrete, sandwich-panel exterior that is set off with dark-brown, anodized-aluminum moldings.

The glassed-in, centrally located foreman's office

serves as a "nerve center." From it, the foreman can oversee virtually all work areas and readily check work in progress. A lighted graphic panel on his wall indicates which of the pre-programmed, timer-controlled heating units are operating. And a similar panel permits lights to be shut off in all areas of the building, except for a skeleton lighting pattern that is always kept on.

Although built to handle 200 buses today, the new garage was designed for the addition of another bay for 60 more buses. All facilities and services have been sized for the ultimate 260-bus capacity.

Land cost was $660,000; architect and engineering expenses added $320,000; and construction ran to $3,950,000 (Canadian).

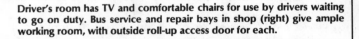
Driver's room has TV and comfortable chairs for use by drivers waiting to go on duty. Bus service and repair bays in shop (right) give ample working room, with outside roll-up access door for each.

Southern California Rapid Transit Dist. West Hollywood maintenance and transportation facility, Los Angeles, Calif.
Architects: Ralph M. Parsons Co.
Contractors: Steed Bros. Construction

Multi-level vehicle maintenance buildings are uncommon these days. But a handsome, four-level structure solved the problem of replacing an obsolete facility for an expanding fleet in the densely populated West Hollywood section of Los Angeles.

Built on a 9-acre site, the new Division 7 headquarters houses, operates, and services 250 transit buses. Measuring 504 ft. long and 81 ft. deep., the reinforced-concrete building, with its textured unpainted concrete and bronzed glass exterior, fits well into its environment.

Combining a fully equipped bus-maintenance shop, maintenance office, bus-operator facilities, and offices, plus two levels of automobile parking, the West Hollywood building has a 32,472-sq.-ft. ground-level shop. Designed with pull-in access to the bus-repair bay through roll-up doors that extend the length of the shop,

Built on a hillside, West Hollywood facility has a large adjoining parking lot for bus storage. Other side of building from photo view borders a major boulevard and has ramps for pedestrian access to the two upper parking levels used by employes.

Billiard tables provide recreation and relaxation for off-duty drivers in driver's lounge area. Tables can be used for eating snacks or writing reports. Room has wall-to-wall carpeting, which reduces the sound level.

the ground-level shop has 12 hydraulic lifts and six pits.

Because Los Angeles occasionally gets some chilly weather (and an unprecedented heavy snow one winter), the shop is equipped with high-bay spot heaters. Overhead exhaust-removal lines at each work location keep the shop free of exhaust fumes.

The second level houses transportation dispatch and administrative offices for the 11 RTD lines that operate from Division 7 and the 348 bus operators based there.

The third and fourth levels provide 220 parking spaces for employe cars; an additional 56 ground-level parking spaces accommodate RTD and visitors' cars.

A separate, four-bay fuel and vacuum building houses the four service lanes, a storage area for cash-vault carts, fuel pumps, the cyclone (vacuum) for cleaning bus interiors, and restrooms.

Yet another separate building houses a tire room, an automatic bus washer, and a high-capacity steam cleaner for cleaning buses and parts. Bus-wash water is clarified and recycled.

A 75-KW standby diesel generator provides full fueling capability and lighting should urgent repairs be needed during emergencies.

Total cost of the facility, which contains 131,348 sq. ft. of shop, office, parking, fueling, and cleaning space, came to $5.94-million, of which $4.42-million was for construction.

The major problems overcome in design and construction were the relatively small, narrow hillside plot, the proximity of residences, and limited access to adjacent streets. Because no additional space is available, there is no provision for expansion.

Central Pinellas
Transit Authority

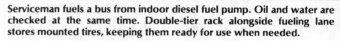
Serviceman fuels a bus from indoor diesel fuel pump. Oil and water are checked at the same time. Double-tier rack alongside fueling lane stores mounted tires, keeping them ready for use when needed.

**Central Pinellas Transit Authority
headquarters and maintenance shop,
Clearwater, Fla.
Architects: Henderson, Ames,
Bortles & Assoc.
Contractors: F.J. Ward & Assoc.**

Well planned expansion provided Central Pinellas Transit Authority with the additional shop, office space, and vehicle-parking area it needed to keep up with its transit-bus-system growth.

The Authority increased shop space by 3,220 sq. ft., and office space by 968 sq. ft. at its headquarters near the St. Petersburg-Clearwater International Airport. The original shop had 9,740 sq. ft., and the office 2,684 sq. ft. in a masonry-and-steel building erected in 1973. The present expansion, completed in January 1979, added two bus-repair bays to the original five bays, and provided needed parts-stockroom area.

Because the 8½-acre site originally granted the Author-

Pleasant, park-like grounds enhance the appearance of the pre-engineered building, improving its community image (below). Mechanic in shop tunes engine of a mini-bus, using modern test and diagnostic equipment (far left).

Bus is raised on hydraulic lift during regularly scheduled inspection and PM service. Lube and transmission-fluid reels alongside the lift speed service and reduce costs by dispensing products from bulk storage. Lift eliminates hazard of in-floor pit.

ity by the County Commission provided ample room for expansion, there was no land-acquisition cost. However, grading, base, and construction work cost $42,485; architectural engineering came to $13,256; and construction ran to $174,407, for a total of $230,148 for the 33.7% increase in building area.

Operating department personnel at the expanded facility include 65 bus drivers, six administrators, five clerical workers, and six dispatchers and local supervisors. Another 12 people work in the bus-maintenance shop, parts room, and other sections of the maintenance department.

Pointing out the value of foresight in planning, Boyd F.

Duncan, superintendent of maintenance for the Authority, says, "The original building was designed for easy expansion." During the expansion, the old outside wall panels of the steel shop section were transferred to the new outside wall, with a significant construction-cost saving.

"The new parts room is designed for easy expansion to double its size at no new cost," says Duncan. "And the building can continue to be expanded as needed."

A security fence surrounds the building site, and its gates are locked at night. The facility operates 24 hours a day, so it is never unattended, reducing potential vandalism and theft problems.

Fleet Designed Shop Proves Its Worth

The new facilities of Schmidt Baking Co., Fullerton, Md., smoothly and efficiently combine the diverse elements essential to a corporate headquarters, a truck loading station, and a fleet maintenance shop.

Designed by Charles E. Marquette, transportation manager, the building is a long, narrow rectangle, dictated by lot size and building code requirements. Located on a hilltop, the land had originally been purchased for the construction of a loading station and a small two-bay truck stop. Corporate headquarters and the main fleet maintenance shop were then located at the main baking plant in Baltimore.

Company expansion and other problems brought a change in plans, and Marquette was asked to revise the original design to include the general offices and main fleet shop at the new location. The final design incorporated the fleet shop attached to the east end of the loading station and general office section.

After Marquette completed the final design, actual construction drawings and engineering details were handled by Faisant Associates, Inc., consulting engineers, Baltimore. The general contractor was Colwill Construction Co., also in Baltimore.

The shop is a rectangle measuring 98 ft, 8 in. long by 58 ft wide. Six vehicle service bays are along the north side of the shop with a modern paint booth behind the last service bay. A two-story service core containing parts and tire storage areas, washroom, and locker room is located along the south wall.

Marquette's office is at the end of the general office area. It overlooks the shop through a large window. His observation and supervision of the shop is further improved by the difference in floor level between the shop and general office area. The shop floor is four ft lower due to the slope of the lot. The window in Marquette's office and the door leading to the shop from the office area corridor are both protected by automatic fire doors.

The adjoining office—occupied by Marquette's secretary, Mrs. Loretta Pearsonette—has two unusual features. There is a large window overlooking the refueling station and an intercom that permits drivers to converse with Mrs. Pearsonette. The fuel pump is equipped with a Tele-Controlator made by Aerotron, Inc., with the controls located in Mrs. Pearsonette's office.

As a driver stops at the pump, he announces his arrival on the intercom and Mrs. Pearsonette turns on the pump control unit and notes the truck number on the daily fuel report sheet. The fuel pumped is recorded on the Tele-Controlator console dial and this is recorded on the report when the driver has completed fueling. In case of trouble with the control unit, a manual back-up system takes over.

Another feature of Mrs. Pearsonette's office is a service drawer similar to those in drive-in bank teller cages. If a driver has a mechanical problem with his truck, he

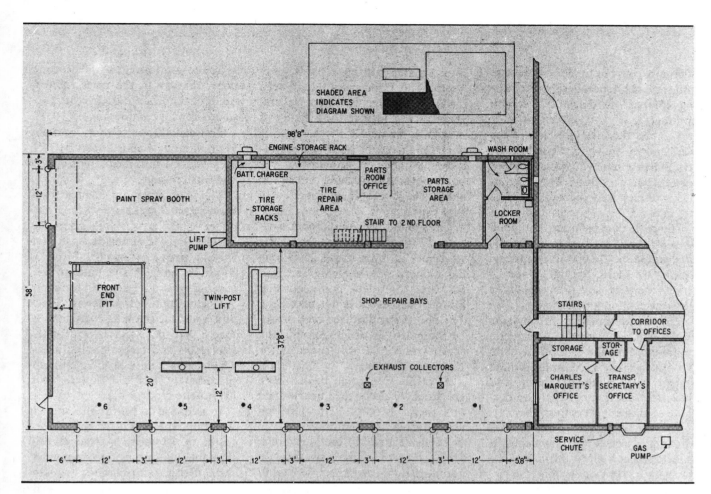

SHADED AREA
INDICATES
DIAGRAM SHOWN

98'8"

ENGINE STORAGE RACK

WASH ROOM

BATT. CHARGER

PARTS ROOM OFFICE

PAINT SPRAY BOOTH

TIRE STORAGE RACKS

TIRE REPAIR AREA

PARTS STORAGE AREA

12'

LOCKER ROOM

LIFT PUMP

STAIR TO 2ND FLOOR

58'

FRONT END PIT

TWIN-POST LIFT

SHOP REPAIR BAYS

STAIRS

4'

37'8"

CORRIDOR TO OFFICES

STORAGE

STORAGE

20'

12'

EXHAUST COLLECTORS

CHARLES MARQUETT'S OFFICE

TRANSP. SECRETARY'S OFFICE

*6   *5   *4   *3   *2   *1

SERVICE CHUTE

GAS PUMP

6'   12'   3'   12'   3'   12'   3'   12'   3'   12'   3'   12'   5'8"

notifies Mrs. Pearsonette over the intercome and she passes him a pad of driver report forms through the service drawer. The driver can complete the form while his truck is being refueled, and return it to Mrs. Pearsonette before leaving.

In the shop there is ample working room in each of the service bays. Marquette pointed out that the service bays are 37 ft, 8 in. long and 15 ft wide. This gives excellent working space around the walk-in van route trucks. The shop also maintains company cars but the leased tractors and trailers are handled by the leasing company under a full service contract.

The first three service bays in the west end of the shop are served by two exhaust removal system outlets installed in the floor. The exhaust

Schmidt's maintenance shop is 98 ft long by 58 ft wide, features two floors and concrete block construction, and has six service bays—three large, three small—on the north side.

hoses retract into the outlets when not in use.

The next two bays are equipped with Weaver twin post hydraulic lifts, rated at 36,000 lb capacity. These are used for all types of chassis repairs and for scheduled

PM services and lubrication.

The Lincoln shop lubrication equipment is portable. Marquette comments that the size of the shop did not justify a centralized lube system with overhead piping and reels, and pointed out that the por-

Small parts and fast-moving items are keep handy in bins or trays at Schmidt Bakery's maintenance shop in Fullerton, Md.

A second-floor parts room, serviced by stairs and a power hoist, is used for storage of heavy parts such as transmissions.

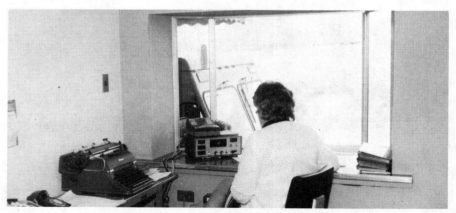

A window overlooking the refueling station and an intercom permits drivers to converse with office personnel. Drivers can also drop-off mechanical defect reports at this window.

table equipment gives flexibility.

The last bay in the shop houses an Ammco wheel alignment rack. It is installed in a pit at the end of the bay with a safety rail around the pit.

Between the front-end rack pit and the outside door, a clear area 20 ft long allows use of this bay for other jobs when the front-end rack is not in use.

At the rear of the lift in the fifth service bay, an Ammco toe-in checker is installed in the floor. Marquette explains that most PM service and driver steering complaints are handled here.

If the mechanic's examination or the reading on the toe-in gage shows the need for a complete front-end alignment, it is easy to move the

truck to the adjoining bay without affecting any other jobs in progress.

A Schildmeier Seal Line wheel balancer is also installed in the sixth bay, near the wheel alignment rack. Wheels are removed from a vehicle, mounted on the machine and spun at high speed to determine the amount and location of unbalance.

Beyond the front-end alignment pit is an area housing a paint spray booth. The Binks booth had been installed within the past several years at the former shop and was moved to the new shop. A separate door for the paint booth allows vehicles to move in and out of the booth without disturbing other shop work. The booth is equipped with Binks spray guns.

The ground floor parts room measures 17 ft wide by 51 ft long. In the west end, an area about 20 ft long has modern steel shelving and bins for parts. Marquette points out that a large parts stock is not necessary.

The fleet is standardized on Chevrolet route delivery trucks except for a small group of Ford trucks at the Tasley, Va. station.

A large Chevrolet dealer with good delivery service is nearby and a General Motors Parts Division warehouse is near Baltimore.

At the east end of the parts room are storage racks for new tires. In addition to those racks, two additional racks located near bays one, two, and three store mounted spare tires. Next to the parts room tire racks is an area where tires are dismounted, repaired and remounted.

Along the south wall of the parts room is a double tier rack for storage of rebuilt engines. Next to the engine storage rack is the Marquette Model 36-100 battery charger. A large exhaust fan in the wall near the charger removes any fumes. Another fan is located at the opposite end of the parts room.

A second floor level above the parts room is reached by a stairway. The second floor area stores bulky, slower-moving parts and components such as rebuilt transmissions. A door opening in the wall overlooking the main shop floor can be used to hoist heavy items to the second floor when desired.

Space underneath the second floor stairway in the parts room is used for the Champion five-hp, two-stage shop air compressor.

Between the parts room and the main building wall is a 10 ft by 17 ft area divided into mechanic's locker and wash rooms.

The shop does not have a truck wash room. Trucks are washed outdoors on the paved area surrounding the shop. If an inside wash area should prove necessary later, it could be built in the parking and loading area or adjacent to the shop.

Custon-built of concrete block and brick, the building cost approximately $10 per square foot for the fleet shop and truck loading areas. The general office section cost approximately $14 per square foot, Marquette reports.

In addition to Marquette and his secretary, the new fleet shop has a roster of 10 men. Marquette said they include one working foreman, three first class mechanics, two second class mechanics, two mechanic's helpers, one combination painter and body repair man, and a parts clerk who helps in the shop when he is not needed in the parts room.

Also, at all but one fleet location, there is a shop to service the route trucks based there. Marquette listed the number of trucks at each location and the personnel based in the branch shops:

• Baltimore, Md.—61 trucks; 1 working foreman, 2 mechanics, 1 washer and 1 utility man.

• Cumberland, Md.—25 trucks; 1 full time mechanic plus a part time mechanic.

• Martinsburg, W. Va.—45 trucks; 3 full-time mechanics.

• Johnstown, Pa.—22 trucks; 1 full-time mechanic.

• York, Pa.—20 trucks; 1 full-time mechanic.

• Forestville, Md.—16 trucks; 1 full-time mechanic.

• The Seaford, Del. station with 16 trucks and the Tasley, Va. station with 8 trucks are handled by a shop in Seaford, staffed by a full time mechanic and a helper.

• Forty-one trucks are based at the new Fullerton station.

Marquette said the new Fullerton shop does all major repairs for the trucks based at the Baltimore plant and the Forestville and York stations. The other shops do most types of maintenance and repairs including replacement of engines or transmissions. But components are not overhauled in those shops; they are returned to the Fullerton shop.

For major body repairs or complete repainting, a vehicle comes to the Fullerton shop. A spare truck is sent to take its place until the repairs are completed.

Since very little work is farmed out, the shop is well equipped. In addition to the major items already mentioned, the shop has these additional items: Marquette oxy-acetylene welding outfit; Marquette electric arc welder; Acco manual geartype arbor press; AC spark plug cleaner; Dayton ¾ hp bench grinder; Weaver headlight tester and aimer; Murphy portable shop crane with 1,500 lb capacity; Murphy hydraulic arbor press with 25 tons capacity; Weaver four-ton floor jack; Gray Mills parts cleaner; Buffalo floor type drill-press; and an AC-GM tune up and diagnostic analyzer.

Marquette credits the analyzer with reducing maintenance cost and labor. "We're not doing any more 'B' inspections," he said. "We put the analyzer on during an 'A' inspection—if everything checks out okay, we let the truck go until the 'C' inspection."

Marquette concedes that he had to disregard some generally accepted tenets during the design of the shop. For example, the shop's six roll up-doors for the service bays are on the north side of the building—the coldest place in winter. But the door location was necessary to avoid interference with the tractors and trailers using the loading dock.

However, he did not neglect provision for future expansion. The building location on the lot gives room to extend the shop on the east end when needed. He points out, "Also, we can make the truck parking and loading area longer without interfering with shop operations or expansion."

YANKEE INGENUITY BUILDS A BUS SHOP

It may still use 'street railway' in its name, but this New England bus fleet didn't indulge in nostalgia when it recently built a modern, efficient shop-and-terminal complex.

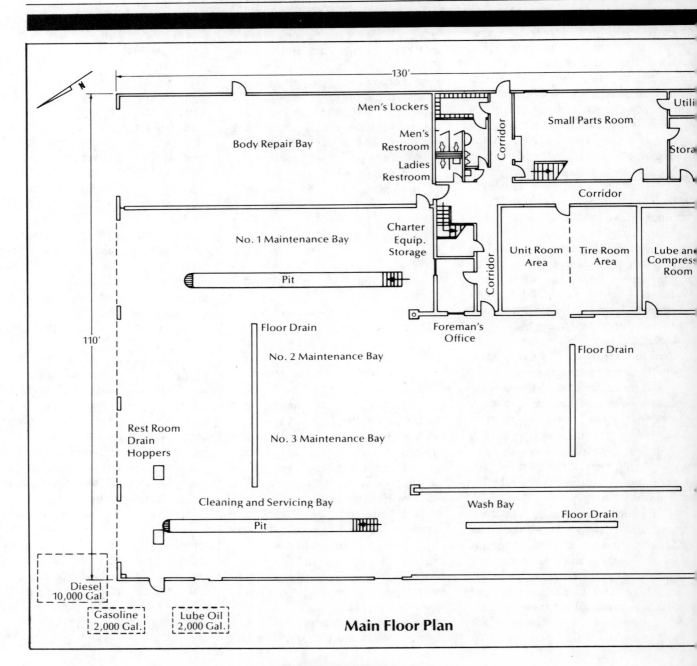

Main Floor Plan

Well-equipped body shop (left) handles all types of body work except major wrecks. View from a hilltop bordering the property (below) shows shop building at right, with general offices and passenger terminal at left. Floor plan of both shop floors and plot plan (left, below) show efficiency of the design.

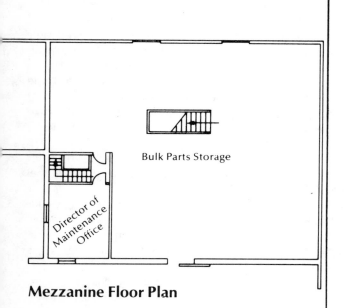

Bulk Parts Storage

Director of Maintenance Office

Mezzanine Floor Plan

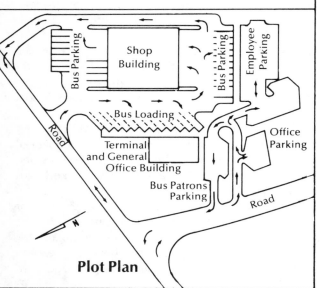

Bus Parking

Shop Building

Bus Parking

Employee Parking

Bus Loading

Road

Terminal and General Office Building

Office Parking

Bus Patrons Parking

Road

N

Plot Plan

The Plymouth & Brockton Street Railway Co., Plymouth, Mass., retains its inter-urban streetcar heritage—but lives in the present. It displayed its contemporary thinking when it recently moved into a highly efficient, handsome shop and terminal complex for its fleet of modern buses.

Operating intercity service from Plymouth to Brockton and Boston and halfway the length of Cape Cod, plus nationwide charter service, Plymouth and Brockton runs 49 intercity and suburban motor coaches plus two shop service trucks and several company cars.

However, the new shop serves a larger "clientele," according to Nate Wilhelm, director of maintenance. The shop does major engine replacement and some smaller jobs for two other charter fleets, Brush Hill Transportation Co., Dorchester, Mass., with 31 intercity buses; and McGinn Bus Co., Inc. Lynn, Mass., with 13. All three lines, plus Brush Hill Autobody Co., Roxbury, Mass., with 124 school buses and North Shore Bus Co., Revere, Mass., with 32 school buses are owned by individual members of the same family. Each of the other bus properties has its own garage and maintenance shop, but Plymouth and Brockton purchases tires and some parts items for all.

The new P & B shop, which replaces an outmoded facility in downtown Plymouth, not far from famed Plymouth Rock, is in a newly established industrial park bordering Mass. Rt. 3. The passenger terminal and general offices building is adjacent to the shop.

The American pre-engineered steel shop building was erected by Atlantic Building Systems, Plymouth Mass. Consulting engineer (and architect) is Richard Rock, Braintree, Mass. Wilhelm himself was also responsible for much of the shop design.

Because of the compact size of the building (see drawing) it was impractical to locate a "service core" in the customary center area, Wilhelm points out. So it was located in a corner but with the foremen's office and Wilhelm's directly above. Both overlook the maintenance bays, for supervision.

Parts stock rooms include a ground floor dispensing

By Jack Lyndall, senior editor/equipment

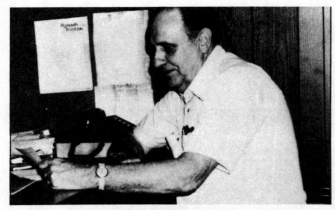

Nate Wilhelm studies a repair order in the foremen's office in shop's service core. Wilhelm's own office is on the second floor.

area for fast-moving small parts, and a second floor room for larger, heavier parts.

There is room in the rebuild area to handle transmissions and differentials plus some smaller components. Engine rebuilding is sent out, and diesel fuel injectors are exchanged for rebuilt or new injectors. Major tire repairs are also sent out.

Somewhat unusual in the bus industry, Plymouth & Brockton and its affiliated fleets own, rather than lease, their tires. Oliver retreading is done on sound, smooth tire casings.

Another innovation appears in the large body repair bay, which gives ample working area around a bus. Wilhelm says that plans call for building a balcony level above the inner 30 or 35 ft. of the body repair bay for storage of bulky body parts and panels and some infrequently used tools.

Along with its full complement of both electric and oxy-acetylene welding equipment and tools, the body repair bay also has a new Kansas Jack "Power Post" chassis and body straightener. Anchors for that equipment were set in the concrete floor.

The No. 1 maintenance bay pit is brightly lighted with explosion proof fixtures and has compressed air, chassis lube, and gear oil piped in. A water drainage system keeps the pit dry and it has an OSHA-required chain guard that is erected when the pit is not in use.

Flanking that bay is a pair of full length, drive-through bays extending the length of the building

The lube storage and air compressor room runs alongside the north end of No. 2 bay, and also has a wide outside door for receiving deliveries of chassis lube, Dexron automatic-transmission fluid, and rear axle or manual transmission gear oil in 55 gal. drums.

Those products are pumped throughout the shop's centralized lube system by three Grover and one Graco air powered pumps. Wilhelm said that motor oil is stored in a 2,000-gal. underground tank.

The shop's two air compressor tanks are interconnected to provide one large air reserve. The primary compressor is a Westinghouse 10 hp. horizontal model; a Gilbarco 5 hp. vertical model operates as a stand-by.

As buses enter from the south end of the shop, they pass over the rest room servicing hopper in the floor.

Another rest room hopper is in the floor at the south end of No. 3 maintenance bay.

Just beyond in the servicing area of the bay are dual diesel fuel dispensing hoses that can fuel a bus from either side. That area also has an in-floor pit, a duplicate of the one in No. 1 maintenance bay.

Located alongside the servicing lane, between that lane and No. 3 maintenance bay, is an overhead bank of hose reels that dispense motor oil, transmission and rear axle gear lube, and automatic transmission fluid. A similar overhead reel set up is located between No. 1 and 2 maintenance bays. Both pits have waste oil drain funnels and swivel piping that carries waste oil to a 1,500 gal. underground storage tank. The waste oil is pumped out periodically by a waste oil collection service.

From the servicing area, a bus moves on to the Ross and White automatic washer. It is a wrap-around brush type that also washes the front and rear of a bus.

A low masonry wall with translucent corrugated panels protects No. 3 maintenance bay from water splash and spray, and also reduces loss of warm air during winter when buses leave the wash bay.

Stored between No. 3 maintenance bay and the servicing-cleaning bay were a "Jenny" steam cleaner and a set of 4 Hywema portable vehicle lifts (one bus). There are also 12 Hywema lift stands (three buses) for holding a bus for extended periods.

In addition to the lube and waste oil tanks, the shop also has underground tanks for 20,000 gal. of diesel fuel and 2,000 gal. of gasoline.

Heating in the maintenance bays and servicing-cleaning bay comes from overhead gas unit heaters; offices, parts room, rest rooms and unit room plus the busy repair bays are heated with forced hot air from a gas fired furnace.

The shop staff totals 20, not including Wilhelm. There are two shift foremen, five first class mechanics, three body repairmen, four washers, two bus interior cleaners, one parts clerk, one purchasing agent, and two lubrication men. The shop operates two shifts.

The modern terminal and office building includes a comfortable passenger waiting room, adjoining ticket office, general offices, a driver's room, and a baggage and package express room. The latter has outside doors opening onto the bus loading area.

Although the shop capacity is adequate, Wilhelm says that an additional small building is planned for storage of rebuilt components such as the four space engines and four space transmissions that are normally stocked, plus rebuilt differentials and other components.

There is room for future additional parking areas for buses, employees, or bus patrons. The bus parking area bordering the shop on the south side has 16 electric outlets for plugging in engine block heaters in winter. Wilhelm notes that all buses in the fleet are equipped with such heaters.

TORONTO'S BUS GARAGE ON THE LAKE

New bus garage has four 20-ft-wide lanes for fast service, and is designed to conserve both worker time and heat-input energy.

Located on a seven-acre site close to Lake Ontario, about six miles from downtown Toronto, Ontario, the new Lakeshore Garage recently opened by Gray Coach Lines Ltd., a private, wholly owned subsidiary of the Toronto Transit Commission, is designed to handle all regular service and repairs to Gray Coach's fleet of 160 intercity buses as well as many "foreign" buses.

The nearby Gardiner Expressway, Don Valley Park-
by Jack Lyndall, senior editor

way, and other major traffic arteries provide good access to the new garage, which replaces the old, recently razed Sherbourne St. garage.

The 165-ft.-wide x 275-ft.-long rectangular garage, a Butler pre-engineered steel building erected by Inter-Construction Co., Mississauga, Ontario, provides 52,000 sq. ft. of garage space plus 4,400 sq. ft. of space on each floor of the two-story office section.

Built at a cost of $4.3-million (Canadian), the facility operates on a three-shift basis, 24 hours a day, under the supervision of Bob Auld, resident superintendent for the Toronto Transit Commission, who was also primarily responsible for the garage's design. T.J. Galinis is director of equipment and garage services for Gray Coach Lines.

The garage's employee roster totals 65, not including office/administrative personnel or drivers.

Three-part maintenance area

The garage's maintenance area is divided into three sections: repair bays, central service area, and bus-servicing area. Each runs the length of the building.

The main bus repair bay area, 66 ft. wide x 229 ft.

long, contains 12 repair bays. Ten bays are 18½ ft. wide, two are 22 ft. wide, and all of them are 66 ft. long, providing ample working space around the buses, even allowing for a walkway area at the inner end of each.

Ten of the bays are equipped with twin-post hydraulic lifts, and there are two portable hydraulic-lift outfits (see list of shop equipment). Adjacent bays in which major inspections and running repairs are made are served by a bank of overhead reels that dispense motor oil, transmission fluid, premixed antifreeze and water, chassis grease, and compressed air.

Roll-up doors for each of the bays are electrically

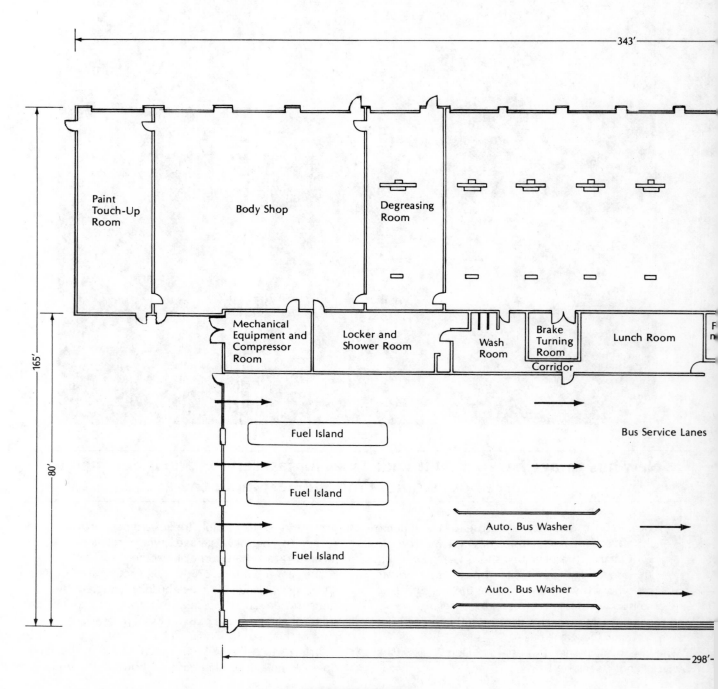

powered with manual controls.

At the north end of the repair bay area is a 24x66-ft. degreasing bay that is fully enclosed and has an exterior roll-up door. In that bay are a steam cleaner (with a long wand for under-body cleaning), a large dip tank for cleaning small parts, and a twin-post hydraulic lift to raise a bus for cleaning the under-body and chassis area.

Next to the degreasing room is a 66x66-ft., three-bay body shop, which is equipped for all minor body repairs. And next to the body shop is a 24x66-ft. paint touch-up room where all repaired body areas are repainted. Complete bus repainting can also be done, if necessary.

Running like a spine down the length of the building is a row of offices and service rooms. At the north end, flanking the body shop, is a 20x26-ft. mechanical equipment room, which houses the shop's two big air compressors, a large hot-water heater, and pumps for the centralized antifreeze- and lubricant-dispensing system.

Then comes a 20x43-ft. shop-mechanics' locker and shower room. Adjacent to it is the men's wash room.

Adjacent to the wash room, and close to the four repair bays where most brake overhaul is done, is the brake-turning room. Here, brake shoes are relined and ground to match brake drums that have been turned on

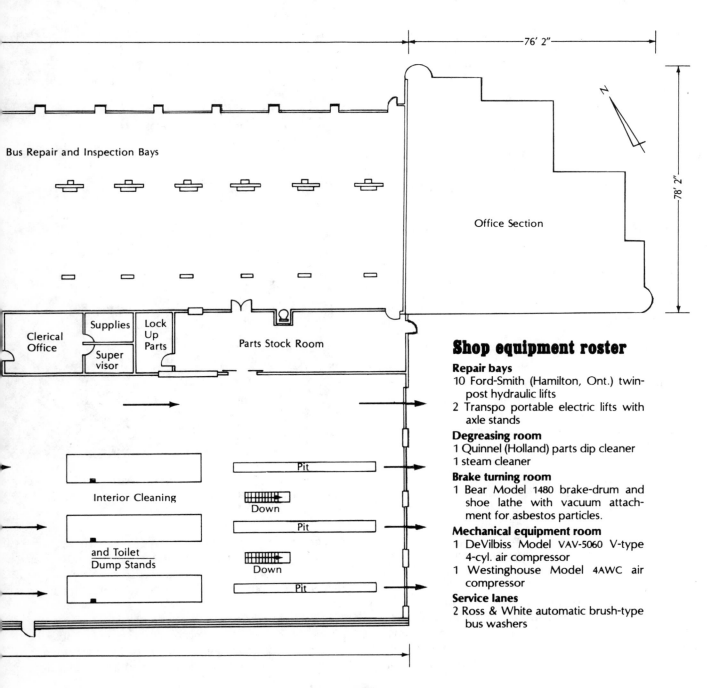

Bus Repair and Inspection Bays

Office Section

76' 2"

78' 2"

Clerical Office

Supplies

Super visor

Lock Up Parts

Parts Stock Room

Interior Cleaning

and Toilet Dump Stands

Pit

Down

Pit

Down

Pit

Shop equipment roster

Repair bays
10 Ford-Smith (Hamilton, Ont.) twin-post hydraulic lifts
2 Transpo portable electric lifts with axle stands

Degreasing room
1 Quinnel (Holland) parts dip cleaner
1 steam cleaner

Brake turning room
1 Bear Model 1480 brake-drum and shoe lathe with vacuum attachment for asbestos particles.

Mechanical equipment room
1 DeVilbiss Model VAV-5060 V-type 4-cyl. air compressor
1 Westinghouse Model 4AWC air compressor

Service lanes
2 Ross & White automatic brush-type bus washers

the drum lathe.

Next comes a 20x38-ft. lunchroom, which has full kitchen facilities for mechanics who wish to prepare their own lunches or heat meals brought from home. (A corridor behind the brake-turning room connects the lunch room and the wash room.)

South of the lunch room is the 10x14-ft. office of the shift foreman, who gets a good view of both the repair bays and the bus-servicing area through windows in three of the office's walls. Facing the foreman's office is the shop clerk's 20x24-ft. office. With windows in three walls, it, too, commands a view of both work areas.

Opening off the clerk's office is a 9x15-ft. private office for the service-lanes supervisor. Flanking his office is a store room for stationary, forms, and various shop supplies.

The remainder of the central spine is occupied by the parts department and is divided into a 20x73-ft. main parts store room, which is equipped with steel shelves and bins, and an 11x20-ft. "lock up" room for locked storage of high-value items.

Four lanes provide fast service

The bus-servicing area, with its four 20-ft.-wide lanes, occupies the entire west side. At present, two lanes are equipped for full bus servicing, with fueling island, automatic bus washers, toilet dump and servicing, and inspection pits. The third lane lacks only an automatic washer; the fourth is used only for refueling. (All four lanes can be converted to full servicing.)

Alongside each service lane are overhead reels that dispense motor oil, transmission fluid, and premixed antifreeze and water.

Buses in need of servicing enter the facility from the main (and only) entrance, drive along the east side of the building past the repair bay area, and then make a U-turn to enter the service lanes.

To save time and heat in cold weather—an important consideration in Toronto—the entrance doors to the service lanes on the north end are controlled by electronic loops and activated by photocells. As a bus approaches a door, the door automatically opens. In case of malfunction, doors can be opened manually.

After buses have been fueled and washed, they move to the interior-cleaning and toilet-dump area. Here, instead of the conventional telescoping funnel for draining the bus' toilet tank (which requires precise bus positioning), there is an easily rinsed, sloped floor area that drains to a sewer outlet. To ensure complete emptying of the tank, special wheel ramps (poured integral with the floor) raise the bus' left rear wheel(s) and tilt the bus to the right.

Next stop is over one of the three in-floor inspection pits, each of which is 3½ ft. wide x 45 ft. long and is linked with the others by a wide sub-floor passageway that makes it possible for mechanics performing inspections or making repairs to move freely from one pit to

another. The passageway is wide enough to accommodate steel workbenches.

Because the underground water table is only 3 ft. or less below the garage floor, special waterproofing techniques were required when building the pits. (The garage site is filled ground that was once covered by the lake.) The waterproofing proved successful: the pits have yet to leak in the ten months the garage has been open.

Ontario law requires carbon-monoxide sensors at strategic locations in the service-lane section. Should a sensor detect a high concentration of CO in the air, ventilating air flow is automatically increased. However, because

of the near-zero CO content of diesel exhaust, the system has yet to function in other than the test mode.

Heating the garage in winter

Two overhead makeup-air heaters heat the bus repair bays during the winter, and a similar heater near the center of the bus-servicing area provides heat for those lanes.

In addition, there is a makeup-air heater above the diesel-fuel pumps. But, because of fire regulations, the heater, whose operation is linked to the door-opening controls, is mounted outside on the roof. When a door opens in cold weather, the heater comes on automatically and directs a curtain of hot air downward to keep cold outside air from entering the service lane.

All of the garage's heaters are fired by natural gas.

On-site traffic flow: a U pattern

Because of the relatively long, rectangular site with single street frontage, bus traffic follows a U pattern. Buses enter the property from the street and move either along the east-side boundary into the repair bays or on around the north end to enter the service lanes.

From the service lanes buses are then driven to the

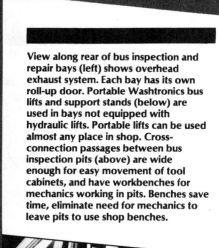

View along rear of bus inspection and repair bays (left) shows overhead exhaust system. Each bay has its own roll-up door. Portable Washtronics bus lifts and support stands (below) are used in bays not equipped with hydraulic lifts. Portable lifts can be used almost any place in shop. Cross-connection passages between bus inspection pits (above) are wide enough for easy movement of tool cabinets, and have workbenches for mechanics working in pits. Benches save time, eliminate need for mechanics to leave pits to use shop benches.

"ready coaches" parking area near the street. From there, they leave via the exit gate.

Buses leaving the repair bays can move around the building into the service lanes or proceed directly to the "ready coaches" parking area.

Buses awaiting repairs or scheduled inspections park along the east-side fence, toward the north, or back, end of the site. Additional bus parking space is located at the north end, opposite the service-lane entrances.

Expansion of the garage, when and if necessary, will take place at the north end, still leaving a large parking area. Also, a tract of land bordering the site on the east may soon be available.

A SMALL SHOP WITH BIG IDEAS

Working efficiency and good design with compact dimensions are hallmarks of the new Hubler Rentals Inc. shop and truck rental facility in Wilkes-Barre, Pa. The neat, moderately sized shop building replaces a facility completely destroyed by the floods of tropical storm Agnes in 1972.

Operating basically as a branch of the main Hubler Rentals headquarters shop in Allentown, Pa., some 65 miles south of Wilkes-Barre, the new shop maintains and services 135 vehicles based there.

The shop was designed and built by Pace Construction Corp., Allentown, Pa. The cost was approximately $90,000, exclusive of land.

According to Michael T. Welles, station manager for the new facility, the Wilkes-Barre fleet comprises 79 transient rental trucks, tractors, and trailers plus 53 long-term, full-service lease units. There are also two shop service trucks plus a company car assigned to Welles. He reports that the truck fleet is composed primarily of Mack tractors powered with Maxidyne engines, Strick trailers, and Ford and International straight trucks.

General Description and Site

Located on a two-acre site on Second Avenue in Plains Township, centered in a rapidly growing light

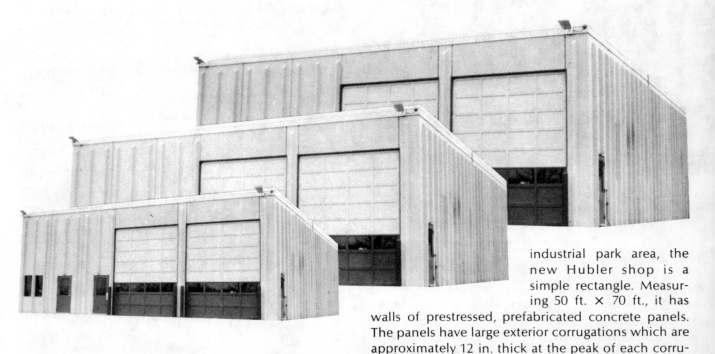

industrial park area, the new Hubler shop is a simple rectangle. Measuring 50 ft. × 70 ft., it has walls of prestressed, prefabricated concrete panels. The panels have large exterior corrugations which are approximately 12 in. thick at the peak of each corrugation. Welles comments that the wall panels were hauled to the site by truck and quickly erected.

The interior shop floor space is divided into approximately 2,350 sq. ft. for two drive-through service bays, 420 sq. ft. for offices, shower, and restrooms, and 540 sq. ft. for an area used for tire storage and repairs, unit overhaul, and storage for shop equipment.

As shown by the plot plan, the building is located close to the northern boundary of the site. This leaves an area 30 ft. wide between the south wall of the building and the other site boundary for the fuel pump island and driveways to the rear parking and storage area.

Drive-Through Service Bays

Two drive-through service bays occupy about two-thirds of the building on the south side. Each bay is 16 ft. wide and extends the full 70-ft. length of the building. This allows each bay to handle two straight trucks, three tractors, or a tractor-trailer unit at one time.

The bay near the center of the building also has an added 1½ ft. of walk space next to the office and restroom section.

Located between the two bays is an Alemite overhead reel system that services both bays. The system has five reels for compressed air, water, motor oil, gear oil, and chassis lube.

Welles reports that the motor oil is pumped from a 2,000-gal. capacity underground tank. The gear oil and chassis lube are pumped by Alemite air pumps

from 55-gal. drums placed against the north wall of the building.

Electrically powered rollup doors are used at both ends of each bay. Welles says the doors are 12 ft. wide and 15 ft. high, enough to provide ample clearance for a 13½ ft.-high trailer. In case of a power failure, the doors can be manually operated.

The bays do not have pits or lifts. Hydraulic floor jacks are used for lifting vehicle wheels or axles for repairs or servicing.

The generous width of the bays allows space for a steel work bench and storage of mechanic's roller cabinet tool chests along the south wall of the shop. Several large windows in that wall plus glass panels in the rollup doors give good daylight illumination for the two service bays.

Office and Restroom Area

In the northwest corner of the building are two offices, each measuring 10 ft. x 15 ft. The one at the front (west) side of the building is for Joseph Pegarella, the truck rental manager.

Behind that office, and linked by a connecting doorway, is Welles's office. Both offices are tastefully finished with walnut paneling and are heated by electric heaters mounted on the wall. Each office also has a window-type air conditioner.

Next to Welles's office is a small private restroom for the office personnel. Measuring 4 ft x 5 ft., its en-

View across shop shows office complex with balcony parts rooms overhead. The shop foremen's desk is next to the service manager's office.

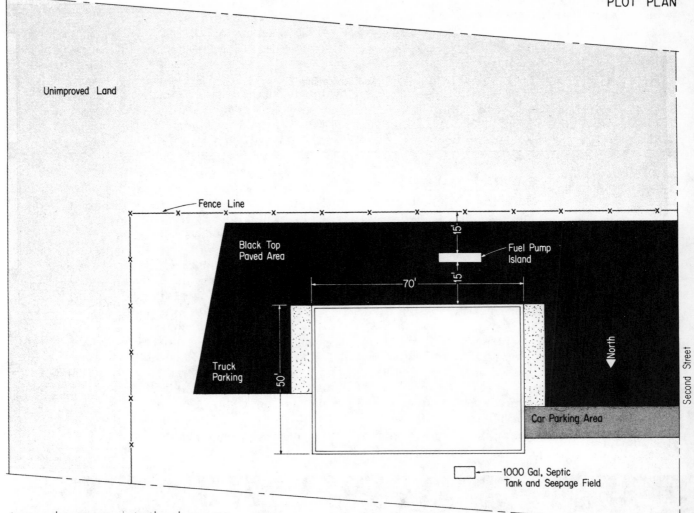

Unimproved Land

Fence Line

Black Top
Paved Area

Fuel Pump
Island

15'

15'

70'

Truck
Parking

50'

North

Second Street

Car Parking Area

1000 Gal. Septic
Tank and Seepage Field

trance door opens into the shop area.

Alongside that door is another opening into a corridor leading to the mechanic's shower and restroom which measures 7½ ft. x 10 ft.

Bordering the mechanic's restroom is a flight of stairs leading to the balcony type parts storage area. Measuring approximately 15 ft. x 30 ft., the balcony extends over the entire main office and restroom area. It is protected by a strong railing and wire fence material on the side next to the shop service bay area and along the stair well.

Parts are stored on modern steel shelving plus hooks fitted into heavy-duty pegboard along the north wall. Mechanics' clothes lockers are next to the stair well since the downstairs shower and restroom lacks sufficient space for the lockers.

Welles estimates the parts inventory at $8,000 to $10,000. He says that is adequate since additional items or replacements are generally quickly available from local truck dealers and parts jobbers plus the stockroom at the main Hubler shop in Allentown.

Adjacent to the stairway leading to the parts storage balcony is a small office for Fred B. Jenkins, the

service manager. Although quite compact, measuring 5½ ft. x 7½ ft., the office has space for Jenkins's desk, a chair, and four-drawer .file cabinet for vehicle records. Like the other managers' offices, it is also walnut paneled.

Placed against the outer wall of the service manager's office is a stand-up desk for use by the two shift foremen.

Heating, Lighting, and Ventilation

Except for the offices and restrooms which are heated by the wall-mounted electric heaters, the main shop area is heated by two large oil-fired overhead unit heaters.

Lighting in the two drive-through bays and other shop areas is by mercury vapor lamps. The offices, restrooms, and parts-garage balcony have fluorescent lamp fixtures.

Both of the drive-through bays are served by an overhead exhaust removal duct and blower system. Engineered and supplied by the National System of

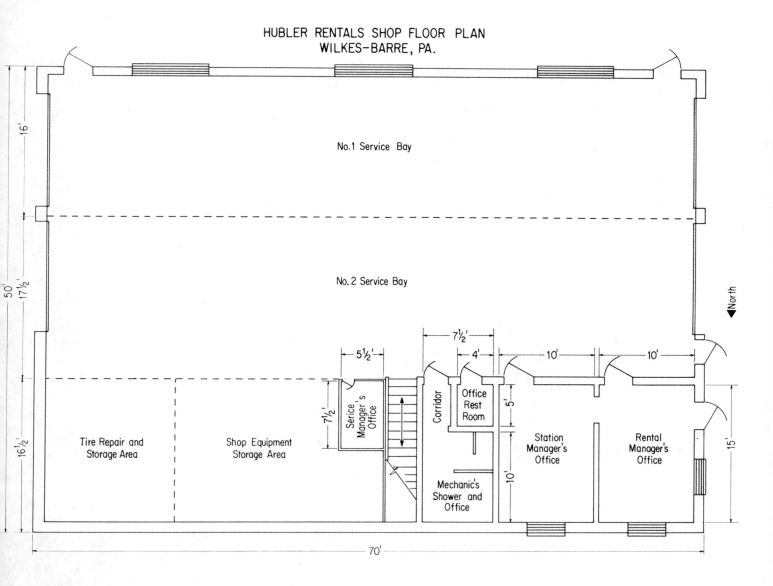

No.1 Service Bay

No. 2 Service Bay

Serice Manager's Office

Corridor

Office Rest Room

Mechanic's Shower and Office

Station Manager's Office

Rental Manager's Office

Tire Repair and Storage Area

Shop Equipment Storage Area

North

Garage Ventilation Inc., Decatur, Ill., the system has four large flexible drop hoses that can fit over the exhaust pipe of a vehicle at any point in either bay.

Tire Repair and Storage/Unit Rebuild Area

Extending along the north wall of the building from the office and restroom section to the rear wall is an open area. Measuring approximately 15½ ft. × 35 ft., this area is currently used for tire repair and storage plus rebuild of such components as engines, transmissions, or differentials.

However, Welles points out that in busy periods or when special equipment or tools are needed, components needing overhaul or rebuild are sent to the main Hubler Rentals shop in Allentown. On some popular items, the Allentown shop can make an immediate exchange for a rebuilt unit from its stock.

Shop Equipment

In addition to the overhead lubrication reel and exhaust removal systems which were installed new, Welles also pointed out a new air compressor. The

Rotunda (Ford) Model 5 TMA horizontal compressor has a 5-hp electric motor and a 2-cylinder, 2-stage pump. It is mounted on an elevated steel framework in the northeast corner of the tire repair and storage area.

The shop is quite well supplied with other equipment that was salvaged and transferred from the old shop. These items include an oxy-acetylene welding and cutting outfit, a Gates Solvo-Sink parts-cleaning machine, Ruger 2,300-lb. capacity portable hydraulic shop crane, Douglass Products Co. hydraulic transmission jack, Marquette 6-12-24-volt battery charger, and a brake lining riveting machine.

The tire repair area also has a tire dismounting machine and a tire inflation cage. Welles noted, as he pointed out the spare tires stacked in piles, that new tire storage racks were on order and would be installed as soon as received.

Personnel Roster

Welles reports that the personnel roster for the new Wilkes-Barre facility totals eight men. In addi-

Wide service bays provide storage room for mechanic's roller tool chests next to wall. Overhead pipe is part of exhaust duct system.

Future Expansion

Some added capacity was designed into the new shop, Welles reports. He says it is easily capable of servicing a fleet of 150 or more vehicles, 15 more than the present fleet size.

However, if expansion becomes necessary, Welles points out that the south wall of the building can be moved, adding at least one more drive-through bay. It would be necessary to move the fuel island nearer to the southern edge of the site but he says that was planned for in placing the underground fuel and oil storage tanks.

In addition, he notes that the existing parts-storage balcony can easily be extended over the entire tire repair and storage and unit rebuild area without interfering with those operations. If not entirely needed for additional parts storage, such a balcony extension could be partly used for a small-unit rebuild room, diesel injector service room, or other specialized repair department. The existing stairway could easily serve such an extension, also, with no problems.

There is also additional land at the rear of the site beyond the present blacktop paved area that can be cleared and paved for additional storage to match any future shop expansion.

Michael Welles; station manager, reviews vehicle records in his office. He has close working relations with the service manager.

tion to Welles, Pegarella, and Jenkins, there are five mechanics divided between two shifts.

There are three mechanics on the day shift and two on the night shift. One of the mechanics on each shift serves as a working foreman—Michael Berish Jr. on the day shift and John Wasta on the night shift.

As a measure of the competence of the shop force, Welles pointed out that the shop is a certified Pennsylvania Vehicle Inspection Station. At least two of the mechanics have passed the necessary qualification tests as vehicle inspectors.

The shop operates from 7:00 a.m. to 12:00 midnight from Monday through Friday and from 7:00 a.m. to 12:00 noon on Saturday.

Two fuel pumps, one for gasoline and one for diesel fuel, are on an island located about 15 ft. from the south side of the building. The island location permits trucks to be fueled when entering or leaving the side and rear yard parking area. The traffic flow pattern past the island also permits vehicles to enter the drive-through service bays from either end of the shop.

Photos by Jack Lyndall

New fleet shop expedites furniture hauls

By Jack Lyndall, Senior Editor

The new Schweiger Industries fleet shop provides the essential maintenance and repair support for a far-ranging fleet of 65 long haul diesel tractors, 139 trailers and 28 miscellaneous fleet vehicles and industrial units.

Located adjacent to Schweiger's new factory in Jefferson, Wis., the new shop replaces an outmoded and outgrown shop complex at the company's original factory nearby.

Drawing on lessons learned in the old shop and long years of fleet experience, original planning for the new shop was the work of a two-man team. These were Val Molzberger, fleet superintendent, and Thomas Lucas, operations manager of the Schweiger transportation division. Also in on the planning was Robert A. Bogan, transportation division controller.

The architect was the Vesperman Association, Fond du Lac, Wis., and the general contractor for the custom-built shop was Maas Brothers Construction Co., Watertown, Wis.

Containing approximately 16,000 sq. ft. of floor space, the shop was started in June, 1971. It was completed and occupied in February, 1972.

Molzberger reports the total cost of the new shop—exclusive of land—at approximately $387,000. He gave a breakdown of different cost items: building—$14,000; electrical system—$68,000; exhaust removal, lube and fuel dispensing systems—$28,000; new shop equipment—$24,000; building site preparation—$48,000.

The shop roster includes 18 hourly employees. Molzberger breaks the roster down into four first-class mechanics, six second-class mechanics, and seven garagemen or mechanic helpers. In addition, there is one lead mechanic who serves as a working foreman.

Salaried personnel includes Molzberger, a parts manager, and an office secretary. The total staff is 21.

The shop is in the shape of a modified rectangle. At the south end, as shown by the floor plan sketch, is a nearly square section housing the tractor repair shop and the central service core. The north end of the building contains the trailer maintenance bays, a body shop, and vehicle wash room.

Entering the "front" door of the shop on the west side, I stepped into the general office area. Measuring about 12 ft. square, it contains a desk for the shop secretary and record cabinets.

From the general office, a door opens into Molzberger's office, which overlooks the tractor shop through a large glass window. After greeting me and some preliminary discussion with basic data on the shop, Molzberger took me on a tour of the entire building.

Leaving Molzberger's office by the back door, we stepped into a wide corridor linking the offices, restrooms, lunch room, and the two main shop sections.

Directly across the corridor, opposite Molzberger's office, was the shop foreman's office. It, too, has a large window overlooking the tractor shop and a door leading into the shop. On the wall of this room, a large control board gives the preventive maintenance status of every vehicle in the fleet at a glance. The shop foreman's stand-up desk and book cases for service manuals, etc.,

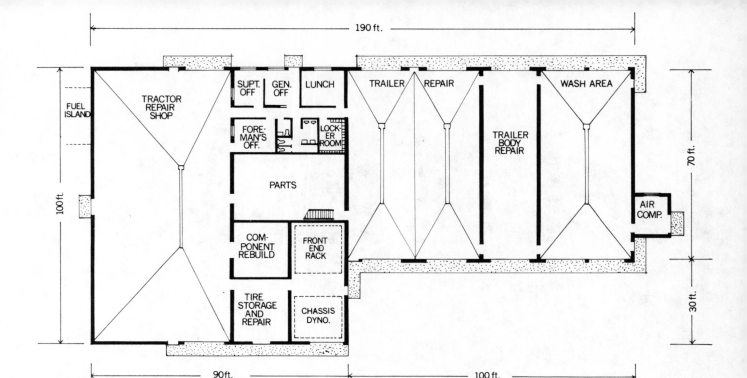

Floor plan drawing shows central service core between tractor and trailer repair areas. A second floor area above the parts, component rebuild and tire rooms stores bulky, slow-moving parts. For future expansion, tractor shop can be extended and end wall of wash room can be moved.

are in this office.

Next, we entered the tractor maintenance and repair area. Measuring approximately 50 x 100 ft., it has seven repair stalls along the south wall and a drive-through lane along the north or inner wall.

While inspecting the tractor shop, Molzberger gave some details on the shop construction and equipment. The building itself, both walls and roof, consists of two steel panels with insulation in between. The roof surface is a built-up type.

To keep the building warm in the rigorous Wisconsin winters, there is a dual heating system. Molzberger explains that the gas-fired main heating unit, mounted overhead in the tractor shop, recirculates air and heats it until the room temperature rises to the setting on the air-powered thermostats. After that, the unit brings in fresh outside air which is heated and fan-forced into all shop areas.

Because of the high doors and possible frequent door openings, the trailer repair shop bays have an additional overhead unit heater supplementing the main system.

All shop lights in the vehicle areas are mercury vapor type except for two night lights. Fluorescent lights

are used in offices and other non-vehicle areas.

The motor driven shop equipment, fuel dispensing pumps, and air compressors operate on 440-480 volt AC current. But all portable shop tools such as drills, sanders, impact wrenches, etc., are air-powered types.

Fire protection is provided by a complete overhead sprinkler system, supplemented by portable extinguishers at strategic points.

There are no pits or post lifts in the shop. Molzberger prefers the portable "bay lift" type and there are five of these portable air powered lifts, made by Walker and Graco, all with five ton capacity.

An overhead reel system serves all of the tractor bays. There is a set of reels between each two bays and the set of reels between bays five and six has hoses long enough to serve the seventh bay. These reels dispense pre-mixed anti-freeze, motor oil, transmission lube, gear lube (for rear axles), chassis lube, and compressed air. The reels and pumps are Graco.

Molzberger explained that anti-freeze is pre-mixed to –40°F. "We use it year around," he said. It is pumped from a 1,000 gal. under-

ground tank below the shop floor. Anti-freeze is poured into the tank through a pipe opening; then a water meter and valve mounted on the shop wall feeds the correct amount of water into the tank. An aerator in the tank mixes the solution.

Motor oil is pumped from an 8,000 gal. underground tank. Molzberger reports the oil used is Amoco 200, SAE 30, used year-round.

Gear lube for both transmissions and rear axles is pumped from 55-gal. drums. The drums and the Graco pumps are located at the west end of the tractor shop. The transmission lube used is Amoco 200, SAE 50, and rear axle lube is Mobil 80/90. Chassis lube is also pumped from 55 gal. drums. The lube used is Mobil Special Moly.

An unusual feature in the tractor shop is the oil drain outlets permanently installed in the floor in each tractor service bay. Each drain outlet is approximately eight in. in diameter with a cover that fits flush to the floor. These outlets are all piped to a 2,000 gal. underground tank.

A plastic adapter fits into the oil drain outlet, somewhat like a large funnel. This eliminates the need to

Val Molzberger, fleet superintendent, uses Thexton oil condition tester at his desk. Large window in his office overlooks tractor repair shop for better supervision of that area.

The Schweiger Industries fleet and the new shop are vital elements in the company's position as a major upholstered furniture producer according to Robert A. Bogan, controller of the transportation division.

The huge, nearly-new Schweiger Industries plant in Jefferson, Wisc., is reportedly the world's largest upholstered furniture factory under one roof. Bogan says the single, highly automated plant gives manufacturing economies not possible with a number of smaller regional plants.

But with the single plant, fast and economical delivery of the furniture becomes absolutely necessary. The highly efficient Schweiger fleet provides that service, ranging from Jefferson into 45 states—all except California, Oregon, and Washington. And the fleet picks up raw materials and supplies on 60% of return trips.

The fleet itself includes 41 Ford and 24 GMC tractors, all powered by Cummins or Detroit Diesel six cylinder engines. All tractors are single drive axle models with 92 or 93 in. BBC. Tandem drive axles are not necessary since outbound loads seldom exceed 45,000 lb. GCW. Some return loads, such as steel wire for cushion springs, can gross heavier.

The fleet of 139 trailers are all drop-frame furniture or electronic vans. Older trailers are all furniture vans with single axles. Newer trailers are the electronic van type with tandem axles and small wheels to eliminate wheel boxes in the trailer.

The shop also maintains 21 miscellaneous vehicles which includes retired road tractors—some gas powered—used as switching tractors at the plant loading dock, local plant service trucks, a Walter Snow Fighter, and several crawler tractors. There are also seven large fork lift trucks used in the furniture plant and the huge adjoining lumber storage yard.

position a truck precisely over the oil drain outlet for an oil change and prevents backsplash on the floor when oil is drained. The adapter is rectangular and is long enough to extend completely under a six cylinder engine. This feature permits the shop mechanic to remove an engine oil pan and all oil drippage will be caught by the adapter, keeping the floor clean.

"With the overhead reel system and the oil drain system," Molzberger comments, "we can lubricate and drain oil in all seven stalls."

Each of the seven tractor service bays also has an in-floor exhaust removal outlet. The flexible metal hose retracts into the floor outlet when not in use.

A neat steel rack mounted on the north wall of the tractor shop stores complete springs and spare spring leaves. Since there is no spring works in Jefferson, the Schweiger shop does all spring repairs or replacements.

Also mounted on the north wall of the shop are two large stainless steel sinks with hot and cold water. Molzberger says the stainless steel sink is more rugged and easier to keep clean than a porcelain fixture. The sinks are there for the convenience of the tractor shop mechanics when washing up.

Located next to the foreman's office, almost in the middle of the central service core, is the parts stock room. It extends from the tractor shop to the trailer maintenance and repair shop, with doors at each end. Parts needed for tractors are stored on shelves nearest the tractor shop door; trailer parts are stored nearest the trailer shop door.

The parts room manager maintains a perpetual inventory with a card file system and pre-established minimum and maximum parts quantities. Molzberger emphasizes, "We buy on quality first and then price."

A large second floor area over the parts room and the rest of the central service core serves as a stock room for bulky, slow-moving parts, rebuilt components, etc. A large rack in the second floor area also stores a wide variety of steel bars, angles, pipe, etc., for use in vehicles repairs.

Adjoining the parts room is the component rebuild room. This room measures about 20 x 20 ft. and is fully equipped to repair or rebuild alternators, starters, cylinder heads, transmissions, or complete engines.

◄Tractor shop has overhead lube service reels. Used oil drains are built in the floor.

"We only send out machining work such as cylinder boring or crankshaft grinding," Molzberger said.

Flanking the component rebuild room, adjacent to the northeast corner of the tractor shop, is the tire room. It measures 19 x 28 ft. Fully equipped with modern tire mounting and demounting equipment, the room also has racks to store new or recapped tires.

The tire room also has a shop-made tire inflation cage. Not surprising in "America's Dairyland," the tire inflation cage is made of old dairy barn stanchions, cut off at the bottom and welded to a steel base.

A door from the tire room leads into a long rectangular room housing a chassis dynamometer and front end alignment rack. This room measures approximately 19 x 48 ft., and has its own entrance. Its location isolates the noise of a vehicle on the dynamometer from the other main shop areas.

The Bear water-type dynamometer is located near the entrance, with the control console next to the wall. At the rear of the dyno rolls there is an in-floor exhaust removal outlet connected to the system serving the seven tractor service stalls.

The dynamometer has 12 in. rolls and has a built-in device for checking odometer accuracy. Molzberger says this feature is needed because Schweiger drivers are paid by mileage recorded on the odometer of Argo tachographs in all tractors.

At the front of the dynamometer room is a large pit-type Bear front-end alignment rack. Molzberger feels that locating the front-end rack in the dynamometer room saves floor space that would be needed for two separate rooms or shop areas. And since both types of work are not in constant progress, he says it is no problem to schedule the two types of work without conflict.

A John Bean wheel balancer is also part of the equipment in the alignment area.

A skilled mechanic performs minor PM and inspection on tractors at fuel island (above.) High pressure portable sprayer cleans a tractor (below) in shop's two-lane wash room.

Heavy duty peg board on the right wall of ▶
parts room stores shop-owned tools neatly.

Moving on to the north end of the building, we next entered the large trailer maintenance and repair area. Measuring approximately 46 x 70 ft., this area has two drive-through bays with a floor drain for each. This keeps the floor clean if it is necessary to bring in a snow-covered trailer or one wet from a rainstorm.

Four ring bolt anchors inset in the concrete floor of the south trailer repair bay are for use in straightening a trailer.

Since all trailer brake work is done in this area, the Bear brake drum lathe is installed between the two lanes. It simultaneously turns a drum and machines the brake lining to the same size.

Another important equipment item used in the trailer maintenance area, Molzberger points out, is a heat gun. He explains that he uses heat-shrinkable tubing on all trailer electrical system splices or connections. "We just don't have any electrical problems anymore; we heat-shrink everything," he said.

Next to the trailer maintenance area is a one-bay drive-through room for trailer body repairs. Measuring about 19 x 69 ft., this bay is used for more extensive body repairs while the other trailer maintenance and service area handles primarily chassis and electrical items.

At the north end of the building is the drive-through wash lane. This gets constant use, Molzberger reports, because all trailers are washed after every trip and tractors are washed at least once a week. The company's color scheme of white with gold lettering makes washing especially important.

The wash lane has two high pressure pumps, each mounted on a 55 gal. drum. One pumps the detergent cleaning solution while the other pumps rinse water. With the frequent washing schedule, very little brush washing is needed. The pump wands deliver about 850 PSI of pressure at the nozzle.

Trailer repair bays (above) handle all jobs except major body work. Dynamometer room (below) houses chassis dyno plus pit type front-end alignment and service rack built in at far end.

Adjoining the north wall of the wash lane is a mechanical equipment room which houses three air compressors. Two of these are Quincy 25 HP compressors with a somewhat unusual hookup. Molzberger reports both compressors run constantly all day, but only pump air on demand. A by-pass valve unloads the compressor when no air is being used in the various shop areas.

At night, when only a skeleton shop crew is on duty, only one of the large Quincy compressors is operational.

The third compressor, a Curtis five HP unit, provides air for the air-powered thermostats in the building heating system.

The compressor room location keeps the compressor noise out of the shop areas. Air intakes eliminate shop dust or dirt.

Retracing our steps back through the trailer shop areas, we again entered the corridor running through the office area.

In the front of the office area, next to the shop general office, was a lunch and meeting room. Attractively furnished, with tables and chairs, the 12 x 15 ft. room had a battery of vending machines for beverages and snacks. Molzberger explained that most of the shop employees bring their lunch to work.

In this same room, a long wooden frame on the wall displays certificates earned by shop mechanics who have attended special training schools.

Across the corridor from the lunch and meeting room are the locker and wash rooms for the mechanics. Like every other area of the building, they were almost immaculately clean. And next to those rooms is a small ladies rest room.

A somewhat unusual intercom system with speakers in two shop areas attracted my attention.

Molzberger explained that it was a Plectron system linked to the Jefferson Volunteer Fire Department. Three of the shop mechanics are members of the fire department; when an alarm sounds on the Plectron system, they drop their tools and rush to fight the fire.

In addition, the shop has fire detection sensors. They are linked to the master fire control warning system located in the nearby furniture plant.

Completing our tour of the building itself, Molzberger next led me to the fuel island alongside the south end of the building, next to the tractor shop.

The island can fuel two vehicles at once if necessary, with fuel hoses on both sides of the two lanes. The high-speed pumps can fuel a tractor at the rate of 75 gal. per minute.

To insure the cleanest possible fuel in vehicle tanks, the diesel fuel pumps are equipped with Fram filters that remove all impurities down to five microns.

The underground fuel tanks have a capacity of 12,000 gal. of diesel fuel. A smaller tank and pump dispenses gasoline for the gas powered fleet vehicles.

The diesel fuel used is Standard Premium No. Two in summer. In winter, Molzberger reports, he uses a blend of No. One and No. Two fuel for better cold weather starting. In addition he says the fuel is treated with a conditioner fixed at five gal. of the conditioner to 7,000 gal. of fuel. No driver purchases of fuel conditioners are allowed on the road.

A comfortable shelter building is on the fuel island between the two lanes. It is a headquarters for the skilled mechanic who works on the island. Molzberger explains that he assigns a skilled mechanic there instead of simply using a fueling attendant because the fuel island mechanic performs a safety inspection and "A" type PM service on each tractor while it is being fueled.

The Graco overhead reel system in the tractor shop extends out to the fuel island. The reels there dispense motor oil, premixed antifreeze, and compressed air.

The fuel island mechanic also checks to see that each tractor leaving on a run has a one-gal. jug filled with motor oil. The jug, carried in the cab, is for adding makeup oil on the road.

In two areas of the large yard surrounding the shop, there are electric outlets on 35 poles for plugging in electric block heaters in cold weather. The dual outlets will accommodate up to 70 tractors.

The new shop has already yielded some measurable economic benefits in addition to improved vehicle maintenance. While still in the old, outmoded shop, Molzberger says that drivers were sometimes called in on week ends to help wash trucks or to help mechanics in the shop. The extra wages for those drivers sometimes got as high as $2,800 per month. In addition, there was considerable overtime for the regular mechanics.

Now, he reports, the expense for the extra driver help on weekends has been eliminated. And overtime for the regular shop force has been reduced at least 15%.

The well planned shop included provisions for future expansion if need be. The rear or east wall of the tractor shop can be moved to allow an addition to the shop and the north wall of the building—the outer wall of the wash lane—can also be moved to permit additional lanes to the trailer repair section of the building. And Molzberger points out that an added second or third shift in the present shop would also increase shop capabilities to service a growing company and fleet.

FLEET GROWTH PACES SHOP EXPANSION

by Jack Lyndall
Senior Editor

Tractor and trailer outlines in blue show PTS fleet size when original shop was built (60 tractors, 500 trailers). Vehicle outlines in red show present fleet size: 200 tractors and 800 trailers plus service vehicles, terminal switching tractors.

Well planned to meet the needs of a growing, ever-busier fleet, a major shop expansion and office addition has more than doubled the size and usefulness of the headquarters location of Paul's Trucking Corp., Woodbridge, N.J.

Paul's Trucking is a subsidiary of Supermarkets General Corp., also headquartered in Woodbridge, and serves as a contract carrier for the network of about 100 Pathmark supermarkets operated by the parent corporation in several mid-Atlantic states plus three other consumer products marketing subsidiaries.

In addition, Paul's Trucking serves other customers, an expanding part of its business. The fleet now totals approximately 200 tractors and 800 trailers.

The Original Shop

From its relatively modest beginning as the contract carrier for the Pathmark stores, Paul's Trucking grew until it was operating approximately 60 tractors and 500 trailers in late 1968. Maintenance and repairs were handled by outside shops or by leasing companies which supplied some of the equipment.

Problems with these arrangements dictated the need for a company-operated shop, which was completed in 1968.

That original or "first stage" shop contained three vehicle service bays, each measuring 20 ft. x 70 ft. At the north end of the shop were two longer bays, each measuring 20 ft. x 93 ft. One of those longer bays was a safety-check and trailer-repair lane while the other was a wash bay.

That shop also included a small balcony area above one of the vehicle service bays for parts storage plus a small shop foreman's office. Fortunately, that original shop was located on a rather large tract of land that permitted the later expansion. Company offices were at another location.

A Major Shop/Office Expansion

Steadily increasing business and fleet size exceeded the capacity of the original shop by early 1973. A major expansion with new corporate, executive, general, and operations offices included, was planned.

The architect was Paul Lyman Trost 3d, Clifton, N.J., and the builders and mechanical engineers were Mahoney and Trost.

The new addition was added on the south side of the existing shop by removing the existing block wall. It includes two tractor service bays with the same dimensions as the original bays, 20 ft. x 70 ft. Each of the two new bays has a below-floor pit measuring 3½ ft. x 26 ft.

Next to the two new tractor service bays is a cleverly designed 3-story office center. (See box included with this report for a description of the office center and its novel features.)

Adjoining the office section on the south side are two "dispatch lanes" or, more properly described, safety check lanes. Measuring 20 ft. x 94 ft. 8 in. each, these lanes are used for a final check of all outbound units. One of the lanes has an overhead catwalk on both sides to permit a fast inspection for any trailer roof damage and to give easy access to upper trailer clearance lamps for bulb or lamp replacement.

When not in use for checking outbound units, which tends to reach a peak in early morning hours, these lanes are used for other trailer repairs.

The new shop additions total approximately 6,600 sq. ft., while the original shop area covered about 8,024 sq. ft. The new office core area measures approximately 40 ft. x 87 ft.; with its three floors, it contains some 10,440 sq. ft. Part of it is devoted to shop operations, housing the main parts room, shop foreman's office, mechanic's restroom, and locker rooms, plus the offices of George Broemmer, director of equipment, and Frank Thune, shop manager.

The new addition, completed in late August, 1973, cost approximately $900,000, according to Paul L. Millian, president of Paul's Trucking (the similarity in Millian's first name and the company name is only a coincidence; the trucking company was established some years before Millian joined it).

Explaining the fleet growth that necessitated the shop expansion, Millian reports, "We now control

Front view shows handsome new office facade with shop adjoining. Tractor parking spaces have electric outlets for engine heaters.

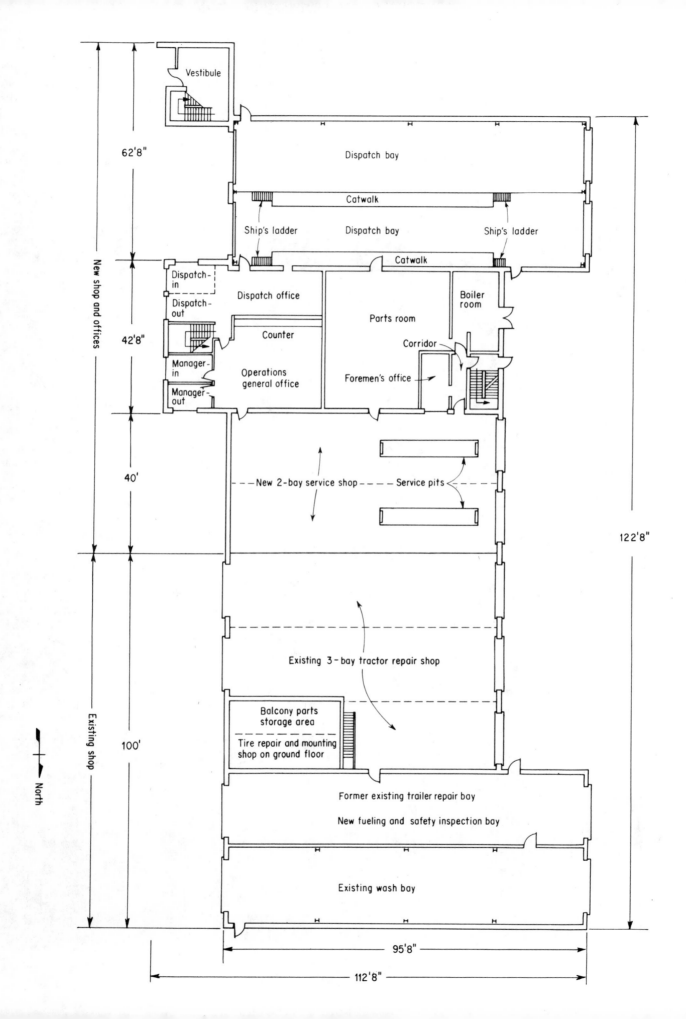

about 200 tractors and 800 trailers.

"Approximately 135 trailers are insulated and have mechanical refrigeration units. This shop maintains about 160 power units (including terminal switching tractors used at the nearby Pathmark distribution center) and maintains all 135 refrigerations units. We also maintain 50 trailers that are on finance lease." He explains that the remaining 750 trailers are on a full-service lease arrangement with the leasing company personnel performing most of the trailer main-

tenance with mobile units at the Paul's Trucking location. Some nonscheduled or emergency repairs on those leased trailers are done in the new Paul's Trucking shop when necessary.

The remainder of the Paul's Trucking fleet is based at two other locations at Mahwah and Cranford, N.J.

Millian comments that the Paul's Trucking shop also occasionally does emergency repairs on vehicles belonging to other Supermarkets General subsidiaries.

New tractor service bays have pits near exterior doors for fast PM work. Major repairs are done in the area ahead of the pits.

Neat, modern parts room includes a rack (at right in photo) for storage of relined brake shoes plus steel shelves and bins.

Tire department is housed on ground floor level of original shop section. Balcony above stores slow-moving or bulky parts.

Safety check and fueling lane has brake test, toe-in check, and headlight-aiming machines. Mounted spare tires are in racks

He also reports that the Paul's Trucking tractor fleet consists of about 30 White tilt cab COE and 125 White conventional tractors. (He notes that the fleet also employs about 50 owner-operator units.)

At the time of my visit to the newly expanded shop in late fall, Millian also commented that he had ordered a fleet of 15 Mercedes-Benz single-axle tractors for lighter loads and multi-stop deliveries.

The trailer fleet consists mostly of Strick and Gindy units except for 30 meat and perishable product trailers produced by Theurer.

Millian comments, "The trailers are all 40 or 45 ft. long; we are trying to standardize on a 12½ ft. trailer height. All trailers are equipped with roll-up type rear doors." He notes, "We have discontinued use of wedge-type trailers." They proved impractical in the Paul's Trucking operation.

In addition to the tractors and trailers, the fleet also includes four walk-in van trucks used as mobile maintenance units plus two road service trucks.

View of shop expansion area from overhead parts storage balcony. Lane in foreground is part of the original shop area. Exhaust-removal system and lube-dispensing reels are mounted overhead. Fluorescent light fixtures provide good light level for 3-shift operations.

Original Shop Modifications

During the shop expansion, which was done without interrupting work in the original shop section, some changes and improvements were made in the original shop.

The former trailer repair bay next to the wash bay was converted to a fueling and safety check lane. This lane was already equipped with a Weaver brake tester, toe-in checker, and headlight tester and aim-

Office and Administrative Center

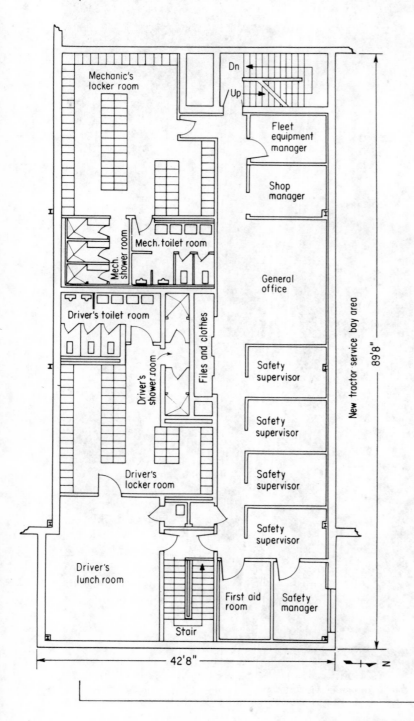

Two outstanding features distinguish the multilevel office and administrative center—the diversity of departments housed and the control of access to each so that unauthorized people do not intrude into departments without specific good reason to be there.

The top floor houses the executive offices, insurance and claims departments, personnel department, accounting, data processing, and employe training rooms. Access to the top floor level is only through the main entrance lobby.

The second-floor level provides private offices for Broemmer and Thune, plus mechanics' locker and restroom, a general office area, and offices for the four roving safety supervisors (who are almost constantly on patrol in their specially equipped cars).

This floor also has the first-aid room and a private office for the safety manager. And it has a large drivers' locker room plus drivers' lunch room and restroom.

The safety manager and the four safety supervisors also conduct the driver-training program. Two additional people in that department are responsible for the OSHA compliance program and the filing of necessary DOT and other safety reports. The effectiveness of the driver training and safety programs was evidenced by the award of a Certificate of Merit to the Paul's Trucking fleet recently by the Hartford Accident and Indemnity Co.

Access to the drivers' part of the second floor, including the safety department, is by a set of stairs leading up from the front of the building, next to the main lower lobby. The access for mechanics to their part of the second floor is by a stairway leading up from the corridor between the shop foreman's office and boiler room on the shop-floor level.

On the ground-floor level at the front of the office section are the inbound and outbound dispatch control offices, together with the private offices for managers of each activity, plus an operations general office area.

Access to the dispatch offices is through a doorway connecting to the outbound dispatch trailer bay. The operations office has a door opening into the tractor repair area.

ing machine. It also had a hydraulic lift for picking up the front axle of a tractor. Two new fueling outlets, one on each side, were added at the end of the lane to permit fueling tanks on both sides of a tractor simultaneously. The pumps have a capacity of 30 gal.

alignment, brake performance, horn, and exhaust system as the unit moves in and stands for fueling.

Tractor Shop Area

Stepping through the connecting door from the

per minute.

With the new lane setup, an incoming unit gets a safety check and is then fueled before it is reloaded and sent out again.

In the large paved yard in front of the building there is a fueling island with pumps and an attendant's shelter building. This can be used for vehicles needing only fuel.

The existing wash bay on the north end of the original shop was already equipped with a Ross and White brush-type automatic washer. A portable high-pressure wash unit with wand nozzle was added to supplement the large washer.

Both Broemmer and Thune, who were accompanying me on a tour of the shop, pointed out the increased usefulness of the original shop section after the improvements. Thune noted that the fueling and check lane allows the fueling attendant to make a safety check of a unit, including lights, front end

fueling and safety check lane into the original three-bay shop section, Thune explained that the former balcony parts-storage level had been retained and slightly enlarged by a more convenient relocation of the access stairway. As we inspected the upper level, two men were busy assembling and erecting new shelving and bin storage equipment. Broemmer noted that the upper deck would continue in use for storage of bulky, slow-moving parts.

The space below the balcony was devoted to the tire department, with modern equipment for mounting and dismounting tires. The shop does not have its own recapping equipment as yet; Broemmer says the volume seems to be inadequate to justify the investment at present.

The two remaining bays of the original shop were largely unchanged by the shop expansion except for the removal of the wall that bordered the south lane. The new shop addition was so well done that only a barely perceptible seam in the concrete floor told me where the old shop ended and the new part began.

New Tractor Repair Bays

Each of the two new tractor service bays has a below-floor pit or depressed service bay at the western end. Meeting OSHA requirements, the pits were protected by a chain guard rail as Thune continued our tour of the shop. The pits, like the other tractor repair bays, are served by the centralized Alemite overhead oil and lube reel system. It dispenses motor oil (from a 1,000-gal.-capacity underground storage tank), chassis lube, rear axle gear oil, and transmission lube. Thune reports that premixed antifreeze is to be added to the system in the near future.

Usage of the shop work bays, Thune reports, is that the two new bays with the pits are used primarily for PM service and inspections or component replacement; the three remaining bays in the shop's center area are mostly for major repairs or overhaul.

The fueling and safety-check lane plus the new outbound trailer-inspection lanes are mostly devoted to daily trip maintenance, with the wash bay, of course, for vehicle cleanliness, so important in food transportation vehicles.

The shop has modern equipment, some of it from the original shop. Included among the original roster of shop equipment were a Nugier 70-ton capacity arbor press plus Marquette and Sun diagnostic and test instruments.

The shop also had both electric arc and oxy-acetylene welding equipment.

Among new equipment bought for the shop expansion were two Greyco portable vehicles and lifts and a Bee Line dynamic wheel balancer.

Main Parts Room

Located on the ground floor level of the office and administration core was a 34 ft. x 40 ft. area occupied by the main parts stock room and the shop foreman's office. The foreman's office, measuring 8 ft. x 12 ft. 8 in., and the parts room both have access doors to the two new tractor-repair bays.

The exceptionally neat, orderly parts room stocks fast-moving parts, with the slower-moving, bulkier items or case lots of smaller parts stored on the overhead balcony. Heavy-duty pegboard panels and hooks on the parts room wall store shop-owned tools.

The foreman's office, tastefully finished with walnut paneling, has a large window near his desk that overlooks the tractor repair bays near the two new pits. A control board on the office wall shows the status of all vehicles in the fleet and which are due for PM or other work.

On the south side of the office and administrative core were the two lanes for a final safety check of outbound loaded trailers. The lane next to the office core, as shown in the floor-plan drawing, has an elevated catwalk on both sides of the lane, as mentioned above.

During the periods when outbound dispatches lessen, these bays can be used for various trailer repairs on those units the Paul's Trucking shop maintains.

The main shop areas are heated by hot air piped through an overhead duct system from the boiler room next to the parts room. But there is a somewhat unusual supplementary heating system, Thune pointed out as we toured the shop.

Above each roll-up door at the end of each of the tractor shop's drive-through bays, overhead unit heaters are mounted. These are controlled by the door-opening switches. As any one of the power-operated doors opens, the unit heater above that door starts blowing warm air to counteract the entrance of cold outside air while the door is open. As the door closes, the unit heater shuts off.

Personnel

Broemmer credits much of the performance of the shop and the good condition of the PTC fleet to the skilled work force. In addition to Broemmer and Thune, there are two shift foremen, two shop clerks, and the parts room manager who are considered as management people. There are 27 mechanics plus two mechanic trainees. The shop operates 24 hours a day, six days a week.

Despite the large shop expansion, only one additional shop employe was needed—a man for the inbound fueling and safety-check lane. Two fueling attendants who formerly worked full time at the outside fuel island were transferred to the inside fueling lane.

The shop crew handles just about all maintenance and repairs on the tractor fleet except major engine rebuilds or major wreck jobs which are sent out. The shop does its own in-frame engine overhauls, however, plus most component rebuilding.

Thune credits the two new pits with saving considerable time and manpower on regular PM service and smaller component replacements.

The shop uses the Mainstem system of maintenance control and data anaylsis for close management control of costs and vehicle efficiency.

Future Expansion

Anticipating still further fleet growth, Millian points out that the shop can be expanded again with additional lanes adjoining the trailer dispatch lanes on the south end of the building.

He also points out that the office space can be expanded as an additional floor level over the new shop additions if necessary.

DSR builds 'Dream Shop'

By Jack Lyndall, Senior Editor

More than five years of careful planning went into this dream shop, a major bus repair and component rebuilding facility recently completed by Detroit Street Railways in Detroit, Mich.

Replacing long-outmoded shops housed in old streetcar barns, the ultra-modern new shop was designed for the Department of Street Railways, City of Detroit; by Smith, Hinchman and Grylls Associates, Inc., Detroit, Mich. The general contractor was Barton-Malow, Inc., also from Detroit. Total cost was $14.5 million.

Identified simply as "the heavy maintenance shop", the new building is located at the intersection of Warren Avenue and I-75 in Detroit.

Starting a day-long tour and inspection of the new shop, I met with T. M. Alexander, superintendent of rolling stock, in his office in the administrative building adjoining the shop. He reported that the new shop does all major repairs and overhauls, plus component rebuilding, for DSR's fleet of 1,048 buses and 137 other vehicles. Among the latter are 43 fleet cars, service trucks, wreckers, road scrapers, snow plows and bulldozers.

The shop roster totals 140 men including Alexander, his assistant, L. J. Grzesiak, and Richard Golem-

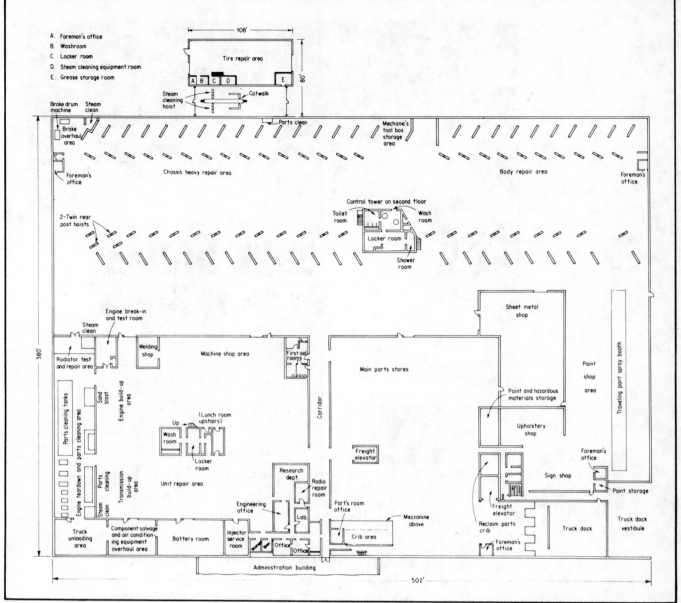

Floor plan shows good traffic flow for vehicles and convenience of parts and component rebuild areas to bus repair departments.

biewski, senior assistant mechanical engineer.

The supervisory staff totals seven, including the superintendent of the mechanical and body repair area, three senior foremen and three sub-foremen. The remaining 129 men are mechanics, helpers, machinists, painters, and radio men.

As we discussed the vast new shop which covers nearly a city block, Alexander noted that the shop building was a rectangle with another smaller rectangle adjoining on the north side.

Measuring approximately 502 ft long and 380 ft wide, the main shop building contains 190,350 sq ft of floor space. The handsome, contemporary administrative office building, faced with tinted glass, contains 35,360 sq ft.

Leaving Alexander's large, tastefully furnished office just off the corridor leading to the shop, we passed a group of four offices and a research labora-

tory. This is the domain of Richard Golembiewski, who heads the DSR engineering and radio departments. Also in this area is the radio repair room that will soon service the all radio-equipped fleet. Two service men work here.

Adjoining the engineering office area on the west side is the diesel injector rebuild room. This room, like the engineering office area, is air conditioned. Alexander pointed out that the main shop itself has a highly efficient mechanical ventilation system, giving at least six complete changes of air per hour. There are no windows in the shop. Interior lighting, so good that I could take photos without flash in most areas, is by modern mercury vapor or fluorescent lighting.

Next to the injector service room is the battery room. Alexander explained that the large battery room and its facilities are needed because DSR does not lease its batteries. He noted that after a study, DSR tightened its battery specifications and switched to a policy of owning its own batteries. In the battery room, batteries are repaired whenever practical and new batteries are stored.

Flanking the battery room in the southwest corner of the shop is the component salvage room and its truck unloading bay.

Trucks bring all defective or damaged components from shops at the three DSR operating garages and unload in this area. Hand trucks or forklifts bring similar items from the bus repair area in the new shop.

Then, all small components go into the adjoining salvage room. There, they are inspected to determine whether they can be economically rebuilt or should be scrapped. This same room also overhauls all of the air conditioning compressors, air cleaners, and heater motors, plus some additional small items. When repairs are completed, items are stored on racks lining the walls of the truck unloading bay and later sent to locations needing them.

Large components such as engines, transmissions, and radiators go from the truck unloading bay into the teardown, cleaning, and radiator repair room next to the truck bay on the north side.

The parts cleaning room, measuring approximately 158 ft long and 36 ft wide, contains four large Magnus cleaning tanks. The first tank, a Model No. 5 ALXH "Aja Lif" is used primarily for cleaning engine

Overhead reels between each two lifts dispense oils, greases, and coolants. All reels are connected to the centralized piping system extending throughout the entire bus chassis and body shops.

Front view of DSR shop with modernistic administration building in front. Office building has tinted glass windows and doors.

blocks, cylinder heads, and the like. The tank has a platform that raises or lowers into the heated degreasing and cleaning solution. This platform raises to receive an engine block for cleaning and then lowers it into the chemical for soaking or agitation.

Alexander reported that the cleaning tank completely cleans the dirtiest engine block in 30 to 45 minutes.

The other three tanks are similar to the first. The second tank, with a different chemical solution, is used for decarbonizing aluminum components. The third tank, with still another type of solution, cleans air cleaners, both oil bath (wet type) and paper (dry type). The fourth tank is used to clean small electrical components such as alternators, starters and generators.

Three additional cleaning tanks for especially greasy components are ranged along the wall adjacent to the unit rebuild room.

At the north end of the parts cleaning room is the radiator repair area. It is equipped with a Magnus cleaning and dipping tank similar to the ones in the adjoining cleaning area.

Radiators are lowered on the power-operated rack into the cleaning solution. Then, air pressure is connected to the radiator and the repair man quickly spots any leaks from the rising bubbles. When the radiator is raised and drained, an overhead hoist lifts it onto the repair bench at the end of the tank for soldering or other repairs.

"The radiator can be lifted, dried, and soldered without moving it," Alexander commented.

While we inspected the parts cleaning room, Alexander pointed out a minor "crisis" that arose during construction. The Magnus cleaning tanks have gas heating burners in the base of each tank to heat the cleaning solution. A local fire ordinance stipulates that any such burner must be located at least four ft above the floor to insure adequate air supply and ventilation.

Since the burners were built into the base of the tanks, the only remedy appeared to be to place the tanks on elevated supports. This would have required a catwalk and platform to allow access to the tanks, with the attendant risk of injuries on slippery catwalk steps.

The dilemma was finally solved when the fire department authorities approved placement of the tanks on the floor with metal ducts to bring in air from four ft above the floor. The burner chambers were completely enclosed at the floor level.

In the parts cleaning room, engines are torn down for preliminary inspection. Non-repairable or broken parts are usually discarded; the parts to be re-used then go into the cleaning tanks.

At each end of the parts cleaning room there is a small steam cleaning booth. These are used mostly to clean parts too small to be immersed in the large cleaning tanks.

From the parts cleaning room we walked into the large unit repair and machine shop area. The unit repair area covers 39,000 sq ft while the machine shop has 5,000 sq ft.

One area of the unit rebuild section is used to build up engines with the cleaned parts whenever possible. New parts are used as needed.

Next to the engine area, transmissions are being completely rebuilt. Both of these areas, as well as other parts of the big new shop, are served with overhead monorail hoists or gantry cranes to lift and move all heavy components. There are eight hoists in the engine area, and six more in the transmission rebuild area.

Along the south side of the unit rebuild area are work benches for rebuilding other bus components. These include generators or alternators, starters, voltage regulators, speedometer heads, engine speed governors, relays, and wiring harnesses. There is an individual bench for rebuilding and testing each of these items.

Adjacent to the engine build-up area is the engine test room. This fully enclosed, virtually soundproof room can test two rebuilt engines at one time. These are not dynamometer tests. The engines are run for a number of hours to check for proper assembly, noise, fuel, oil, or water leaks, and any other defect before installation in a bus.

Motor oil and fuel are stored in tanks in the engine test room and both are filtered before going into an engine under test. Cooling water flows into a standpipe for cooling, supplemented by fresh make-up water as needed.

A wall-mounted control panel monitors engine RPM, oil pressure, water temperature, and engine maximum speed. If any malfunction occurs, the panel automatically shuts down the engine and sounds an alarm.

"This engine test room was designed so it does not have to be monitored by any personnel," Richard Golembiewski reported. "Formerly our engine run-in would take a lot of man-hours."

Near the engine test room is the welding room. It is

Traveling paint spray booth runs on rails in the floor. Two painters work on elevating platforms inside the booth.

fully equipped for every type of soldering, welding, and flame cutting including a line cutting machine.

The machine shop area is fully equipped with lathes, milling machines, and other machine tools needed for the jobs done here. Many of the machine tools were transferred from the old shop, but have been well maintained and are still serviceable.

At the east end of the unit repair area is a screened-in tool crib where repairs are made to shop-owned tools such as air impact wrenches, hydraulic jacks, gasoline pump meters, and other small precision devices.

In the center of the unit rebuild area is a service core. This is on two levels. On the ground floor is a large washroom with "bird bath" type wash stands, toilet, and locker rooms. On the upper level is a lunch room with access stairways on both sides.

Next, we moved on into the vast bus chassis and body shop area. It extends across the entire north half of the shop building and contains 54,700 sq ft.

There are 28 twin-post hydraulic lifts in the chassis repair areas plus 19 more lifts in the body repair area—47 in all. The lifts were supplied by Joyce-Cridland Co., Dayton, Ohio. There are no pits in the building. One extra lift is also used for work on the fleet cars and trucks.

The lifts are located on centers spaced 14 ft apart, allowing ample working room. Each lift bay has an outlet for the in-floor exhaust removal system.

At every second lift bay there is an overhead reel system. They supply automatic transmission fluid, motor oil, chassis grease, rear axle gear oil, engine coolant (pre-mixed water and Nalcool 2000 cooling system treatment), permanent anti-freeze, and compressed air. Each bank of overhead reels also has three drop lights. The overhead reel setup allows complete preventive maintenance to be done at the lift.

The chassis and body shop area has a broad center aisle running its full length. Buses come into the aisle and "peel off" into the angled lift bays. At each end of the long aisle, next to the entrance and exit doors, are offices for the two foremen. One is in charge of the chassis repair area, the other supervises the body shop.

In the northwest corner of the chassis repair area, next to the foreman's office, is the brake overhaul area. Superintendent Alexander pointed out that DSR is still continuing its highly successful use of bonded brake linings so that no shoes are relined.

T. M. Alexander, superintendent of rolling stock, reviews maintenance records in shop office atop "control tower."

View of bus chassis repair shop shows area for brake overhauls in foreground. Truck is DSR armored money van.

Heavy duty peg board on screen partition in main parts store room keeps gaskets neat and orderly, yet easily accessible.

In the corner of the shop is a Star Transformatic brake drum and shoe lathe. It simultaneously machines a brake drum and a set of relined brake shoes to the same size.

Adjacent to the brake drum lathe is a steam cleaning booth. All metal chips, dirt, and old grease are steam-cleaned from a drum and wheel hub after the drum has been machined.

Several lifts next to the brake drum lathe area are reserved for brake overhaul work.

At the mid-point of the long aisle, between the chassis and body repair areas, is the elevated superintendent's office. Resembling a modern airport control tower, it gives an excellent view of the entire length of the two repair areas. On the ground floor beneath the superintendent's office is a utility area including locker room, wash room, shower room, and toilets for the mechanics in the chassis and body repair sections.

Directly opposite the "control tower" is an area enclosed by a strong wire mesh screen wall. This area provides secure, locked storage for mechanic's roller tool cabinets when they are off duty.

In addition to the hoists, overhead reels and in-floor exhaust removal system, the chassis repair area has several small Magnus parts cleaning machines. These allow mechanics to quickly clean the parts or components they are working on without taking them all the way to the parts cleaning room.

A compressed air line with numerous outlets runs around the perimeter of the chassis and body repair area, and Alexander noted that air lines are connected to many points in the unit rebuild, machine shop, and other departments, wherever needed.

Electric service is extensive, too. Alexander said: "We needed 220 and 440 v, three-phase ac current for large motors. We also had to install a 600 v, dc motor-generator set to provide current for the older machine tools transferred from the former Highland Park shops."

In addition, the benches in the unit rebuild room that rebuild and test electrical components such as starters, alternators, and relays were equipped with 12 v, dc outlets.

As we walked down the boulevard-sized aisle in the chassis and body repair area, Alexander noted another advantage of the ample space designed into the building: "In severe winter weather, we can park up to 85 buses inside."

The aisle has another noteworthy feature. It, and the entire vehicle repair area, has an epoxy coating on the floor. Light gray in color, the coating gives a smooth surface that is easily cleaned.

Next to the body repair area, in the southeast section of the building, is the sheet metal shop. It has 6,000 sq ft of floor space and is fully equipped to make almost any sheet metal part for a bus except those requiring forming on a die. Alexander said that the sheet metal shop fabricated much of the various types of duct work in the new building.

Alongside the sheet metal shop, bordering the east end of the building, is the paint area. It has floor space for several buses while sanding, masking, or other preliminary work is going on.

A major feature of the paint area is the De Vilbiss Type SER 28992 traveling spray booth. It moves on tracks set in the floor and has elevating platforms on both sides to allow painters to reach every part of a bus. The paint booth has built-in lights and a "waterfall" water curtain to trap paint overspray particles in the air before they are exhausted outdoors.

The air from the traveling booth discharges into a large ceiling-mounted duct that runs the length of the paint booth track. With the paint booth, Alexander reports that two men can paint a DSR bus in 1½ hours or less.

Entrance doors to the paint area are next to the body repair area. As body repairs are completed on a bus, it rolls directly into the paint room. The exit doors from the paint room open into a large covered vestibule area which also serves the truck dock for incoming parts and supplies.

Alongside the paintroom are the upholstery and sign shops. These areas, together with the paintroom, total 15,000 sq ft.

The upholstery shop has two power-driven sewing machines. Three men work full time on repairs to upholstered seats. The DSR fleet is predominately equipped with upholstered seats. Alexander estimates vandalism damage to seats and upholstery runs about $1,500-$2,500 per month, with a similar amount for glass breakage.

The sign shop makes destination signs for the buses plus other signs for street corner bus stops.

At the end of the sign shop area, next to the paintroom, is a small storage room for paint used in both departments. Next to this is a small office for the foremen in charge of the paint, upholstery and sign departments.

Almost centrally located in the building is the main parts stockroom, which has 24,800 sq ft of floor space. Modern steel bins and racks store the vast stock of replacement parts needed for the DSR fleet.

On the east side of the main stockroom is a walled-off storage room for inflammables. It stores larger quantities of paint and other volatile products which are dispensed in smaller quantities as needed to the other paint storeroom next to the paintroom and other departments.

Near the storeroom for inflammable products is an enclosed area or "crib". In that area, parts being sent to outside companies for repairs and reclamation are stored until shipped or picked up by the vendor's truck. This same area is also used to inspect all such rebuilt or reclaimed parts received before they are accepted and placed in inventory.

A large truck unloading dock and receiving area adjoin the main store room. It has 5,000 sq ft and all incoming parts and supplies are delivered here by vendor's or carrier's trucks. There are spaces for three trucks, and each space is equipped with an elevating dock board. The dock is fully enclosed within the building, with a sloping ramp up to street level in the vestibule area.

Standing on one side of the truck dock is an office for the dock supervisor, and there is another office in the parts room for the parts supervisor.

Directly opposite the dock supervisor's office is a large freight elevator. This is used to transport heavy drums of cleaning materials and other supplies to a storage area in the basement. A second freight elevator located near the center of the main storeroom also serves the basement storeroom area.

Also located in the building basement is the fare box repair room, driver's training class room, a large lunch room, printing shop, and stationery stores.

Also centrally located in the building, at the intersection of the main aisle and the vehicle repair area, is the first aid room, even though the term "first aid room" is somewhat of a misnomer. It is actually a suite of four rooms—a waiting room, eye treatment room, medical treatment room, and the "ward". This is a room equipped with beds and a private wash room. The first aid facility is fully equipped to handle any emergency or minor injury and has a full-time attendant.

The rectangular "annex" on the north side of the building measures approximately 80 ft wide and 108 ft long. It contains two rooms or bays.

Located next to the main shop wall is a drive-through steam cleaning room. It has two hydraulic twin-post lifts to permit steam cleaning the underside of a bus and chassis.

Alongside the two lifts are elevated platforms, or catwalks, seven ft, six in. above the floor level. The platforms permit access to the upper part of a bus and the roof.

The steam cleaning room also accommodates two additional buses in an area ahead of the two hoists. Buses that have been cleaned can be parked there to dry, or cleaned if desired.

The other room in the "annex" was originally planned as a tire repair and storage department. However, Alexander plans to use the 4,000 sq ft area for a chassis dynamometer and a research and test facility. He pointed out that it is well suited for that purpose, being separate from the main shop and is already equipped with a foremen's office and me-

chanic's locker and rest rooms. It also has an elevated balcony that can be used as a parts room. Alexander also said that the proposed research and test room has sufficient space to set up a service bay for the fleet cars which are now serviced along the main aisle in the chassis repair area.

He also noted that "We are planning to install a brake analyzer and the chassis dynamometer to enable a mechanic to check out a brake job without going out on a road test."

Located in the paved yard area on the north side of the building are three service buildings. One contains the electrical transformers, main switches, and circuit breakers.

The second building, called the mechanical services building, has fire fighting system pumps and controls, plus water controls for the shop.

Also housed in this building are two big Ingersoll-Rand air compressors rated at 600 cu. ft. per minute, powered by 150 hp motors.

The third service building is an incinerator to dispose of the trash and refuse collected daily in the shop and offices.

Although there was a brief drop in productivity during the move to the building, the shakedown period went quite smoothly, Alexander said. The new shop has already proven one of the benefits it was designed for, Alexander said: "The way it is laid out, it takes less people to supervise it. We have three less foremen than in the old shop."

Future fleet expansion can be handled by the new shop, thanks to the spacious dimensions planned into it. According to Alexander: "This shop is projected to handle the heavy maintenance and component rebuild for up to 2,500 buses. That is anticipated if present plans go through for DSR to become part of the Southeastern Michigan Transportation Authority (a six-county regional authority)."

Offering well-founded advice to any fleet superintendent planning a new shop, Alexander cautioned: "Put at least 8% of the estimated cost in a contingency fund. We spent at least $325,000 here when we moved in to install items that were overlooked, such as overhead monorail conveyors for the brake drum lathe, overhead hoists in the unit rebuild and machine shops, the modification of the gas burner intakes on the parts cleaning tanks and overhead compressed air lines. We had $325,000 in our contingency fund and it was all used."

Alexander pointed out that many architects are not familiar with all the specialized requirements of a fleet shop, and he advised: "The superintendent of maintenance should stay with the architect all the time during the planning, especially for major equipment items like hoists. The superintendent of maintenance should be fully involved." 🚌

Shop savvy on Michigan's shores

by George Snyder, associate editor

Part of the "yard fleet" (left to right): A White salt spreader, a Mack dumper, a White refueling tanker, and an FWD snowplow.

In the early 1920s, when brothers John C. and August J. Lindner bounced Federal and Available trucks, respectively, over rough Wisconsin and Illinois roads, little did they know the seeds of one of the Midwest's most successful trucking companies had been planted.

In 1923, for example, both operated one-man trucking businesses, but the next year, due to a proposal from another company to take over its hauling, they borrowed $950 and joined in the trucking business. By 1928 they had incorporated as Lindner Bros. Trucking, Inc., and two years later purchased Advanced Transportation Company, a Milwaukee meat hauler.

Today, August Lindner serves as chairman of the board of the company he helped establish; an organiza-

tion that currently operates more than 800 trucks and trailers and 50 automobiles. His brother, unfortunately, is deceased.

In spite of growth and sophistication, however, Advance Transportation's philosophy remains the same as that of Lindner Bros. Trucking Company: To provide superior service and operate the best fleet possible. Even though the company evolved into Wisconsin's largest common carrier, one rule remained constant — "keep the vehicles operational."

Maintenance was the name of the game then and still is, although the setting has changed. Today, Advance Transportation operates out of an architecturally-efficient home terminal that is the envy of many other fleets.

After almost five years in the new terminal, director of maintenance Bill Fischer still takes pride in the free hand he was given to design the service facility. He says, "Because the top management group understands the need for maintenance and repair flexibility under one roof, I was almost able to have the facility built to my specs."

On the other hand, Jim Joppe and the management group consider Fischer an economy-minded maintenance supervisor who keeps the fleet in the best possible shape at the least expense. For that reason alone, they were willing to give him the type of shop he needed. A familiar figure at RCCC meetings and a former winner of a FLEET OWNER Maintenance Efficiency Award, Bill Fischer makes one thing clear—that his procedures work best for his particular operation, but they aren't necessarily the ones he'd advocate for all fleets.

Shop layout

In helping design the service department, Bill Fischer paid particular attention to parts and traffic flow, incoming parts shipments, and storage-free work areas. As a result, the shop is completely departmentalized for work efficiency and quick parts availability.

The lubricating room, for example, features automatic metering of oil from bulk storage as well as an oil pipeline to the service island outside. As a result, the lube room is free of the clutter of drums and containers. Used oil is collected for recycling.

The 40,000-sq.-ft. service department also includes a wash rack at the south end of the building with automatic door openers, an automatic trailer wash at the east end, and high-pressure automatic washers for tractors and cars at the west end. Wash water is collected in an 850-gal. underground storage tank, where contaminants are settled out to prevent them from entering the sewer system.

The trailer repair shop is 107 ft. from door to door and 21 ft. high for easy access to the top of any of the company's 504 trailers. The shop also includes a frame-rail straightener, portable scaffolds for work on rolling tarps and trailer roof repair, and an overhead crane for reefer removal and installation.

Temperature in the tire storage room is kept at 70°F. for longer rubber life. Fischer also incorporated a unique

Opened five years ago, the terminal is located on Milwaukee's south side, a few miles from the General Billy Mitchell airport.

Situated on a 30-acre site, the facility boasts 150,300 sq. ft. under roof. Over a million and a quarter sq. ft. of the area is blacktopped, the equivalent of 18½ highway miles. The 102-door loading dock alone measures 100 ft. wide and 635 ft. long.

During the initial planning stages, Advance Transportation management solicited ideas and suggestions from the employes who would eventually use the new facility. As a result, company president James L. Joppe says, "We came up with improvements that would have been overlooked had we failed to consult our people."

elevator cage for tires in the shop; tires now can be stored in a room above the shop floor and don't take up valuable work space. Three men work full time on tire repair.

Two stalls in the shop are used for trailer PM, with another two designated as areas for minor repair and safety checks on all equipment. A separate area with an overhead crane is used for removal of any power train component. One stall is used to rebuild and repair electrical components; another for reefer repair. In this shop, two three-ton cranes are overhead for engine removal, while a steam rack with two high-pressure water heaters is available for parts cleaning.

In addition to 4,000 sq. ft. of parts storage space, batteries are kept in a special room with a ventilating system, wash sink, and floor drain, all installed for safety purposes.

Finally, a separate chassis dynamometer room with exhaust system and sound-deadening walls permits Advance Transportation mechanics to tune tractors to the road conditions they face each trip.

Amenable to change

Bill Fischer exemplifies the entire organization in his willingness to experiment with and accept new methods. He says, "I've got to be convinced it's best for the company, but once I'm convinced, it's full speed ahead." For example, he went from radiator shutters to viscous fan clutches with outstanding success and is now using Lipe-Rollway self-adjusting clutches, increasing clutch life from 180,000 to 250,000 miles.

He currently is testing automatic brake slack adjusters and is of the opinion they're going to be beneficial. He is specifying the Rockwell slack adjuster and admits he didn't favor them until they became comparatively trouble-free.

He also is keeping a close eye on the bias-vs.-radial tire situation and says, "I hear the pros and cons at RCCC meetings and I'm staying with bias until something more definitive comes out." If nothing else, that statement shows the value one common carrier maintenance supervisor places on the RCCC sessions.

Standardization

Advance Transportation's linehaul tractors are tandem and single-axle Whites and Fords, while the straight trucks and automobiles are all Fords. Linehaul units range in horsepower from 270 to 290; city tractors are rated at 210 hp and straights at 175 hp. The road tractors are powered by Caterpillar high-torque-rise economy engines coupled with 9-speed transmissions. In fact Fischer says, "in 1963 Advance Transportation purchased the second or third Cat truck engine ever made and has been completely sold on them ever since."

Standardization also includes the use of multigrade 15W-40 oil, wheel oil seals on all vehicles, ThermoKing reefers, and Dorsey linehaul and Trailmobile city trailers.

Fischer says the multigrade oil has solved problems in the spring and fall when it always had been a chore to get lightweight oil out and heavy in, or vice versa according to the season. Also, during the coldest months, Fischer blends 25% No. 1 oil with standard No. 2 diesel fuel.

Fischer prefers the constantly circulating Fleeter Heater anti-freeze system for cold starts as opposed to electrical systems. He says, "This system controls temperatures better than electrical methods and still assures a full radiator. I feel it's better for the engine block as well as the cooling system."

Fleeter Heater circulates ethylene glycol throughout the engine blocks of all tractors, returning it to a unit for quick recovery of the heat lost to the wind-chill factor as it passes through the connecting hoses. (FO—8/78, p. 90).

Fleeter Heater is actually a constant-flow, temperature-controlled system consisting of a 40-gallon reservoir, a constant-circulating pump, and the quick-heat-recovery boiler. It allows the anti-freeze to flow at 140°F. during the warmer fall months and at 190°F during protracted cold spells.

The anti-freeze enters the engine block on the low side and returns on the high side. Each tractor exterior is equipped with quick-connect fittings for easy hose hookup. Pressure in the line is held at 6½ lbs. in conjunction with a 7 lb. radiator cap. This keeps the radiator full at all times, avoiding cavitation. Although anti-freeze circulates primarily through the engine block, Fischer says at 160°F the thermostat opens and it flows through the radiator.

While admitting the system has been around for some time and is no great discovery of his, Fischer does note that with easier winter start-ups "the former spring ritual of replacing blown head gaskets and clutches, worn out before their time, has been happily discontinued."

"In the old days," he says, "it would take six men beginning work at midnight to push and pull the equipment and introduce ether. Even then we wouldn't have all of the tractors on the road until 10 or 11am Monday morning. Now, two men begin start-up at midnight and have all 218 tractors out of the yard by 8am each Monday."

Although city straight trucks are not on the Fleeter Heater system, the ethylene glycol in all vehicles is reconditioned with Zecol rust inhibitor, manufactured by Lubaid Enterprises. The cooling system drain interval for straight trucks is set at two years.

Vehicle life expectancy

Advance Transportation plans on extracting 10 years of life from a linehaul tractor, using two engines. That figure is upped to 12 years for city-delivery units and trailers. Trailer life is based on a 5-year period of rebuilding, during which units are relined, sandblasted, and repainted. Power equipment is scheduled for 4-year repainting cycles.

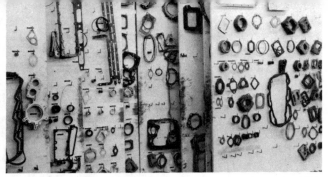
Unique arrangement of eight sliding panels makes instantly visible every engine gasket and component gasket used in the operation.

The company does all of its truck and trailer repair and rebuilding, with the exception of boring or sleeving blocks and rebuilding Bosch pumps. Caterpillar ejectors and ejector pumps are rebuilt on the premises.

Preventive maintenance

Advance Transportation puts line-haul units through minor PM cycles at 50,000 miles, and major PM overhauls—when wheel bearings are checked and brakes relined—at 100,000 miles.

City trucks and tractors are minored every six months and majored every two years. Linehaul and city trailers also are majored every two years. With this program Fischer obtains 350,000 miles from a Cat road engine and

Bill Fischer checks the tire elevator that allows rubber storage on an upper floor, in a temperature-controlled atmosphere.

Rebuilt engines and transmissions are stored in a clean, dry area. Caterpillar models 1674, 3208, 3306, and 3406 are used.

One of Advance Transportation's Ford 9000 city tandems with the Caterpillar 3306 engine (6-cyl., 250-hp.) and the Fuller RT910 manual transmission.

Volvo F86 city tractor (below) has been tested by Advance Transportation for seven full months. Company reports that the truck's performance has been listed as "very satisfactory."

says, "We only go into the engine once during the lifetime of a tractor."

Linehaul equipment is lubed at 7,000-mile intervals, including oil and filter change, while city equipment is similarly serviced every 45 days.

As with many other fleets, the Advance Transportation fuel island is becoming passé; instead, a tanker is used to refuel the fleet. Fischer says this method, designed to save endless hours of yard jockeying, paid for itself almost at once.

Today, president Jim Joppe, who began as a salesman for the company in 1946, says Advance Transportation as a common carrier moves over 40% of the truck cargo between Chicago and Milwaukee, handling at least 50,000 individual shipments each month. In addition to Milwaukee and Racine in Wisconsin, the company maintains terminals in Aurora, Peoria, and Chicago, Ill. In fact, a considerable portion of the freight emanating from Peoria consists of Caterpillar products.

In addition to August Lindner and Joppe, the company is currently under the direction of Ronald G. Lindner, executive vp and treasurer; Richard H. Lindner, first vp and secretary; and Glenn Carroll, vp-operations.

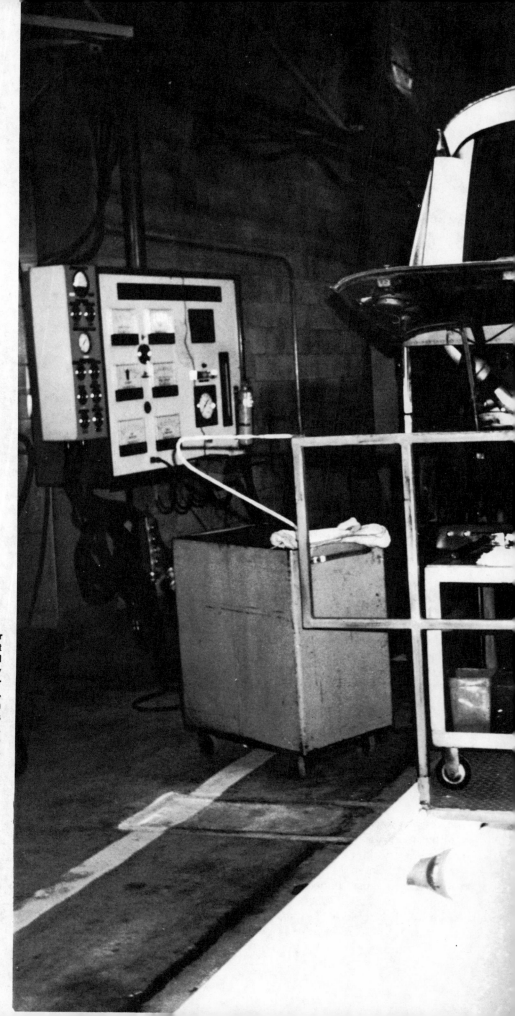

Shop-built safety rail and platform for mechanic's tool toter spans brightly lighted pit in dynamometer room (right.) Control and gauge panel at left of photo is within easy view and reach. Exterior view of garage (far right) taken from atop one of the grassed, landscaped berms shielding the building from sight and hearing of adjoining residents, shows handsome exposed aggregate exterior walls. Matching finish aluminum fascia above the walls masks roof-mounted ventilation fan ducts and other unsightly equipment.

Imagine yourself the general manager of a large transit bus fleet. You have in your hand a detailed study that points clearly to the need for a new, modern operating garage. But the only feasible site is a piece of undeveloped land with three big handicaps:

☐ The land is partly wooded, partly swamp.

☐ Handsome residences abut the land on two sides.

☐ Corridors must be left open for a projected rapid-transit rail line that would run alongside the property.

Those were the problems facing Hector Chaput, general manager of the Ottawa-Carleton Regional Transit Commission (OCRTC), in planning the Commission's new Pinecrest bus operating garage in Ottawa, Ontario, Canada.

The unfavorable soil conditions could be overcome by the architect through use of piling and special floor engineering.

The next problem, predictable opposition by the resi-

Fitting a bus garage into the community

dents abutting the property on two sides, was a thornier issue. After preliminary plans were drawn, OCRTC met with the residents to inform them of the plans and the garage design, and of OCRTC's desire to be a good neighbor and not to degrade the residents' life style or property values.

After the first meeting, with some residents' opposition still evident, a table-top scale model of the proposed

by Jack Lyndall, senior editor/equipment

garage was made for showing at a second meeting. With the model clearly showing berms, tree plantings, and the tasteful building design, and with OCRTC agreeing to several minor design changes, a majority of residents approved the garage plans.

The last problem, to leave open projected rapid-transit corridors along the Queensway (an expressway through Ottawa), was solved by locating the shop at an angle on the site. That change also contributed to operating efficiency by eliminating the need for buses to make a double turn when entering and leaving the garage.

The OCRTC Pinecrest garage performs three main functions for the 190 buses based there: daily servicing and cleaning, storage, and preventive maintenance plus repairs. It is not staffed or equipped for major vehicle or component rebuild; that is done at the OCRTC main St. Laurent shops.

A walking tour of the facility, in the company of two of its principal planners—R.M. Weitzel, equipment engineer, and Peter J. Newgard, plant and equipment engineer—shows how well the garage does its job.

The handsome building, with vertical rib, sandwich-panel walls with exposed aggregate finish, measures 312 ft. wide and 418 ft. long. Total floor space is 132,016 sq. ft., less walls and partitions.

From the main driveway entrance, buses returning from runs drive through the gate and along the north wall to an offset with doors in each end (No. 3 on floor-plan drawing). Just inside that main jack-knife door is a small, glassed-in booth. As each returning bus comes to that booth, a man inside directs the driver to a parking spot in one of the three bus-storage bays (20) or in the turning-area bay (19), which is used for night parking when all other storage areas are full.

Each storage bay measures 75x262 ft. A 50x418 ft. transfer aisle extends across the north side, and much of it is used for parking after the storage bays are full.

During evening or night hours, a garage attendant drives the buses from storage, through the big roll-up doors along the south wall, and into service lanes (27).

Actually, there are two service lanes. As a bus enters the regular service lane, the one nearest the west wall, it stops at the fueling location and for interior vacuum cleaning. The OCRTC-designed diesel-fuel dispenser combines several components: a 40-gpm pump, a recording meter made by RNG Equipment Ltd., and a Buckeye 690 nozzle with long extension. From the pump, fuel flows through two 5-micron filters supplied by 3-L Filters Ltd. (Weitzel comments that, even though the fuel dispenser can deliver 40 gpm, bus fuel tanks normally will only accept fuel at a rate of 30 gpm.)

The fuel dispenser draws fuel from two 10,000-gal. underground storage tanks adjacent to the outer wall of the service lane. Piping and valves for those tanks are arranged so fuel can be shut off from inside the lane or outside and either tank can be isolated as desired.

Next to the fuel dispenser is a portable vacuum cleaner. Made by Dustbane Enterprises Ltd., the Model DC-8

cleaner mounts on top of a 55-gal. drum, which serves as the dirt receptacle. With its two high-performance motor-blower units and its long flexible hoses, which are pulled in through the bus door, the vacuum quickly removes all dirt and trash from the buses.

Also at the fueling station is a low-pressure pump that dispenses windshield washer fluid. On the opposite side of the service lane is a hose that pumps transmission fluid. The windshield washer fluid and transmission fluid are checked together on a weekly schedule.

Beyond the fueling station, where the Duncan fare box vault is also located, is an automatic brush-type washer made by Washtronics, Winnipeg, Manitoba.

Major inspection bays (10,11,12 on floor plan) have hydraulic lifts plus overhead lube and grease reel system (left). Close-up view of Z-duct heat exchanger in garage ceiling (center) shows heat transfer unit in center which transfers heat from outgoing air in upper duct to incoming air in lower duct. View of tire and brake area (7,8 on floor plan) shows tire equipment at rear (right).

After passing through the washer, a bus is returned to the storage bays by a garage attendant unless it is scheduled for preventive maintenance inspection or repairs when it goes to the shop area.

Alongside the main service lane is a second lane used primarily for bus inspections and minor repairs. This lane has an in-floor pit with snow-white painted walls. Newgard points out that the lighting for such pits was studied carefully in an attempt to put enough light on the underside of a bus so that mechanics' drop lights would be unnecessary. The 200-watt, explosion-proof lights are staggered along the pit walls and do give better lighting, but some areas under a bus still require a drop light.

Shop and repair areas

Ranged along the western end of the building, flanking the service lanes, are eight areas or departments for bus inspection, maintenance, and repairs.

At the north end of the shop area, adjacent to the wall, is the steam-cleaning area, which is equipped with a modern, high-pressure steam cleaner that cleans all components removed from a bus as well as the bus itself.

The steam-cleaning area was especially busy as FLEET OWNER inspected the shop. Weitzel explained that OCRTC conducts a "demudding" program each spring to remove all of the winter's accumulation of mud and

dried salt from the bus undercarriage, door hinges, and other areas where it collects. Prompt and thorough removal reduces corrosion damage.

Next to the steam-cleaning area, at the northern end of the shop area, is a fully enclosed chassis dynamometer room (6), which is equipped with a Maxwell Model 7512 water-brake dynamometer. In addition to testing rear wheels for bus power, road speed, etc., the dynamometer can test front wheels for brake performance, wheel balance, or shimmy at speeds up to 60 mph.

An auxiliary dynamometer panel, built by the shop, has gauges for engine intake manifold pressure, fuel pressure at the filter, fuel pressure at the manifold (those two gauges show pressure drop across the fuel filter, which is the determining factor in filter replacement), air-box exhaust pressure, torque pressure (with separate gauges for turbine-inlet and turbine-outlet pressure), and gauges for the main, hydraulic, and direct-drive sensing line. There is also a portable engine-coolant temperature gauge.

The dynamometer room has a floor pit, which is as brightly lighted as the pit in the inspection/service lane. Newgard points out an interesting safety feature: Fresh air is pumped into the pits and stale air or fumes are drawn out by a 2,000-cfm exhaust fan. Because the

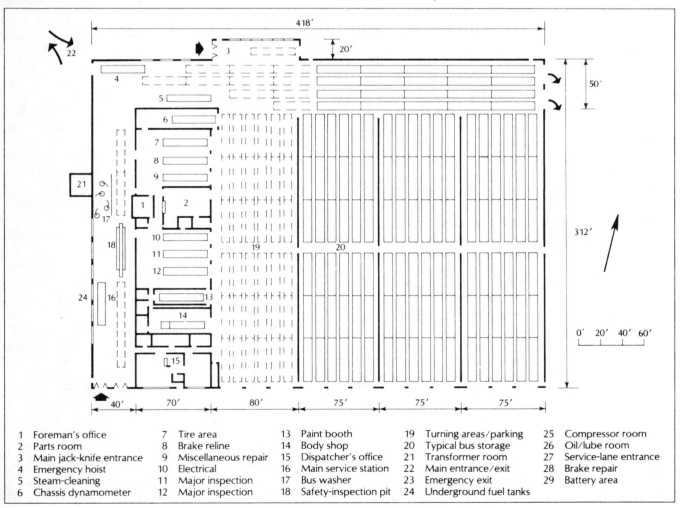

1	Foreman's office	7	Tire area	13	Paint booth	19	Turning areas/parking	25	Compressor room
2	Parts room	8	Brake reline	14	Body shop	20	Typical bus storage	26	Oil/lube room
3	Main jack-knife entrance	9	Miscellaneous repair	15	Dispatcher's office	21	Transformer room	27	Service-lane entrance
4	Emergency hoist	10	Electrical	16	Main service station	22	Main entrance/exit	28	Brake repair
5	Steam-cleaning	11	Major inspection	17	Bus washer	23	Emergency exit	29	Battery area
6	Chassis dynamometer	12	Major inspection	18	Safety-inspection pit	24	Underground fuel tanks		

incoming fresh air is pumped in at 2200 cfm, the pit is mildly "pressurized," thus preventing accumulation of the heavier-than-air fumes.

Next to the dynamometer room is a large triple bay equipped with three Dover Rotary hydraulic lifts, (7, 8, 9). Lift No. 7 is used for tire work; No. 8 primarily for brake relines; and No. 9 for miscellaneous repairs.

A long rack along the north wall of that room holds tires ready for mounting. Behind the lift is tire equipment, including a Bishman tire-mounting and demounting machine and a large tire-siping machine (FO-9/77, p. 85). OCRTC regularly sipes its tires.

The brake department removes bus wheels, drums, and brake shoes, and sends them for steam-cleaning before re-use. Cleaned brake shoes are dipped in Sunko-rite rust-proofing compound in a shop-built dip tank with drainage rack. When the compound dries, shoes are relined and rollers replaced as necessary.

Brake drums are turned on a Van Norman drum lathe. The relined shoes are mounted on a bus and are ground to the size of the drum by a Gordon grinder.

The brake department also reconditions axle radius rods, using a 60-ton Nike hydraulic arbor press to remove and replace rod eye bushings. The radius rods receive the same rust-proofing as the brake shoes.

Next to the parts room is another three-bay area (10, 11, 12). It, too, has three hydraulic Dover Rotary lifts. The lift nearest the parts room (10) is used primarily for electrical-system work; the others are used for major pm inspections.

Centered in the repair shop area along its west wall is the foreman's office (1). Through glass windows in all four walls, the foreman supervises the service lanes, the two main bus repair and maintenance bays, and the parts room, which is directly across the aisle.

Next to the major inspection bays is a modern DeVil-biss paint spray booth (13) that measures 16 ft. wide, 60 ft. long, and 10 ft. high. Across the aisle (behind the spray booth) are fireproof rooms for storing paint and thinners.

The last room or bay in the shop is the body shop (14), which has a capacity for one bus at a time. Among its full set of body repair equipment is a Snap-on hydraulic body-ram set.

An electronic precipitator in the body shop serves as a "smoke eater" for fumes from the welding area along the north wall. The precipitator makes it unnecessary to have a flue and fan to vent welding fumes to the outside.

All of the bus repair bays, from the dynamometer to the body shop, have roll-up doors opening into the turning-area bay (19). Those doors help maintain comfortable working temperatures in the repair bays in winter, when the turning-bay doors are open for bus movements.

Building utilities

Heating and ventilating are vitally important in Otta-wa's rigorous winters. To conserve natural gas used for heating, the three storage bays and the turning bay are equipped with four Z-Duct heat exchangers. Those units take heat from the air exhausted through roof vents and transfer it to recirculated air drawn in from the building space. Some fresh air is drawn in from outside and heated, but Newgard reports the heat exchangers recapture up to 70% of the heat in air being exhausted from the building.

Because of the local electric-utility's generally excellent reliability record, the Pinecrest Garage is not equipped with its own stand-by generator. There are, however, approximately 30 battery-powered emergency lights (with trickle chargers) throughout the building. Those lights have a life of approximately 30 minutes if power fails, ample to evacuate the personnel if necessary.

But local power outages can occur due to an isolated transformer failure or a vehicle knocking down a vital line pole, so OCRTC is arranging to provide emergency power protection for Pinecrest and several other facilities. An engine generator is being mounted on a service truck, and the OCRTC facilities are being equipped with receptacles so the engine-generator unit can be almost instantly plugged into a building's electric system.

Should power fail, the portable generator will be dispatched immediately and, within a few minutes, provide power until commercial power is restored.

The entire Pinecrest garage is protected against fire by an automatic sprinkler system. Sprinkler pipes near the building doors are filled with anti-freeze to prevent freezing if the doors are open for an extended period in bitter cold weather. Anti-drainback valves prevent the anti-freeze from migrating backward into the system and possibly contaminating the drinking water.

The Pinecrest garage is open 24 hours per day, five days per week. Weitzel reports that in the total staff of 58 people there are 17 first-class mechanics, two of them body mechanics. Eleven mechanics, including those body men, work the day shift. The remaining six mechanics are divided between the second and third shifts.

Two semi-skilled men work the day shift, doing such jobs as cleaning brake shoes and bolting on new linings.

During the day shift, seven garage attendants shuttle buses through the service lanes, clean (including interior "shampooing" of all buses regularly, and handle other bus movements. Twelve other attendants are on the second and third shifts to handle the heavy night schedule of washing and servicing the Pinecrest fleet.

In addition to the 185 large transit buses based at Pinecrest, there are five Deutz diesel-engine-powered minibuses assigned to "Dial-a-Ride" service, and about 10 miscellaneous service vehicles, including snow-removal equipment, wrecker, and other utility vehicles.

Proving the value of the long and careful planning prior to construction, Chaput reports there have been no complaints about the garage from the nearby residents. And its efficiency has helped achieve a good record of fleet availability. Weitzel reports the OCRTC fleet operates regularly with only a little over 5% of its buses out of service for maintenance or repairs. 🚌

Private fleet builds award winning shop

by Lee J. Rocheford,
associate editor/technical

A layout to accommodate the needs of the job, plus siting to serve the market, are the two halves of the success of National Tea Co.'s shop and distribution center at Hodgkins, Ill., near Chicago

National handles foods, many of them perishable, so minimum delays are desirable, both in accepting incoming shipments and in dispatching loads to retail outlets. A spacious warehouse and a modern controlled-temperature and humidity facility give further protection to produce and refrigerated items.

The distribution center and shop, designed by the Austin Co., Chicago, was deliberately placed so departing trucks can be on an Interstate in less than five minutes.

Typical of the modern design of the plant is the fuel island, which handles two lane traffic, and serves up diesel, gas—leaded and unleaded—anti-freeze, and motor oil. The fluids are dispensed from over-

Photo by Jim Bald

head lines, to keep them out of the roadways, and flow through automatic dispensing nozzles, for faster handling. The liquids are maintained in underground storage tanks: 20,000 gal. for diesel; 10,000 gal. capacity for regular gasoline and 2,000 for lead-free; 1,500 for anti-freeze; and 1,500 for the motor oil. The island is sheltered by a canopy.

The shop—from the top

While the distribution center is the core of the National operation, it is the shop that makes it go. The shop is divided into three major sections: trailer

Photos by Lee J. Rocheford

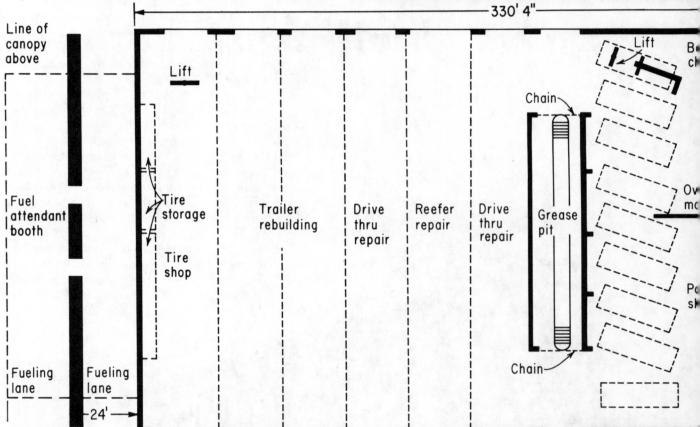

rebuild, service and PM; major maintenance; repair and repainting. It begins at the north end of the shop with seven drive-through lanes, each 20x130 ft., and devoted to separate functions.

Lane 1 is the tire shop, with racks along the north wall that can store up to 200 tires. Equipment includes an 18,000-lb. end lift for speeding tire changes, a tire breaker, dip tank and twin 10 hp. air compressors that also supply air for the rest of the shop. The tire shop does all its own work except for recaps and section repairs.

Lanes 2 through 4 are devoted to trailer maintenance, the first two for heavy work, the last for fast drive-through repairs like lights, mud flaps, and springs.

The two heavy-duty repair lanes, with their 130-ft. length, can take two trailers at a time with no crowding. The trailers come in from each end, with the center area occupied with heavy woodworking machines, welding equipment, and stacks of plywood sheeting for doors, panel, and roof repairs. Ed Vanderheyden, shop manager, says he can rebuild a trailer from the ground up in his shop.

Lane 5 is home territory for the reefer crews, who can handle "all major and minor refrigeration repairs," according to Vanderheyden. They keep 150 refrigerated trailers in shape from their lane. (The regular fleet of dry freight trailers numbers 277.)

Lane 6 is another drive-through type, this time for power equipment. Repairs handled include lights, air

Grease pit equipped with rolling oil drain pan can handle up to three tractors at a time. Walls protect the perimeter of the pit.

Wash rack for the interior of the vans and trailers feature open grating to eliminate water build-up while still catching debris.

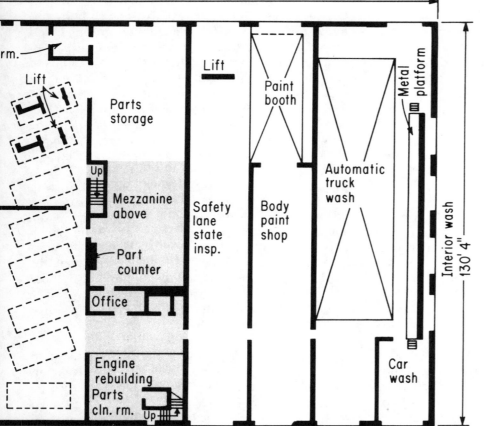

rm.

Lift

Parts storage

Up

Mezzanine above

Part counter

Office

Engine rebuilding Parts cln. rm.

Up

Lift

Paint booth

Safety lane state insp.

Body paint shop

Automatic truck wash

Metal platform

Interior wash 130' 4"

Car wash

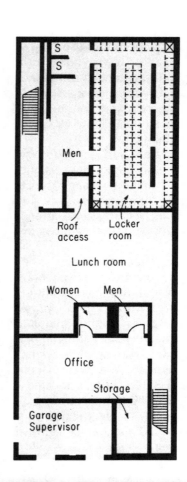

S
S

Men

Roof access

Locker room

Lunch room

Women   Men

Office

Storage

Garage Supervisor

Protection from the weather is offered in this ideal fueling location. Note how the overhead hose will keep the ground area clear and safe.

Spacious well lit trailer shop allows the shop personnel to do all trailer repairs including rebuilds from the ground up if needed.

leaks, tuneups and starters. Drivers who find minor mechanical faults when they make their own pre-trip inspections also use Lane 6.

Lane 7 has a 70-ft. pit that can handle grease jobs on three tractors simultaneously. The pit has a rolling drain pan and recessed lube reels that feed both the pit area and the neighboring drive-through lane. Scheduled PM work is done in the pit, along with lube work.

Safety and good housekeeping practices abound. The pit, for instance, is enclosed on two sides by a 4-ft. concrete wall and the ends are chained off to keep personnel safely away. In the main shop, the next main section, the battery room contains an OSHA approved shower and eyewash basin.

Seventeen at once

The main shop area, where major overhauls are taken care of, measures 85x130 ft. (see drawing) and is entered through two overhead doors at either side of the area. The shop maintains 182 power units and 118 company cars, and can handle as many as 17 units at a time with ample working room.

Hoists are well-placed and available. One, a 36,000-lb. unit is located just inside the east door; near the battery room are two 24,000-pounders; and a 4,000-lb. electric hoist is mounted on a monorail for use by mechanics in the middle of the main shop area.

Vanderheyden and his crew of four working fore-men, 16 journeymen mechanics, and three apprentices work on a 24-hour/day basis, as do six body and trailer men with one apprentice, two tire men, and nine washers and fuelers. The office is run with a staff of two. The major overhaul section is completed with the parts room, parts cleaning room and engine rebuild shop, the office and the locker room section.

National Tea does all its own state required inspections on the spot, with one drive-through lane equipped with all state-required equipment, Weaver safety lane devices, and another hoist (18,000 lb.).

The final area, devoted to body repair, includes a pre-paint area, a complete paint spray booth, with vehicle identification, and a car wash.

The truck wash is a model of good design. From the same dock, four trailers can be washed out in succession without the cleaner having to climb up and down into the units. He merely walks along the dock and into the trailers, handling one unit about each 6 min. A wash wand handles stains with high pressure and a brush attachment. Dock lights ensure a clean and safe job.

Heat is provided during winter with hot water units that reportedly recover quickly when the doors are opened to the Illinois weather. Lighting is mainly fluorescent, with smaller lamps in necessary areas for safety and precise work. An exhaust system works with 12 drop hoses spread throughout the shop. 🚚

Clean equipment is a must when you carry food products so National installed an truck washing machine to do the job right.

Riteway: Two operations, one roof

Because their functions overlap, Riteway Rentals and Riteway Repair and Equipment, Inc., were able to combine their operations, plus a warehouse, under a single roof.

Located in East Brunswick, N.J., Riteway Rentals is a fast-growing truck rental and leasing firm. It serves New York, New Jersey, and Pennsylvania, specializing in trailers and heavy-duty trucks and tractors.

The affiliate company, Riteway Repair and Equipment, offers complete truck and trailer body repairs and painting, and distributes and installs truck equipment.

The Riteway Rentals fleet based at the new headquarters includes about 155 tractors and 200 trailers, according to David Dondershine, president. He said other major Riteway Rentals shops are located in Elizabeth and Camden, N.J.

Situated in a rapidly-growing industrial park near Exit Nine on the New Jersey Turnpike, the handsome new building was designed by Chapman-Biber, architects, Summit, N.J. In addition to the two shops and company offices, the building also includes warehouse space which is rented.

The basic configuration of the building is two rectangles, a

By Jack Lyndall,
Senior Editor

smaller one adjoining the larger. The smaller rectangle houses the offices and Riteway Rentals shop; the larger rectangle contains the Riteway Repair and Equipment shop and the warehouse.

Dondershine said the entire building covers approximately 46,000 square ft. The rental operation has 6,000 square ft of office space and 7,000 square ft of shop. The repair and equipment operation has 11,000 square ft of shop space, and the warehouse takes up 22,000 square ft. The building cost a little over $600,000.

The truck and trailer repair shop area measures 60- by 77-ft, about two-thirds of the total shop area. The balance is partitioned off for the tire shop.

Because of the adjoining warehouse, the truck and trailer shop does not have drive-through bays. George Zorn, maintenance director, said the layout includes three long repair bays, with a pit located in the center bay near the outside doors.

Since the three bays are 77 ft long, Zorn uses the space at the inner ends of the bays for major repair jobs. The area near the doors is used for minor repairs and PM work. "Every piece of equipment gets a PM service once a month without exception," Zorn said. "We have an ABC inspection set up. On a minimum cycle, we perform the A inspection and service twice in succession, followed by a B service. The major C service is done once a year as a minimum.

"As vehicle mileage goes up, we shorten the cycle. For a vehicle that is running over 6,000 miles per month, we go to an A-B cycle with a maximum of 12,000 miles between oil changes. As soon as mileage goes over 8,000 miles per month, we go to a straight B service each month, by-passing the A inspections."

In addition to the PM system, the new East Brunswick shop does

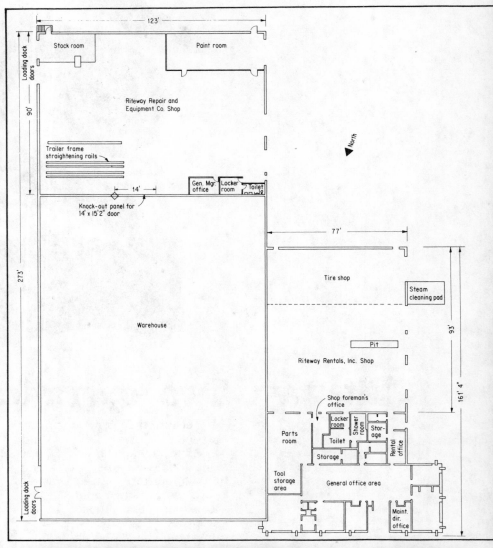

George Zorn with wall charts that aid Riteway in determining its exact cost per mile.

A Riteway Rental COE in the shop for PM. Major work is done at one end of the bay, minor work at the other.

Riteway Rental's parts room has modern steel shelving and racks for storing small parts, gaskets, and hoses. ▼

A Riteway Rental unit is positioned over a pit for lubrication and oil change.

Shop foreman checks repair order before starting work on a Riteway Rental unit. ▶

all routine repairs and removal and replacement of all major components. This includes a limited number of out-of-frame engine overhauls. Zorn said replacement schedules for most Riteway Rentals tractors are set up so that the vehicle is replaced before the engine requires overhaul.

Transmission and rear-axle overhauls are farmed out to the Riteway Repair and Equipment shop, as are major body repairs and wreck-rebuild jobs. All electrical component rebuilding is farmed-out to specialists.

To speed up body repairs, the shop stocks components such as front fenders and pre-painted cab doors. As soon as the new parts are installed, the vehicle is back in service with no delay for painting.

"Because we recognize the value of mechanic training," Zorn said, "we hold schools right here on the property. He said most of the schools are scheduled on Saturday morning because the rental mechanics work a 5½ day week, and the schedule allows attendance by at least two shifts that overlap.

Zorn said the shop arrangement also offers the option of a U-shaped flow of vehicles through the shop around the pit. Work stalls for tractors can be located along the west and south walls of the shop.

There are no hoists in the shop. Zorn said he prefers to use Greyco bay lifts, which give complete flexibility for hoisting a vehicle anywhere in the shop. The pit is used for servicing large straight trucks and tractors.

An Alemite overhead reel system supplies oil and chassis lube for the pit. The oil is pumped from a 3,000 gal. underground bulk storage tank. The grease is pumped from drums.

An office for the general foreman is located on the south side of the Riteway Rentals shop. It adjoins the parts and tool storage room which has doors opening into the foreman's office and the maintenance shop.

Also located on the south side of the shop are the mechanics' lockers and rest rooms. There is a large locker for each of the 11 mechanics. The shop supervisory force includes the general foreman and two shift foremen. The shop operates 24 hours a day.

With the around-the-clock operation, shop lighting is important. Zorn said the large mercury-vapor overhead lights are spaced on 15 ft centers.

Two important emergency features were designed into the shop. There is a separate group of emergency fluorescent lights, operated by battery power. The entire building is protected against fire by a high capacity overhead sprinkler system.

An Engwald in-floor exhaust removal system extends to all three truck repair bays. This type was chosen, Zorn said, because a horizontal exhaust system is "standard" on Riteway Rentals units.

Along the north side of the truck repair shop a wire mesh screen serves as a partition between the truck shop and the tire repair area. On the truck shop side of the partition, a bank of large shelves stores heavy components, mounted spare tires, and a variety of shop tools.

The tire repair area measures approximately 30- by 77-ft. It has a roll-up door since it was originally planned for an additional truck repair shop bay. But Zorn felt that it was more important to move the tire department from the former main shop at Elizabeth, so it could better serve the entire Riteway Rentals shop system.

The tire shop makes all repairs to tires and mounts all new tires as needed. Recapping is sent out. High racks on both sides of the tire repair area store mounted tires

ready for use or shipment.

Similar high racks are outdoors, ranged along the north wall of the tire repair area and the adjoining east wall of the warehouse section. These racks store scrap tires and those waiting to be sent for recapping or adjustment. The neat racks eliminate the unsightly piles of scrap tires so often seen at some shops.

Located next to the tire shop's roll-up door is an outdoor steam cleaning stand. It measures 14- by 21-ft, and has a rounded concrete curb to keep the steam and water from running over the black-top paved yard. The Jenny steam cleaner is portable and can be rolled outside when the pad is in use for other jobs.

Barton Satsky, president of Riteway Repair and Equipment, said his company operates from 7:00 a.m. until 4:30 p.m. for body repairs and painting. But, he added that there is a second shift to do PM and other repairs for other fleets that are not Riteway Rental customers. He said Riteway Repair also offers towing and wrecker service.

The main shop of the "Repair Company," as it is called by the employees, measures 90- by 120-ft, less the space occupied by the parts stock room, the paint room, and the office of Raymond DelSol, general manager.

The repair company is also a truck equipment distributor for several lines, including the Leyman Ley-Vador. The staff includes two shift foremen and 11 mechanics. Three of the mechanics specialize in vehicle repairs and road service; the other eight men are body and paint specialists.

Along the south wall of the shop is DelSol's office, the lockers, and rest rooms for the mechanics. At the southwest corner of the shop are two sets of steel I-beams set in the concrete floor. The I-beams are 40 ft long and 5¼ in.

wide. They are used as anchorage points for straightening trailer frames or bodies.

The northwest corner of the repair company shop is occupied by the parts room. It measures approximately 15- by 30-ft, with steel mesh walls which are easily moved. There are two roll-up doors at the rear of the parts room and a loading dock.

At the northeast corner is the modern paint spray room that measures approximately 20 by 55-ft. It meets all applicable fire safety code rules.

"With the major equipment in the shop," Satsky said, "the repair company mechanics can do anything from straightening a tractor frame to painting a 45 ft trailer."

Other items of equipment in the repair company shop include an Airco MIG welding machine, an Ausco bay-lift rated at 10,000 lb capacity, a Nye pipe-threader, a Hendey 12 in. swing-lathe, a Bridgeport bench grinder, a Star brake shoe service machine, in addition to an Ausco 15 ton hydraulic arbor press.

Heating for both shops is by gas-fired overhead unit heaters. The repair company shop also has mercury vapor lights.

With Riteway Rental's rapid growth since its beginning in 1966, future expansion figured in the shop plans. Although the shop occupies all available land at the site, future shop expansion will take over space now devoted to the warehouse. In fact, a knock-out panel for a 14- by 15-ft door opening was built into the wall between the repair company shop and the warehouse.

Dondershine said the warehouse space is rented under a comparatively short-term lease. But he also points out that the new facilities can handle fleet growth up to 250 tractors and 450 trailers before additional expansion may become necessary. ◼

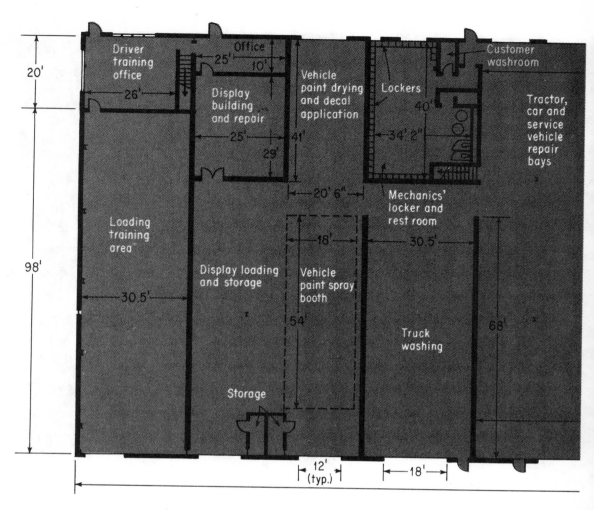

Mayflower builds shop for second half-century

by Jack Lyndall

With only a year to go to complete its first 50 years in business, Mayflower Corp. has recently completed a new international headquarters at Indianapolis, Ind. The twin building complex includes a 63,000 sq. ft. vehicle maintenance building and the headquarters and administration building.

The move to the ultra-modern new facilities on a 57-acre site just off I-465 on U.S. Rt. 421 meets a precept stated by the giant moving firm some years ago, "We do things first because our customers come first." The new facilities replaced two smaller, outmoded locations near downtown Indianapolis (also see State Trucking Closeup).

Located toward the rear of the property, the vehicle maintenance building is a steel pre-engineered

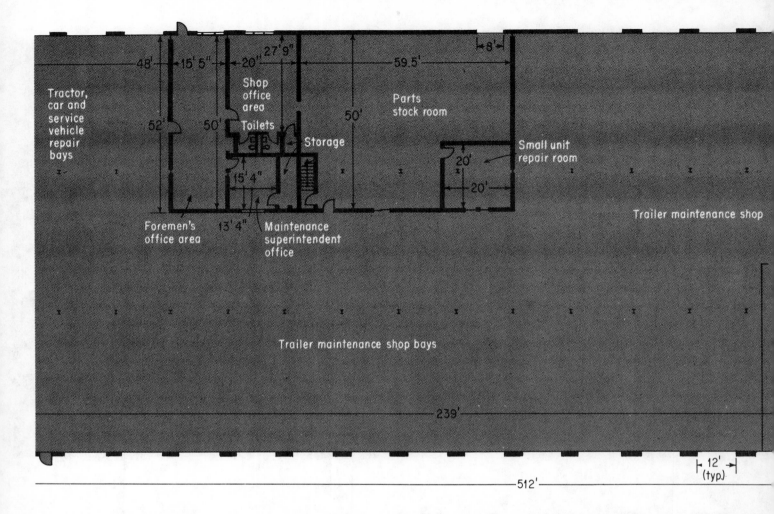

Butler structure with adaptations to fit the needs of Aero Mayflower Transit Co., Inc., the principal subsidiary of Mayflower Corp., and operator of the world-wide moving business.

The shop was designed by Everett I. Brown Co., architects and engineers, Indianapolis, (who also designed the new headquarters building.)

Much of the planning for the new shop can be credited to Fred J. Grumme, chairman of the board of Aero Mayflower, according to Robert L. Hart, assistant vice president-maintenance. Hart points out that Grumme had served as maintenance superintendent for Aero Mayflower in Irvington, N.J. from 1938 to 1941, and then transferred to the same position at company headquarters in Indianapolis from 1941-47. So Hart says that Grumme understood and fully supported the need for the best possible maintenance facility.

Hart says, "At about the time we decided to design the shop, we saw a picture of a wide shop roof overhang in a copy of FLEET OWNER. Mr. Grumme believed that to be a very useful feature. It would permit us to leave the shop doors open in summer rainstorms, and vehicles could be parked lengthwise or backed under the wide overhang for minor maintenance or repair jobs outdoors in mild weather, but still be protected in case of rain. So the wide roof overhang was designed into the building."

Hart says, "We found from our review of many published shop layouts that the most popular shop width seems to be 100 ft. But because of variations in our tractor and trailer lengths, we designed for a 60-ft. long bay on one side of the shop and a 50-ft. bay on the other with a 10 ft. wide aisle offset from the shop center line."

Mindful of rigorous midwest winters, Hart points out, "All floor drainage is toward the edge or rear of the bays to prevent snow droppings in winter from creating a water problem on the bay floors."

The general configuration of the shop is a long, narrow rectangle (see floor plan.)

Hart noted that the new shop is the sole company-operated facility for maintenance and repair of the approximately 2,000 company-owned trailers.

There are approximately 5,600 vehicles in the Mayflower system, with approximately 3,600 owned and maintained by affiliated Mayflower agents. Hart says that, in addition to maintaining the company owned

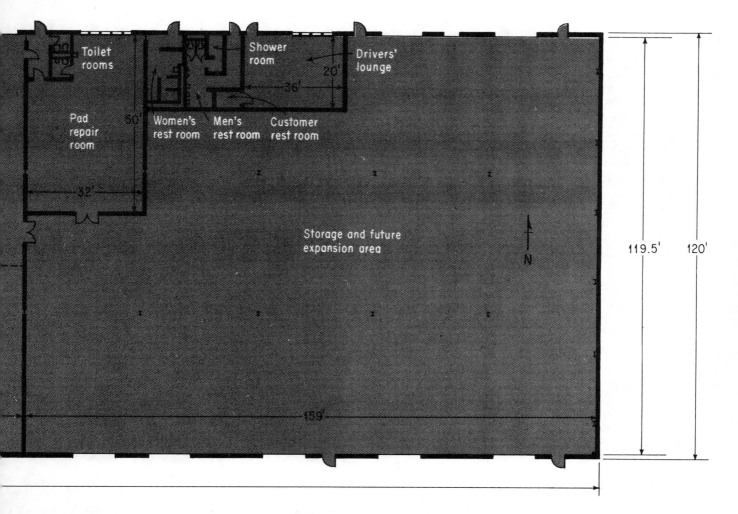

trailers (700 are domiciled and assigned to the Indianapolis headquarters), "We take care of all the agent's trucks that want or need service as they come through here. We average about 450 repair orders a month, which includes both company-owned and agent's units, but does not include a scheduled refurbishing program on company-owned trailers. We have approximately 14 company-owned tractors that operate from the U.S. into Canada and back; the rest are all owner-operator units."

Although the tractors are nearly all owner-operator units, Mayflower exercises close supervision of those tractors for safety and dependability reasons, Hart stresses. "We do not permit any work to be done on a tractor away from this shop except in the shop of an authorized franchised dealer."

"All maintenance is controlled from here; all emergency work on trailers anywhere in the U.S. is authorized from here; and we purchase all tractors and trailers from here."

Although the owner-operators are responsible for the maintenance and repair costs on their own tractors, Hart says the new Mayflower shop will do most maintenance or repair (except major engine rebuilds)

on owner-operator units, and bill the owner for the cost.

Also, the Mayflower shop must inspect and approve all owner-operator tractors before they are permitted to go into service for Mayflower.

In addition to the tractors and trailers, Hart notes that the shop services some 60 to 70 fleet cars required in business by company executives, district managers, salesmen, etc., and several shop service vehicles.

The personnel roster at the shop totals approximately 64, including 16 first class mechanics, four mechanic's helpers, three shift foremen, 19 trailer body men, two painters, three lettering and decal men, six shop office personnel, two furniture pad repair people, and four utility men. The shop operates two shifts, with 10 of the total roster assigned to the second shift. The oldest employees in years of service started in 1935; many more have 15-25 years of service.

Parts layout follows demand

Besides Hart's office, facilities in the central service core include a shop office where vehicle maintenance records, job costs, etc. are computed and kept, a room for the shift foremen, and rest rooms for both men and women employees.

The largest part of the service core is devoted to the parts stock room. Here, Hart explained two time-saving and efficiency improving ideas. "For a year, we kept a record of every item dispensed through the parts room window and how often the part was used. That's how the parts are arranged now in the parts room, according to frequency of use. Those used most often are nearest the window."

But some rows of parts shelves and bins are devoted to a complete parts category. For example, one row of shelves and bins houses all parts used in a trailer brake system. A parts room man or mechanic can push a supermarket type cart down the aisle, picking every part for a brake overhaul in one pass.

Similarly, all parts needed to overhaul an air suspension are stocked in another row.

In a mezzanine area above the central service core and parts room, large and bulky parts, like trailer doors, side or roof panels, axles, landing gears, etc., are stored.

Adjoining the foreman's office on the west side are three drive-in bays for tractor service. Each has its own roll-up, translucent fiber glass door, as does each shop bay. The bay nearest the foremen's office has a large overhead canopy type exhaust removal system that eliminates flexible tubes to a vertical exhaust stack when running the engine in the shop. The bays also service the fleet cars or service vehicles.

The modern paint spray booth can accommodate

Long center aisle traverses entire trailer repair bay area. Each bay has its own power operated roll-up type exterior door.

Shop supervisor's desk just outside maintenance vice president's office wall (below, left) also is near parts room that flanks center aisle just beyond desk. Interior view in parts room (below, right) shows bin row containing all air brake system parts.

Modern paint booth can handle any Mayflower van. After painting and initial dust-free set, van goes into adjacent drying room where decals are put on.

Tire shop, which occupies one trailer repair bay area, has modern air-powered equipment. Auxiliary make-up air heater is overhead at rear of tire shop.

the largest Mayflower van. To speed up production, the paint drying and decal application room is directly opposite the paint booth. As soon as a freshly painted trailer can be moved, after the initial paint is set, it is moved directly into the drying area where it completes drying and where decals and hand lettering is done. The completed job then rolls out through the roll-up door for the drying room.

Beyond the paint and drying rooms, an area is currently being used by the operations department for making up and loading of industrial displays and for a school area where drivers are taught proper loading and packing methods for furniture or other items hauled by the Mayflower system.

Trailer and body shop bays

Twelve trailer service bays are ranged along the south side of the long shop, plus five additional bays along the north side wall behond the central service core. The trailer bays are equipped for any job from rebuilding a major wreck to a minor door hardware fix.

Hart explained that in case of damage or unexpected repair need to a Mayflower van on the road, an authorized dealer for the particular trailer make, if available, is given the okay to make emergency repairs sufficient to get the trailer safely back to the main shop, where permanent repairs are made.

The tire shop is equipped with modern air-powered tire handling equipment and has racks for storing new, used, or recapped tires. Hart says that while

the Mayflower trailers use mostly new tires, some Bandag recapped tires are used, and are also supplied to owner-operators of tractors.

In the tire shop area, a large auxiliary air heater mounted on a steel frame above the floor supplies heated make-up air. That compensates for lost heated shop air when the paint spray booth exhaust fans are operating. It's location near the far end of the shop ensures that the warmed make-up air is distributed evenly through the vehicle work bays.

plied by a Model 2012, Type 30 Ingersoll-Rand air compressor with 25 hp. electric motor.

There are also two Westinghouse Model 3YC-1 stand-by compressors; one has a 7½ hp. motor while the other is a 5 hp. unit.

In addition, a Johnson compressor with ¾ hp. motor supplies air for the shop's air operated heating system thermostats.

The shop itself is heated by overhead hot water unit heaters. The water is piped underground from

View of shop from northwest corner shows wide roof overhang on both sides of the Butler pre-engineered steel building.

At the end of the trailer work bays and tire shop, a cross partition wall encloses an area now used for storage of trailers waiting repairs, incoming parts shipments, etc. This area has roll-up doors for five more trailer repair bays along the south wall, plus two more doors and bays on the north side.

In this same area is the furniture pad repair and storage area. A skilled seamstress with a large sewing machine makes minor repairs to the thousands of pads used by Mayflower; Hart also notes that more badly damaged or worn pads are sent out for repairs and cleaning. All pads ready for service are stored in the pad storage area ready for issuance to trailers.

Alongside the pad storage and repair room is a comfortable driver's lounge, used by drivers waiting for dispatch or while minor repairs are done to a tractor or trailer. Since some of the owner-operators are husband-wife teams, the lounge has complete restroom facilities for both men and women. The only access to the lounge is an exterior door, with no door into the shop area from the lounge.

Equipment to support the job

Hart says, "We transferred most of the portable shop equipment from the former shops to this new one." But he notes, "We did get a new automatic tire changer. Also, a new automatic cab air conditioner system servicer; it evacuates the system, puts in new Freon, etc., automatically."

The large number of air powered tools used in the trailer repair work and the paint spray room are sup-

the heating plant for the new corporate headquarters building. The make-up air heater in the tire repair area uses a hot water heat exchanger.

All overhead piping in the shop is color coded. The steam heating system pipes are grey, cold water lines are green, and fire protection sprinkler system pipes are red. Compressed air lines are blue.

Security was provided for in planning due to the somewhat isolated shop location on the large tract of land. Hart points out that both doors to the parts stock room have ultrasonic burglar alarm systems. All exterior shop doors and doors to the various shop departments are protected by an ADT system.

Always a mark of good planning, provision was made for future expansion in both the shop and the new International Headquarters buildings.

As need for more shop space develops, Hart points out, "We have storage space on the east end of the building and we have display and training areas on the west end. We designed them so we can quickly knock down the walls."

He also notes that blank wall areas between several of the door openings in that storage area would permit installation of at least three more roll-up doors, making ten additional service bays instead of the seven now existing.

As pointed out by John B. Smith, president of Mayflower Corp., "The entire complex is designed for a continuing expansion program. Both the office space and the 57-acre site give Mayflower practically unlimited expansion capability in the future."

A shop, a training school and a parts depot

by Jack Lyndall,
senior editor

The recent completion of a huge world headquarters shop by North American Van lines on a 113-acre site at Fort Wayne, Ind. marks a unique combination of efficient layout and skilled management, to gain full utility of the location. The shop has nearly 106,000 sq. ft. of floor space. Completed cost for the complex was about $5 million.

The facility, which combines a tractor and trailer shop with a two-story office and training section, a driver training course, plus support buildings for packing pads and blankets, is as attractive as it is utilitarian.

The complex was designed by Schenkel and Schultz Inc., Ft. Wayne, and built by Construction Control Corp., an affiliated firm.

The shop is officially owned by Fleet Service, a di-

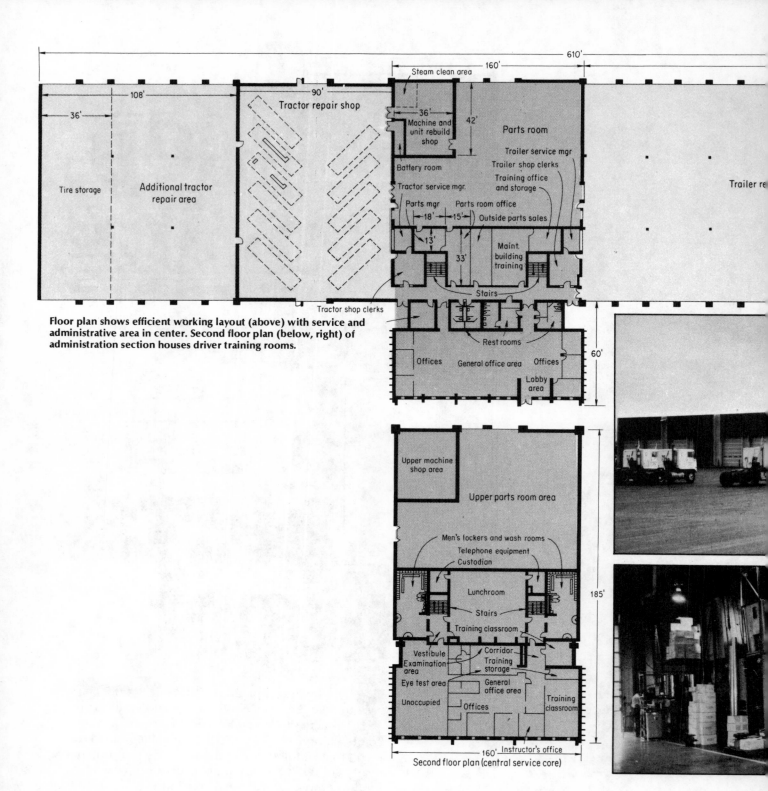

Floor plan shows efficient working layout (above) with service and administrative area in center. Second floor plan (below, right) of administration section houses driver training rooms.

First floor plan labels:
- 610'
- 160'
- Steam clean area
- 108'
- 90'
- Tractor repair shop
- 36'
- 42'
- 36'
- Machine and unit rebuild shop
- Parts room
- Battery room
- Trailer service mgr
- Trailer shop clerks
- Training office and storage
- Tractor service mgr.
- Tire storage
- Additional tractor repair area
- Parts mgr
- Parts room office
- 18'
- 15'
- Outside parts sales
- Trailer re
- 13'
- Maint. building training
- 33'
- Stairs
- Tractor shop clerks
- Rest rooms
- 60'
- Offices
- General office area
- Offices
- Lobby area

Second floor plan labels:
- Upper machine shop area
- Upper parts room area
- Men's lockers and wash rooms
- Telephone equipment
- Custodian
- Lunchroom
- Stairs
- 185'
- Training classroom
- Vestibule
- Examination area
- Corridor
- Training storage
- Eye test area
- General office area
- Unoccupied
- Offices
- Training classroom
- 160'
- Instructor's office
- Second floor plan (central service core)

vision of North American Van Lines. Operations are under the direction of Wayne Thompson, vice president-fleet maintenance, Pepsico Transportation Div. (Pepsico is the parent company of North American.) Max Hetrick is maintenance supervisor for the "Maintenance Center."

North American maintains a 7300-sq. ft. parts area, with offices and sales room, where parts and accessories are sold (at fleet discount prices) to owner/operators.

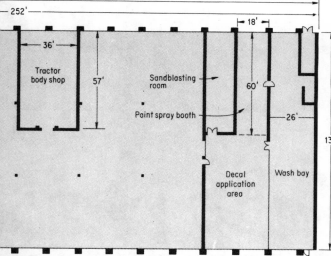

Center aisle extends full length of trailer repair wing (below). Each trailer repair stall has roll-up doors for easy access.

Component rebuild room and machine shop (below) is well equipped. Steam cleaning room adjoins unit rebuild room.

Tractor repair wing at left in photo flanks central office and training center. Trailer repair bays and wash bay extend from office core as shown in floor plan.

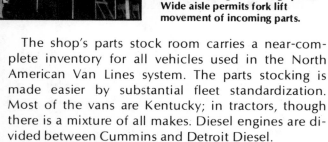

Modern steel bins and shelves in parts room (left) store smaller, fast-moving parts. Upper deck area above shelving stores large parts. Wide aisle permits fork lift movement of incoming parts.

The shop's parts stock room carries a near-complete inventory for all vehicles used in the North American Van Lines system. The parts stocking is made easier by substantial fleet standardization. Most of the vans are Kentucky; in tractors, though there is a mixture of all makes. Diesel engines are divided between Cummins and Detroit Diesel.

In the parts room, modern steel bins and racks go two tiers high, with bulky items such as trailer rear doors, cab roof panels, etc., stored in upper racks. At the rear of the parts room is a receiving area with its own exterior door for incoming parts deliveries.

Completing the central service core is the machine and unit rebuild shop. It rebuilds both gasoline and diesel engines, cylinder heads, and transmissions, relines brake shoes, welds broken castings, etc., and handles complete rebuilding of numerous small components. Machine shop includes a Sioux Model 680 valve refacer, two Kent-Moore engine stands that handle any diesel engine, a Dake Model 6-375 50-ton arbor press and a Blackhawk AP-50 hydraulic arbor press, a Buffalo Model 18 drill press, a Van Norman Model 30xH brake drum lathe, a brake shoe riveter from Chicago Riveting Machine Co, and a cabinet type sand blaster.

In one part of the machine shop area is the steam cleaning room, equipped with a large capacity Jenny steam cleaner. And next to that area, fully walled for OSHA compliance, is the battery storage room.

Tractors in "the bay area"

In the tractor shop, a center aisle, with a 13-ft. wide roll-up door at each end, gives drive-through access. From that aisle, tractors "peel off" into the 12 work

Wash bay (above) cleans all vehicles before leaving. New model Ross and White gantry type washer travels on tracks and wand nozzles are used for detail washing.

Tractor shop (below) has drive-through center aisle with roll-up door at each end. Overhead monorail system extends to all work stalls and into adjoining parts room.

bays arranged at a 60° angle.

Two of the tractor work bays are equipped with twin-post hydraulic lifts. Exhaust removal on the west side of the tractor shop is in-floor, while an overhead system with drop hoses handles the east side bays.

An overhead piping system, with reels located between each two bays, dispenses compressed air, pre-mixed anti-freeze, motor oil, transmission lube, and chassis grease on the east side. On the west side, a

Tractor body shop (below) handles any type of cab or chassis damage, including major wreck rebuilds. Cab parts and components are kept well stocked.

Van equipment building (below) stores furniture pads, dollies, etc. and has its own loading dock where drivers learn dock procedures.

Reinforced steel I-beam columns and floor tracks are installed in one trailer repair bay (left) for straightening bent trailer walls or understructure.

Training track (below) includes different types of roads plus off-street parking area to train drivers for all driving situations.

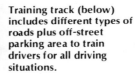

similar battery of reels dispenses air, motor oil, and chassis grease. The motor oil comes from a 6,000-gal. underground tank while the other lubricants are pumped from 55-gal. drums. Anti-freeze is pre-mixed in an elevated tank in the southeast corner of the tractor shop.

Waste oil outlets in the shop lead to a 6,000-gal underground tank, which is periodically pumped out by a waste oil collection service.

Equipment in the tractor shop includes a Walker mechanical transmission jack, Walker dual wheel dolly, a portable shop crane, Lincoln electric arc welder, and complete air conditioning service outfit.

In the shop Max Hetrick pointed out the efficient overhead crane system serving the tractor shop and parts room. The traveling crane, with a capacity of 4,000 lb., runs the full length of the tractor shop. At midpoint, a monorail track leads into the parts room.

The electrically driven crane can be aligned with the monorail track and then run into the parts room to pick up heavy objects such as engines or transmissions, and move them where needed in the tractor shop, or into the steam cleaning room.

Next to the tractor service shop is a large area, divided into three 36-ft. wide bays, each equipped with roll-up doors at each end. Two bays are used for additional capacity for tractor repairs, and contain an Ostradyne chassis dynamometer. Presently under construction is a 15,000-sq. ft. building on the site nearby to be used for a tractor display area (showroom.) All tractors are completely checked by the Fleet Service shop and put into virtually new-tractor condition. After the reconditioning, such tractors will go into the tractor display building "showroom" for examination and purchase by graduating students (see below) or regular drivers wishing to move up to a better, later model tractor.

At the time of FLEET OWNER's visit, approximately 300 tractors were waiting for reconditioning and display in the "showroom."

The third bay of the section is used for tire storage, with hundreds of new or recapped tires stored in racks behind a steel mesh partition.

The entire west wing of the big shop building is mostly devoted to trailer repairs, service, painting, and washing. The main trailer repair area has 14 drive-though bays, each equipped with roll-up doors 14 ft. wide. Work bays are 18 ft. wide, giving ample working room.

In the area, several trailers could be seen stripped down to virtually nothing but floor and axles. The rebuild shop can literally take a trailer all the way down to the axles and rebuild it like new.

Shop equipment includes Solar Industries Model S-1400 air-hydraulic trailer end lifts, eight Airco and Lincoln electric arc welders, acetylene welding outfits, and a large radial arm saw with table, plus a Webb Iron Worker.

One of the trailer repair bays has specially reinforced steel columns, floor hooks, and other equipment; this is used for straightening trailer frames.

Near the mid-point of the trailer shop, on the south, or back, side, is the tractor body shop. It has two exterior roll-up doors. (An additional double bay off the trailer shop area next to the tractor body shop can be used as a staging area for tractors waiting for parts or pending the start of repairs.)

Opposite the body shop are four bays used for chassis service on complete tractor-trailer units. Four bays are equipped with hydraulic lifts to lift the tractor and trailer together.

One lift has seven posts with a lifting capacity of 140,000 lb., one has five posts and a capacity of 100,000 lb., and the other two have twin post lifts with a capacity of 40,000 lb. each. Over the front end of those lifts, suspended from the roof girders, is a large canvas enclosure resembling a large straight-wall tent. The "tent" catches exhaust fumes from tractors when they are being positioned on the lift, or running, while on the hoist. A large exhaust fan in the roof, at the apex of the tent, vents the fumes.

At the end of the trailer shop is the wash lane, where vehicles enter from the south side door, pass through a pre-soaking arch and then through a new Ross and White gantry type washer. Portable high pressure wands at each end of the bay wash wheel wells, fuel tanks, and frame rails not reached by the washer brushes. The wash bay cleans approximately 300 vehicles (tractor and trailer) per week.

Behind the main shop building is a small concrete block building housing the shop's air compressors, all made by the Le Roi Div., Dresser Industries. There are three compressors with 25-hp. motors, rated 100 cfm, which alternate automatically to supply the normal air demand.

The air from the compressors goes through a large Kellogg American refrigerated air drier before it is piped underground to the main shop building.

Personnel and shop services
The roster of shop personnel is approximately 200, consisting of tractor and trailer mechanics, body men, parts men (and women), clerks, shop office clerks, janitors, etc., plus six men for moving vehicles in and out of the shops and adjacent yards.

Cleaning of the shop is by two Tennant motorized floor sweeping machines. Hetrick says the cleaning job is made easier by the clear urethane finish on the concrete floors of all shop working areas including the machine shop, tractor shop, body shop, and trailer shop.

The shop is heated by big hot water heaters in trailer repair and hot air in the tractor shop. The office and training school section has Singer heat pumps, which provide both air conditioning and heat.

Van equipment building
Approximately 400 ft. north of the main shop building is an important supporting structure in the complex-the van equipment building. In that building are stored the thousands of furniture pads plus hand trucks, dollies, straps, etc. that are used in most of the North American trailers (the fleet includes car carriers for auto transport).

The south side of the van equipment building has a row of loading doors so trailers can be backed in easily to load necessary equipment. The van equipment building is heated by radiant electric fixtures. A dry cleaning set-up is being installed to clean the furniture pads.

Alongside the van equipment building in the main driveway serving the shop is a Toledo platform scale 70 ft. long with a capacity of 120,000 lb., and a fueling island.

On the fueling island are both gasoline and diesel fuel pumps. There is one gasoline storage tank with 10,000 gal. capacity, and two diesel fuel tanks with capacities of 10,000 and 12,000 gal.

Breaking-in the newcomers
In the northeast corner of the 113-acre site, a training track of three loops of blacktop-paved "road" is built. Together, they total nearly two city blocks. Two sections have offset parking areas to train students how to park in off-street docks, alleys, etc.

A row of electric outlets on poles in the lot provides tractor engine heaters in cold weather.

Because of the sometimes large inventory of tractors awaiting reconditioning and the somewhat seasonal nature of household goods moving, large paved parking areas were provided.

Paved parking areas inside the main fence total 620,000 sq. ft., providing capacity for 500 tractors and 600 trailers, and space for 200 employee's cars.

Mechanics Tom Cummings and Angelo Paccione checking out necessary engine repairs on a typical small company truck.

A new look for an old shop

by
Jack
Lyndall,
senior
editor

Judicious investment in modern shop equipment together with minimal changes in an existing but sound building are key elements in a greatly upgraded fleet maintenance program in the New York City-Brooklyn Region of the New York Telephone Co. Combined with a revamped, expanded program of vehicle maintenance in company shops, they have achieved substantial cost savings and better vehicle availability, according to Earl C. "Buzz" Barry, superintendent-motor vehicles, for the region, which operates nearly 5000 vehicles.

The "keystone" of the improved fleet maintenance procedure is the Nostrand Avenue Plant Work Center at 1580 Nostrand Ave., Brooklyn, N.Y. The solidly-

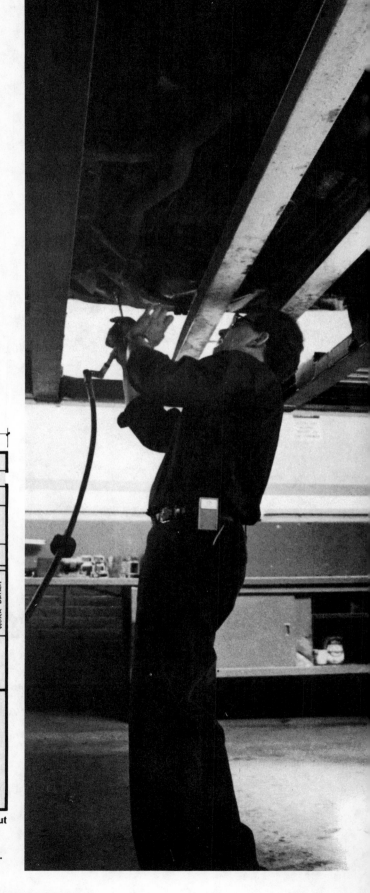

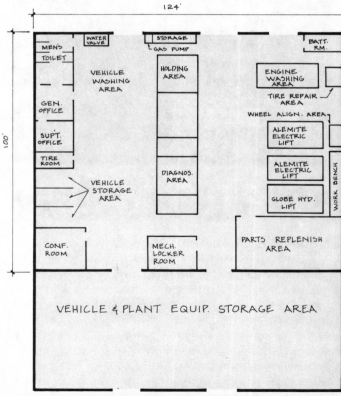

Diagram of phone company's Nostrand shop shows how shop layout was revamped for efficient maintenance and repairs on 500 units.

Working under electric vehicle lift, mechanic performs lube job. Lube reel system dispenses oil, grease, air and water.

Stewart-Warner front end alignment machine, and a wheel balancer are conveniently located in front of electric lift to save time.

Blue and white fleet vehicle colors brighten remodeled Nostrand shop area, along with fluorescent lights and new shop equipment.

built, utilitarian brick building was previously devoted mostly to storage of about 110 fleet cars and telephone service trucks based there, and for storage of telephone equipment.

One mechanic did work there, mostly doing light repair and PM services. Major repairs and overhauls were farmed to outside garages and vehicle dealers. A similar arrangement exists in most of the 86 garages in the New York City-Brooklyn Region.

Barry says "Changes in that system were needed because of increasing outside repair costs, to get better work efficiency, and reduce operating costs and downtime." After discussions with Ted Marr, general superintendent of buildings and motor vehicles for the region, who approved the concept and detailed plans, the Nostrand Avenue facility was chosen as the first in the projected new system of company-operated fleet maintenance centers. That garage was selected due to its central location relative to eight satellite garages whose 450 vehicles would come to that shop.

Once the decision was made, necessary changes in the building itself were minimal, according to N.T. Cianflone, division motor vehicle supervisor in charge of the center. An existing partition wall separated the projected shop area from the storage area where vehicles are stored at night.

The major element was approximately $40,000 of new modern shop equipment.

Additional new fluorescent lighting was installed, and the new shop area painted in colorful tones by New York Telephone personnel, Cianflone says. "The colors, which are based on the fleet vehicle colors of blue and white, seemed to be a major factor in gaining employee acceptance of the remodelling."

FLEET OWNER's visit to the shop began at an aisle in the holding area used for vehicle washing.

Between the two main aisles, near the center of the shop (see drawing), is the diagnostic area with three main equipment items. A Stewart-Warner portable tune-up console includes a cylinder balance tester, ignition timing advance tester, electrical system tester, oscilloscope, and vacuum pump with gauge.

A Fox Valley infra-red exhaust gas analyzer checks engines for compliance with New York City's stringent exhaust emission regulations.

—And a new Hamilton Standard Autosense diagnostic computer had just been uncrated. Barry says he expects the Autosense to greatly speed the accuracy of diagnosing vehicle problems.

The battery room, enclosed in heavy steel mesh, has both conventional slow and fast chargers and testers for checking battery condition.

Alongside the battery room is the engine wash area. All vehicle engines are cleaned prior to tune-up or other engine work, by a high pressure wand type washer made by Nobles Industries, Inc., used with a detergent spray.

In the engine cleaning area there is a Tempe "gasoline tanker" used for pumping out and storing gasoline from vehicle fuel tanks prior to tank repairs.

In the electrical repair area, a headlight tester, a voltmeter, and other instruments check electrical system problems.

The tire repair area is also adjacent to the electrical repair bay. Equipment includes a new Coats Inflat-Air Model 10-20 tire changer. Tire storage is next to the office section.

Ranged farther along were two new Alemite-Bradbury electric vehicle lifts, supplied by Stewart-Warner. Cianflone noted that the lifts, rated 8,000-lb. capacity each, required no digging or other floor alterations for installation. A Stewart-Warner front end alignment machine was positioned in front of the first electric lift, together with a wheel balancer.

In front of the second electric lift, which is primarily devoted to lubrication, is an overhead Stewart-

N.T.Ciaflone, division motor vehicle supervisor, operates from improved work center.

Mechanic uses brake drum lathe to handle drum turning job. Note the use of safety eyeglasses, a "must" for all maintenance department workers at this vehicle shop.

Garage foreman John Caminiti and mechanic use Hamilton Autosense diagnostic equipment to check vehicle performance and problems.

Warner Alemite lube reel system. It dispenses motor oil, automatic transmission fluid, chassis grease, gear oil, compressed air, and water. The oils and greases are pumped from 55-gal. drums at present, but Cianflone says a 250-gal. bulk oil storage tank is under study.

Waste oil is put in a 275-gal. above-ground storage tank. A waste oil removal service pumps it from the tank and hauls it away.

At the end of the area is a single-post Globe hydraulic lift, which was part of the original shop setup.

The hydraulic frame, lift is used mostly for brake work. But brake work is also done on the electric drive-on lifts, which have built-in adapters to lift wheels free of the lift ramps.

In the parts room, Cianflone explained, since the fleet is quite highly standardized, only fast moving parts are stocked since dealers are nearby. A two cylinder, two-stage Kellogg-American air compressor is mounted on an elevated platform in the rear of the parts room.

Located along the parts room wall, which is steel

mesh screening, are a Safety-Kleen drum type parts washer and an Ammco 4000 Series brake drum and disc refinishing lathe.

With the extensive complement of new shop equipment, the shop now handles virtually everything but major repairs and overhauls on the approximately 450 vehicles from the satellite garages plus its own 100 units with seven skilled mechanics. They work from 5:00 pm to 1:00 am. five days a week.

Two mechanics perform the diagnostic work while two more are assigned to chassis lubrication, oil changes, and all underneath repairs such as muffler and tail pipe replacements.

Two mechanics are assigned to brake work, and one to electrical service and repairs, wheel alignment and balancing.

There is also a garage utility man who does engine washing and other supporting jobs to assist the mechanics.

Barry reports that the shop now does at least seven complete bumper-to-bumper preventive maintenance jobs per night. The schedule per vehicle is one or two PM services per year, depending on mileage and the vehicle application.

Furthermore, Cianflone intends to reduce the level of major outside repair jobs by obtaining new or rebuilt engines, transmissions, and rear axles, which will be installed by his mechanics. Looking toward eventual company-operated shops for such unit rebuilding, Barry says, "We now have a smaller component rebuilt shop for such items as alternators, carburetors, fuel pumps, etc., in the Bronx. It will help cut the cost of outside repairs."

With its complete equipment and qualified mechanics, the shop is now certified to perform its own New York State vehicle inspections, which formerly were also done by outside garages or vehicle dealers.

In addition, Cianflone notes with justifiable pride, "We hardly ever get any road calls here anymore." Road calls and downtime for the fleet are under 1%, he says.

Building on the success of the Nostrand Avenue Work Center, which was the prototype for his region, Barry says, "We plan to open a similar shop in Manhattan and another in Brooklyn. That will then put the remaining 500 or so vehicles in Brooklyn that are now serviced in satellite garages under the control of another such work center as this."

The goal, in addition to reducing the cash flow to outside repairs, is maximum uninterrupted availability of the telephone company fleet with its many highly specialized service vehicles. Barry says, "When a vehicle comes out of our work center now, we can be confident it will run efficiently and trouble-free for four to six months, at least."

NEW TERMINALS

Terminals and shops range from ultramodern to utilitarian. Whichever way you choose to go, professional planning will pay off.

PROFESSIONAL PLANNING PAYS

Whether your new terminal is going to cost $100,000 or run into millions, advance planning—with professional help—pays for itself in the long run

When you're building a trucking-terminal complex costing upwards of $8.6-million, spending 2.8% of the total for the services of a topflight architectural firm is no extravagance. It's good business.

The rewards are a massive construction job done correctly, prospects of an improved operation, room for expansion, most contingencies taken into consideration, and, last but not least, peace of mind.

The alternatives can be jerry-built structures made of inferior materials, poor traffic flow, the threat of early obsolescence, inadequate room for expansion, and a

by George L. Snyder, associate editor

parade of craftsmen correcting mistakes.

One owner of a new terminal recently told FLEET OWNER: "We've got a serviceable installation here, and we designed it all ourselves. Naturally, we made some mistakes along the way, but they'll be corrected."

He didn't say, however, what it would cost to correct the mistakes. Probably much more than professional planning would have cost in the first place.

A multi-million-dollar case in point

Commercial Carriers Inc., Southfield, Mich., the nation's largest highway common carrier of new automobiles and trucks, recently spent the aforementioned

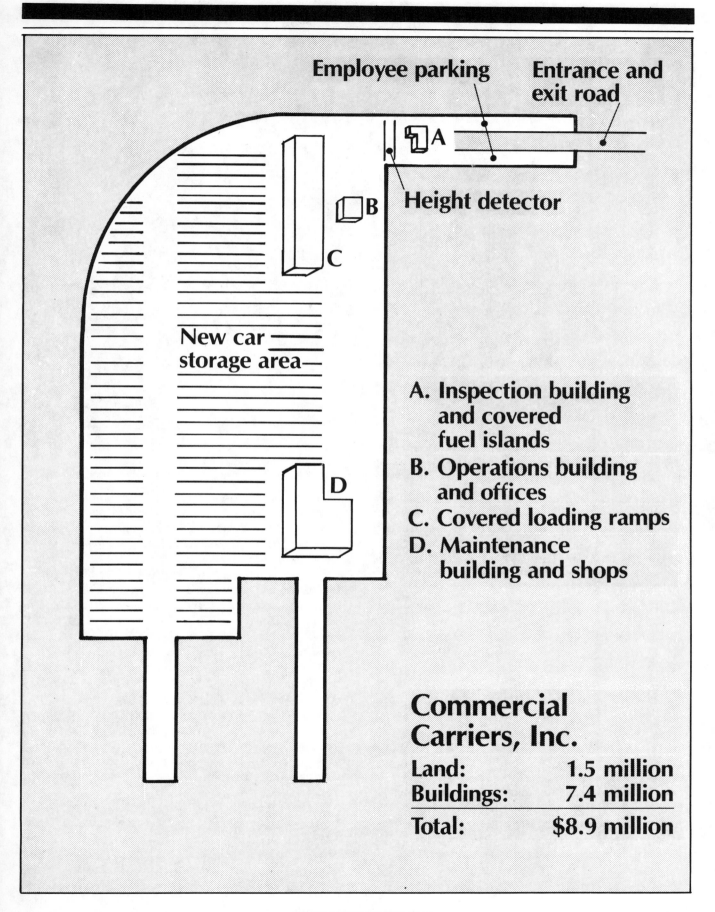

Employee parking

Entrance and exit road

A

Height detector

B

C

New car storage area

D

A. Inspection building and covered fuel islands
B. Operations building and offices
C. Covered loading ramps
D. Maintenance building and shops

Commercial Carriers, Inc.

Land:	1.5 million
Buildings:	7.4 million
Total:	$8.9 million

CCI president James G. Skala (left), vp-operations J.W. Kelly (center), and vp-administration E.M. MacDonald at planning session.

$8.6-million on a new terminal on the outskirts of Detroit. Not only were all of the above advantages inherent with the help of an architectural firm, but the project came in on budget—a cherished goal in inflationary times.

Commercial Carriers Inc. (CCI) is part of Texas Gas Transmission Corp. Based in Owensboro, Ky., that conglomerate lists gas-transmission services, inland-waterways services, trucking services, and oil and gas exploration and production as separate divisions. In addition to CCI, the trucking services division includes American Freight Systems and Midwest Coast Transport.

The teamwork concept pays off

According to CCI president James G. Skala, the builder, Etkin, Johnson & Korb Inc., was contacted about the proposed terminal simultaneously with the retaining of the architectural firm, Ellis/Naeyaert/Genheimer Assoc., Troy, Mich.

"The essence of a successful building project, we learned," Skala says, "is establishing a rapport between the client, the builder, and the architect-engineer. The teamwork we achieved, I believe, is the main reason the project was so successful. And, I have no doubt that it was responsible for bringing the job in on budget."

Skala also pointed out that in the former terminal in Romulus, Mich., maintenance was deployed into three separate operations. "During the waning months of that terminal's existence," he says, "we tried different maintenance and operational concepts to see what would work best in the new shop. Some we retained; others were discarded."

Skala also stressed that the project was faced with a severe time limit. Site clearance began on June 26, 1978. Concrete and asphalt paving was completed by September 1, 1978, and 1979-model-year car and truck shipments commenced immediately at the new terminal. The construction of the operations-building loading dock, fuel and inspection building, and maintenance building was completed by June 1, 1979, and the project was fully operational for the 1980 model year shipments.

CCI handles Cadillac new-car production directly off the assembly line for highway shipment. For that reason, the new 50-acre site had to be located as near as possible to that manufacturing plant. The new Dearborn terminal serves people in seven states, operating 350 tractor-trailers.

Bruce H. Etkin, vp of Etkin, Johnson & Korb, says: "When we were retained by the client as construction manager, we immediately met with Ellis/Naeyaert/Genheimer Assoc. to establish a sequence of construction activities. The client agreed. From that point on, the project moved swiftly. We got to work even before the

The maintenance building is most complex structure within the new CCI terminal area. As evidenced here, there are numerous engine-exhaust outlets to protect workers.

Few shops do as much complex machining as CCI. Here, one of the company's skilled machinists reconditions a transmission.

Car-carrier's superstructure just about rules out use of automatic truck-washing systems.

plans were complete. While the architect was designing it, we proceeded with site work. Another major reason for the uninterrupted work flow was that, working in concert with the architect, we were able to agree quickly on subcontractors and to put the various jobs on the street for restrictive competitive bidding. Another advantage of construction speed is that the customer has quicker use of his money; he doesn't have it tied up in lengthy proceedings."

Architectural planning—in depth

A. Robert Bliven, project manager for the 180-person architectural and engineering firm of Ellis/Naeyaert/Genheimer Assoc., says every available source of information was used to implement the planning.

For example, the firm's Industrial Group went to the old CCI terminal to learn how the car-carrier processed its work. Other trucking installations were studied, and GMC Truck & Coach Div. was contacted for advice. Bliven says J.G. Skala and J.W. Kelly, group vp-operations for CCI's Central and Southern Division, made many valuable contributions to the building of the complex truck operation and maintenance facility. CCI employes were interviewed for suggestions and made many worthwhile points.

After the cram course in truck maintenance and oper-

ation, the architects produced "a dozen layouts."

At the outset, CCI leaned toward a two-story, one-building concept in which employe facilities and parts storage would be on the upper floor. That was finally deemed uneconomical, although the present structures can be expanded to incorporate lateral additions.

The architects submitted eight proposals for the maintenance building alone. "Proper shop/work flow and location of the maintenance department was one of the keys to the entire project," Bliven says. "For example, a mezzanine for tire storage was once considered, but we had to know how many tires CCI wanted to buy at one time and how many it wanted to store at any given time. That posed a question almost impossible to answer, because of changing supply and demand conditions. So, we didn't incorporate upper-level tire storage.

"If we had gone to a multipurpose building, the structure could have been L-, T-, or U-shaped. But our final dispersion of separate buildings was done in the interest of good over-all work flow, good traffic flow, and the need to meet specific CCI requirements. The whole point is to prevent the client from being 'locked in' to an unchangeable installation."

The final, workable solution

The completed 50-acre CCI project includes a 3,342-

CCI hauls one of the nation's most prestigious automobiles, the Cadillac. In lower photo, a load of new Cadillacs are "nested" on a truck and trailer.

Commercial Carriers Inc. is part of Texas Gas Transmission, a conglomerate headquartered in Owensboro, Ky.

sq.-ft. vehicle-storage area, a 33,790-sq.-ft. loading-dock structure, a 5,292-sq.-ft. operations building, a 5,302-sq.-ft. fuel and inspection building, and a 54,696-sq.-ft. maintenance structure (see drawing p. 82).

A tour of the premises brings the architectural drawing to life in terms of how the area functions and why. For example, the employe parking lot is to the left inside the main gate—remote from all work areas to reduce traffic and protect new cars from in-yard damage.

Several yards inside the main gate is the fuel island and vehicle-inspection structure. Beyond that is a truck lane leading to a sophisticated electronic height indicator.

The multi-lane fuel island contains what CCI terms "the most sophisticated underground system," which delivers 60 gpm with a dual card/ticket printout. The printout, computerized at the moment of dispatch, controls driver road-fuel purchases by telling how much can be bought away from the terminal and where. That information eventually goes into a master computer and is charged back to the truck.

Upon entering the yard, every rig passes through one of the two inspection lanes in the building adjacent to the fuel island. Each inspection bay has pits for checking undercarriage wiring and the condition of all tires and springs. If a vehicle needs repairs, it doesn't go back on the road; it goes back to the maintenance shop.

CCI originally intended to complete minor repairs, such as headlights, tail-lights, windshield wipers, etc., in the inspection area. But that idea was abandoned for two reasons. First, because any type of repair could impede inspection procedures and, second and most important, because it was felt that any repair should be a thorough procedure at maintenance and not a pass-through operation at inspection.

Car heights on a carrier are not fixed, as on a van-type trailer, necessitating the electronic height indicator. A CCI load cannot be higher than 13½ ft., nor wider than 96 in. to comply with state legal limits. Weight and length laws vary by state, as they do for any other type of carrier, but some states won't permit the overhang that places a new car directly over the truck cab.

Car meets carrier in comparative safety

As indicated on the drawing, the 26-bay loading dock is located in the front right corner of the new-car storage area (3,342-car capacity). Cars are driven from the lot, up rear ramps, and onto the covered dock. Carriers then back up to the front of the dock to receive the cars. The new automobiles never are endangered by trucks maneuvering in the same lot.

Also, the maintenance building is positioned at the facility's extreme left, which removes that flow of traffic from the vicinity of the new cars.

In its finished state, the maintenance shop incorporates 21 tractor bays, 12 trailer bays, and 5 drive-through bays. The drive-through bays are divided into two for lubrication, two for quick repairs, and one for washing.

The maintenance building required driving 90-foot piles because of poor soil conditions. "We could have built it more economically in another area at the site," Bliven says, "but it would have destroyed the traffic flow that had been agreed upon." The maintenance shop was constructed of metal upper walls (for economy) and masonry lower walls (for protection).

The building is equipped with insulated doors, and both forced air and radiant heat. Rather than diffuse to all areas, the radiant system "heats down" on workers. "Even so," Bliven says, "there is inevitable heat loss. You can't avoid it when giant doors are constantly opening and closing in cold climates. In fact, drive-through bays are not overly advantageous in cold climates."

Outside areas are illuminated by 1,000-watt, weather-proof high-pressure-sodium lights, mounted on a total of 41 poles. Site paving consists of 15,000 sq. yd. of concrete and 143,000 sq. yd. of asphalt. Another "deep strength" asphalt-paved area encompasses 71,500 sq. yd., used for areas of heavy truck traffic.

The entire CCI installation is protected by a chain-link fence and soon will be additionally guarded by closed-circuit TV surveillance system incorporating three cameras with zoom lenses in a pan and tilt operation, each with its own monitor. Ernest M. MacDonald, CCI vp of administration, who supervised the project from the customer side, says: "We find the extra protection pays for itself by reducing cargo theft to a minimum."

Areas in the yard are also provided for piling snow and storing salt. The yard must be kept plowed and clean at all times so new cars don't get banged up.

The yard is wired with cold-start plug-ins to handle a third of the Dearborn-based fleet, the approximate amount that is in the yard at any one time.

Maintenance tailored to the operation

MacDonald credited the insight and input of maintenance personnel as being the chief factor in the success of the new maintenance installation. "They knew what their operation required and helped tailor the building to meet those needs," he said.

To understand the building, it is necessary to understand the operation. At present, the structure can service 37 tractors at any given time, and has the capacity to service 60.

The new maintenance building houses an engine-rebuild shop, which not only services Dearborn's 350 power units but also rebuilds for other CCI terminals. The facility is 90% self-reliant and can "match any distributor's quality." The structure also includes the latest in exhaust-removal equipment and complies with OSHA, state, and federal safety requirements.

They call it instant trucking

Not only is the 26-bay loading dock covered and well lighted, but the new cars are receiving additional CCI protection in the form of a new type of hauling. Termed "instant trucking" by CCI, the new method incorporates a trailer and superstructure that holds seven automobiles in a drive-on position, all facing forward, thus eliminating nesting and dovetailing. It also reduces the need for many of the hydraulics on the trailer, and provides a much better ride. According to Vernor L. Caide, vp of the Central Division, a Cadillac can now be driven directly from the assembly line to its drive-on position on the trailer, with no backing and maneuvering. Hence, the term "instant trucking." At its destination, it is merely backed off.

Some 40% of the CCI fleet is currently considered fuel efficient—with fan clutches, aluminum componentry, radial tubeless tires, 6-speed Spicer 1010-2A or B transmissions, and Detroit Diesel 92TT or Cummins Formula 290 engines. There is, of course, no chance to use air deflectors.

CCI policy calls for a 375,000-mile depreciation on a tractor, but the increased volume of business has recently made purchasing enough trucks and trailers difficult. MacDonald says: "Replacement lead time in the car-carrying industry is entirely different from that in general freight. Our equipment is 'married' 90% of the time, and the lead time for obtaining our special trailers and cabs with superstructures is 90-100 days.

"The superstructure determines the trailer configuration, and the two together determine wheelbase configuration. MacDonald points out that since 1960 the car-carrying industry went from hauling four standard-size cars to eight, and then up to ten compacts. During that period, the size of automobiles grew, but finally shrank with the advent of the energy crunch.

An average CCI trip approximates 240 miles one way, with possibly three "drops" in various locations. Caide points out that drops are time-consuming. "Three in Chicago, for instance," he says, "takes a lot of unloading time, and that can get nervewracking. For that reason, we must have excellent drivers who are, or can easily become, acclimated to this type of hauling."

**DeCarolis Truck Rental Inc.
Terminal and
maintenance complex
Rochester, New York**

**Architect:
G. William LaDue**

**General contractor:
Frank F. DiBattisto
Construction.**

Even without the addition of a new maintenance building to its existing facility, DeCarolis Truck Rental Inc. of Rochester, N.Y., would have been an eminent candidate for an award.

An on-premises inspection, however, turned up well thought-out innovations that clinched the honor for one of America's fastest growing truck-leasing companies.

Such attention to detail as channeling hot air from a rotary air-compressor system into the shop during the cold months and out of doors in summer places this installation a notch above the usual static vehicle repair shop planned by someone remote from the problems.

The new facility cost $1,290,000 and occupies 15 acres. It is an 18,000 sq. ft. edifice used to repair 450 fleet trailers as well as customer trailers. It also handles paint and collision work for 250 DeCarolis power units.

Strategically located a short distance from the older DeCarolis facility that primarily services power units, the new building also houses corporate offices, which frees up office space in the older building for possible rental to outside interests.

Energy efficiency and productivity were paramount in the planning. For example, insulated overhead doors and foam-filled cinder blocks are basic ingredients of the construction. All materials specifications comfortably exceeded those required by the New York State energy code.

In the newer building a 54-ft. paint-spray booth is incorporated with drive-through doors to permit multi-vehicle painting regardless of weather. A central fabrication area, containing woodworking and metalworking equipment as well as welding apparatus, comprises a work facility for trailer rebuilding and repair.

A mezzanine above the fabrication location provides storage for bulk items, utilizing otherwise wasted space. A lubrication room is remote from shop operations, with oil and grease being fed to required service areas via overhead reels.

Building heating and cooling is accomplished with a combination of air rotation and zoned forced-air systems. The shop area is heated with an air rotation unit and the aforementioned recycled warm air from the rotary air compressor.

The zone forced-air systems provide heating and air conditioning for the service and parts departments, general offices, and employee convenience areas. Timers are used to maintain minimum preset temperatures when the facility is unoccupied. Shop air purification is aided by an exhaust system that carries the fumes of running vehicles out of doors. Dual roof fans have also been installed in the new building to help eliminate heavier fumes emitted during diesel startup.

The light and power system for the shop was spec'ed with the appropriate voltage for minimum draw when in operation, in the interest of energy efficiency. Voltages, single- and three-phase, are 460, 230, and 115. Metal halide and energy-saving fluorescent fixtures pro-vide the lighting. Because of wiring configurations, any area fixtures not in use can be turned off without creating safety hazards.

All hand tools, lifting equipment, spray paint, and sandblasting apparatus are powered by dual 25-hp. rotary screw compressors. Sloped air lines in a loop configuration and a receiver-drier assure dry, constant air pressure throughout the shop. Shut-off valves are placed so that sections of the air system can be shut off for maintenance and repair.

What little waste oil is produced is fed to an oil-water separator and then to an oil holding tank, from which it is sold. Waste scrap metal is stored in palletized metal baskets before being sold for recycling.

Because the new construction took place on a landfill, caissons set on bed rock were used to support the foundations. Although the property allows for future expansion, plans for further building at present will be directed toward satellite expansion in other areas of the county and state.

The original DeCarolis terminal building (1) now services the company's power units and also contains office space that can be rented to outside interests. The new building encompasses over 18,000 sq. ft. and features a 54-ft. paint spray booth (2) that incorporates drive-through doors to permit multi-vehicle painting, regardless of weather. The new building is also used to repair and refurbish 450 DeCarolis trailers and is equipped to handle paint and collision work for the firm's 250 power units. Customer trailers are also repaired on contract in this facility. The covered fuel island (3) handles a steady stream of company trucks, customer vehicles, and contract work, such as large school-bus fleets.

**Metropolitan Transit
Commission
South garage
St. Paul, Minnesota**

**Architects/engineers:
Smiley Glotter Associates
Contractor:
Bor-Son Construction**

The new South Garage of the Metropolitan Transit Commission filled a gap in the vital bus maintenance and storage facilities serving the Minneapolis-St. Paul Twin Cities area. Supplementing three early 1900s garages acquired in a 1970 takeover of a private bus system and a garage added later in the northern parts of MTC's service area, the new garage accommodates 200 buses.

It provides indoor parking (a must in Minnesota's frigid winters), a service area for fueling and washing, and a shop area for maintenance and light repairs. The 106,000-sq.-ft storage area includes 20 lanes in four bays for MTC's 40-ft. standard buses and its 67-ft. articulated buses.

The 49,000-sq.-ft. maintenance and repair shop has four bus lifts and four bays for lubrication and minor repairs, in addition to inspection pits. An engine cleaning area is provided adjacent to the two pits used for bus-defect inspection.

The service area, 38,000 sq. ft., has three fueling stations, a parts cleaning section, and areas for storing batteries, alcohol, and lubricants.

The dispatch/driver areas encompass 10,000 sq. ft., and support areas (locker and lounge areas for drivers and mechanics, plus parts storage) occupy 10,000 sq. ft.

Built on a 12½-acre site adjacent

to the Minneapolis-St. Paul International Airport and I-494, the new garage is integrated with its surroundings by earth berms at portions of the building facade to minimize its apparent size.

Consistent with the needs of the times, MTC and its architects worked toward use of energy efficient materials and design, with an eye on lowering overall operating expenses. Insulated glass and walls and a computerized control center for all ventilation and heating equipment provide efficient operation and reduce energy consumption.

Bus movement and traffic flow are predominantly within the building, another big energy and time saver,

especially during the winter season.

Designed in a somewhat unusual, roughly triangular plan, the building had to meet Federal Aviation Administration regulations because of its proximity to the airport. The site was selected because it offered economies in operating expenses and a minimum of deadhead miles.

Building protection includes door security, a fire alarm system, wet and dry sprinkler systems, and good lighting. To cope with emergencies, the garage has standby electric generators and air compressor.

Architectural engineering costs were $449,000, vibro-flotational land preparation came to $97,000, and construction $7.1-million. 🚌

Dispatch area (1) has bank-type counter and glass partitions. Drivers lounge (2) for drivers waiting to go on duty offers comfortable seats and a variety of vending machines for candy and snacks. View of south end of maintenance garage (3) with bus storage bay doors beyond shows modern design. Twin-post lifts in maintenance garage (4) are used for bus inspections and chassis repairs. The maintenance garage also has two sets of pits for bus inspections and minor defect repairs.

**Schuster Express Inc.
Terminal and shop
Cinnaminson, New Jersey**

**Architects/engineers:
Edmund Cox 3rd,
and Roland Aristone Inc.**

Replacing an old, outmoded terminal in Philadelphia, the new Schuster Express terminal and shop at Cinnaminson, N.J., serves the heavily industrialized Delaware River valley area, including Philadelphia and Chester, Pa., Wilmington, Del., and the Camden-Pennsauken area in New Jersey.

Located in a new industrial park on US 130, a major north-south truck artery, the terminal is only a few minutes away from major Interstate highways and bridges spanning the Delaware River.

Not especially large as motor-freight terminals go, the Cinnaminson terminal is nevertheless efficient. Handling approximately 7-million lb. of freight per month, 90% of it LTL, the terminal's centralized location in its service area assures swift customer service. Meassuring 58x195 ft., the 36-door dock covers 11,842 sq. ft. and can be lengthened to 300 ft. if necessary.

Located on a 7¼-acre site, the terminal and shop cost $940,000. That breaks down into $150,000 land cost, $30,000 for architectural engineering, and $760,000 for construction of the custom-built facility.

Paved yard area totals 197,616 sq. ft., with an additional 98,808 sq. ft. left unpaved.

Good supervision on the dock comes from the centrally located dock office. Adjoining the general office section, at one end of the dock, are the dispatch office and

driver's lounge. Flanking the dispatch office is an OS&D room, with an OS&D bay on the dock immediately in front of the dispatch office. A heated and air-conditioned room, depending on season, is for storage of freezable and perishable freight.

The 4,225-sq.-ft., three-bay shop services and maintains the 10 road tractors, 40 road trailers, 17 city tractors, 11 city trailers, and three straight trucks based at the Cinnaminson terminal. Fully equipped for PM service plus minor and major repairs, the shop can be expanded by adding three more bays.

A well organized parts room stocks fast-moving items, and the area above the parts room provides added storage.

Utility services include public wa-

ter and sewage plus 800-amp electric service. There are 29 electric plug-in connections for engine-block heaters in winter.

Ample storage capacities were provided. There is a 10,000-gal. storage tank for domestic oil for heating, a 10,000-gal. tank for diesel fuel, and an 8,000-gal. tank for motor oil. A 5,000-gal. tank collects waste oil from the shop.

Personnel include six dockmen, 44 drivers, nine administrative, five clerical, and two mechanics.

Any future expansion will have continuity of design with the original building. All Schuster terminals have commonality of design, for all are designed by an architect who has worked closely with Schuster Express management for years. ■

Terminal garage (1) is of cement-block construction, has three drive-through bays opening onto the street and the rear of the property. Parts room and parts-cleaning equipment (2) and a small office are located within the 4,225-sq.-ft. garage. Outbound freight in cart bays (3) surrounds dock office in the 58x195-ft., 36-door dock. One of Schuster's tractor-trailer rigs take on fuel (4) at covered fuel island adjacent to the garage. The Cinnaminson, N.J., terminal located on a 7¼-acre site, handles 7-million lb. of freight a month.

**Tri-County Metropolitan
Transportation District
Main garage and
administration buildings
Portland, Oregon**

**Architects/engineers:
URS/Madigan-Praeger;
Art James, Engineers;
Koch, Sachs & Whittaker
Architects; and
Peterson Associated
Engineers**

**Contractor:
Todd Building Co.**

Replacing a badly outmoded facility built in 1911, the new main garage and administrative buildings for the Tri-County Metropolitan Transportation District of Oregon (Tri-Met) embodies modern design principles, including solar heating.

Built on a 400x1300-ft. site centrally located in Tri-Met's operations area, and on land already owned by Tri-met, the actual construction posed a major logistics problem. The new facility had to be built in phases to allow bus maintenance operations to continue in the existing buildings, which were scheduled for demolition after the new facilities were completed and occupied.

The four-floor administration building, located at one end of the site, contains 65,000 sq ft of floor space. The basic space planning is an open office concept for maximum flexibility. There are 120 administrative personnel plus 20 clerical employees in the new building. Also, 425 drivers work out of the new facility, which operates 300 GMC, Flxible, and AM General transit buses. Shop personnel include 108 mechanics and eight supervisors.

The mild Portland climate permits outdoor storage of buses between the administration building and the new main shop at the other end of the site.

Measuring 90x210 ft. long, the new main shop has 42 service bays for buses plus two bays for Tri-Met fleet cars. A central service core contains the main parts storeroom, a separate tire storage room, a secured storage room with adjoining shop foreman's office, a paint stor-

age room, and a tool storage room. Two parts-cleaning rooms, one for steel parts and the other for aluminum parts, are served by an overhead chain conveyor for lifting heavy components.

The second floor of the new shop houses employee locker rooms, additional parts storage, lunch room, an exercise room, and offices. The second floor is served by central passenger and freight elevators.

Reflecting the planning for energy efficiency, the solar collectors for the administrative office building's solar heating system are on the main shop roof. That system primarily satisfies the winter space heating and domestic hot-water heating requirements for the administrative building.

A gas-fired radiant heat system provides more comfortable and more efficient heat for the main

shop than a space heating system originally considered.

Planning for emergencies was not overlooked. A standby electric generator is wired to handle 80% of the shop area and from a third to 100% of the operations level.

For fire protection, the entire facility is equipped with sprinklers. An incinerator burns waste materials.

Land cost and preparation amounted to $1.8-million. Architectural engineering amounted to $291,271. Construction cost was $3.0-million for the administration building and $4.8-million for the new main shop, for a grand total of $10.9-million, which included some necessary change orders.

Two subsidiary structures, a washing module and a fueling module, flank the bus storage area, at the end of the shop.

Tri-Met's four-floor administration building (1) houses 120 administration and 20 clerical personnel, and provides bullpen space for the 425 drivers working out of this new facility. The 90x210-ft. main shop (2 and 3) has 42 bays for buses and two for fleet cars. Shop's first floor houses the main parts storeroom, foreman's office, storerooms for tires, paint, and tools, and two parts-cleaning rooms. On second floor are locker rooms, additional parts storage, lunch room, exercise room, and offices. Solar collectors on shop roof provide space heating and hot-water heating for the administration building.

ECONOMIC CONSIDERATIONS

Forward thinking—weighing today's construction dollars against tomorrow's needs—is the basic challenge confronting the shop designer. Energy use is a prime example. For years, fleets were spoiled on cheap fuel: diesel was 19 cents a gallon, and heating oil even less. Today, fleets have to make staggering investments in fuel to keep their trucks running and their shops heated. Consequently, there is a concerted effort underway to save fuel and reduce operating costs. This often requires additional expense. For example, many existing fleet shops have re-insulated to conserve heat. New shops make extensive use of heat-retaining construction materials. A few are investigating—and investing in—air-recirculating systems and even solar heating. While it can hardly be considered a general trend, we are seeing an increasing number of shops turning to waste-oil heaters as a means of keeping the temperature up in cold weather.

Despite the fact that the maintenance shop is usually regarded as a cost center, there are grounds for arguing the wisdom of that approach. Look-ahead fleets have taken novel accounting tacks, setting up their shops as closed corporations and charging back the repairs to save on taxes. Others solicit outside work with the goal of creating a shop profit center, since outside work can eventually become profitable rather than merely help to cover garage overhead. By calculating flat rates and multiplying them against the labor cost for outside work, you can quickly see how much cheaper it is to perform your own work. The challenge, in a nutshell, is to continue controlling your shop costs in relation to the price of those outside services.

—Stewart Siegel

CLIMATE CONTROL FOR COST CONTROL

We used to talk casually about 'waste heat.' No more. Now the design must accommodate new heat sources, old heat distribution

Space-heat economy is a growing concern in many truck-fleet maintenance-shop operations—especially in cold-weather climates—for two main reasons. One, of course, is the need to provide a healthy working environment for mechanics, but the overriding motive is to save money by curbing ever-rising heating-fuel costs.

Until the recent dramatic increases in heating-oil prices, planning for space-heat efficiency was generally a low-priority item in many fleet-shop operations. Now, however, cost-conscious truckers say they either are looking for fuel-efficient ways to heat their existing shops or at climate-control systems and designs for new shops they are planning to build.

Naturally, fleets hit hardest by soaring heating bills are those with terminals and maintenance facilities in cold-weather regions, where the opening of a bay door can send a blast of frigid air through the shop, forcing furnaces and heaters to work overtime to compensate.

But interior building heat can be lost in other ways, as well. Heat continually escapes through poorly insulated floors, walls, and ceilings, and through drafty doors and windows. Exhaust blowers positioned to remove smokey and dirty air from a shop can take a good deal of warm air out with it at the same time. All of which means furnaces, oil-burners, and heaters must operate longer and more frequently to keep re-heating the air and maintain the desired building temperature.

"We never really thought much about it before," says

by Thomas W. Duncan, Western editor

T. Richard Swennes, president of The Convoy Co., an auto-transport fleet based in Portland, Ore. "Heating-oil was relatively cheap, and we simply burned as much as we needed to keep our shops warm. That's a practice we no longer can afford."

Like a growing number of his colleagues, Swennes is looking at ways to control his heating-fuel costs, yet maintain an adequate working climate inside his shop.

Using heat that's already there

Shop-heating methods are as varied as truck-fleet types and sizes, themselves. Everything from solar-paneling and electronic air-control systems to old-fashioned pot-bellied coal and wood stoves either have been or are being tried. In some cases, new, lower-cost fuels such as propane and natural gas have been substituted for home-heating oil. The effectiveness and cost-efficiency of a heating system depends in great part on the size and type of building to be heated and the payback in terms of heating-fuel savings sought by the fleet operator. Many fleetmen are finding, however, that shop heating can be improved and fuel bills reduced simply by not wasting building heat they've already got.

At the Advance Transportation fleet shop in Milwaukee, Wis., maintenance director Len Wirkus has installed seven electric ceiling fans. That doesn't sound much like a heat-efficiency move until Len explains: "The fans push the warm air trapped at the ceiling back down toward the shop floor where it's needed. We've probably doubled the heating efficiency in the shop without burning any additional heating fuel." The fans, 250-rpm units each capable of covering 2,500 sq. ft., have enabled Wirkus to heat his shop comfortably by using heat that was there all along.

Jim Boylan, who helps plan dealer maintenance facilities at the General Motors Service Research Center in Detroit, agrees that ceiling fans can promote economical space heating. "One of our dealers had five blower-type hot-air furnaces heating his shop area. By installing ceiling fans and recapturing the warm air trapped at the top of the building, he was able to turn two of his furnaces completely off—a cutback of 40% on the fuel heat required to keep the building warm."

Boylan says, "More and more interest is being shown in this area—fleets are looking for a relatively low-cost installation with a quick pay-back time."

Electronic air cleaning comes to the shop

Another space-heating concept catching on in fleet and machine shops involves electronic air cleaning. The idea is to remove dirt and fumes from the air in the shop, then recirculate the cleansed air, rather than exhausting dirty air outside the building and losing heat along with it.

One such industrial air-cleaning system, the Coanda Airflow, has been developed by Honeywell Inc., in Minneapolis, Minn. The air cleaner removes indoor pollution—from welding fumes to grinding particles—by electrostatic precipitation.

Bill McDonnell, vp and director of Honeywell's Residential Controls Center, says electronic air cleaning can save substantially on a shop's energy costs as it improves air quality—a necessity in complying with OSHA work-environment standards. "It reduces the number of air turns needed in the shop and eliminates the need to ventilate," he claims.

Air-cleaning units are suspended above the shop floor, out of the way of shop traffic and shop equipment. Dirty air is drawn in through the bottom of the unit, and clean air is continuously circulated from all four sides in a top-to-bottom movement.

Another approach: radiant-heat pipes

A different method of radiating heat from the ceiling down toward the floor is found in the Briggs Transportation fleet shop in St. Paul, Minn. There, John Johnstone, vp-maintenance, has installed a system of radiant-heat

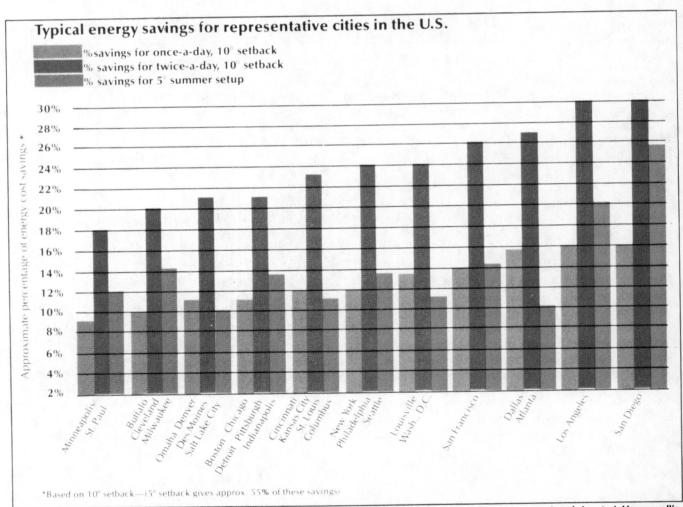

By lowering a thermostat for eight hours, you can save from 9% to 30% on heating costs, depending on where your shop is located. Honeywell's Fuel Saver thermostat can be programmed much like a pocket calculator for wide range of setbacks and cycles.

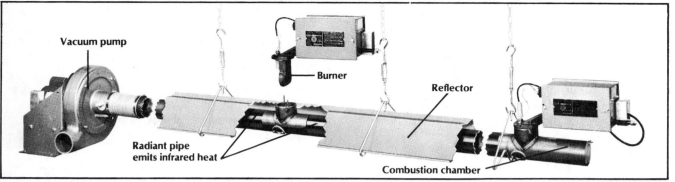

Co-Ray-Vac radiant gas heating system consists of burners connected by pipes that radiate heat. Entire system is suspended from ceiling. Metal reflectors direct heat downward. Vacuum pump draws heat through system, exhausts combustion by-products outdoors.

pipes along the side wall, 7-ft. above the floor, of his vehicle check lane. The Briggs installation, a Co-Ray-Vac system developed by Roberts Gordon Appliance Corp., Buffalo, N.Y., is designed to reduce fuel consumption by up to 50%.

The radiant-heating system at Briggs consists of a series of burners—miniature furnaces, actually—connected by pipes. Aluminum reflectors above the pipes direct heat downward evenly, with no blowing of air to stir dust or create warm and cold spots on the floor. An exhauster at the end of the system expels combustion by-products outdoors. Heat created by the burners is drawn through the pipes by a pump that closes the system when it is not firing, eliminating heat loss through the exhaust pipe.

The system's combustion-efficiency rating is 90%, compared with space-heater ratings of 75% and central-heating system ratings of approximately 60%. And, unlike the other systems, radiant-heat-pipe systems turn nearly all available Btus into usable heat, rather than sending them out the chimney. A 20-ft.-high building can expect a difference of only 4°F. between floor and ceiling temperature with radiant-heat pipes, say Co-Ray-Vac engineers, enabling building thermostats to be set 5° to 10° lower than normal. The infrared heating principle also helps provide fast heat recovery after bay doors have been opened, they claim.

In addition to the Co-Ray-Vac installation, Johnstone says he has turned back his shop thermostats to 60°-65°, has placed plastic sheeting over all shop and office windows, and is controlling exhaust fan operations in other parts of the shop to reduce heat loss.

Getting heat from the floor

Radiant heat of a different nature is being used to warm the Safeway Stores fleet shops in Portland, Ore., and Seattle, Wash. Marsh Burton, Safeway's maintenance director, says radiant-heat floors not only help reduce central-heating costs, but also are "great for mechanics who spend a lot of time on a creeper underneath a truck."

Radiant-heat floors involve a network of pipes beneath the shop floor. Hot water is pumped through the pipes by a large boiler unit, and heat is radiated upward. "The system provides fast heat recovery after

bay doors have been opened, and it dries the floor quickly after a snow-covered truck has been driven into the shop," says Burton.

Installation of such a system is involved and expensive, however, says Burton, and should be considered only during the construction phase of a new shop facility. "You also have to be careful not to allow water to lay in the pipes for long periods," he adds. "Mineral deposits can build up and plug or rot the pipes. That's what happened in our Seattle shop, and we've had to switch to space heaters in the repair bays." To prevent that from happening in the Portland shop, water is treated and softened before it is pumped through the system.

Insulating against drafts

Swennes, whose Convoy fleet has several shop locations throughout the Northwest, is undertaking several simple homeowner-type energy-efficient measures he hopes will make the heat pumps and gas-heater/blower units now operating in his shops more effective.

"One of the first moves we made was to remove the five wood-and-glass doors at our new metal-maintenance shop in Laurel, Mont., and replace them with insulated doors to prevent heat from escaping. We then installed ice-cream-parlor-type ceiling fans to keep the warm air down on the floor, put up storm windows, and have substantially lowered our heating costs there."

The next step, says Swennes, is to insulate the shop ceiling with a layer of insulating foam, topped with a new roof. "Maybe then we can live with 65°F. in the shop," he adds. "It's tough right now because there are too many drafts and too much hot air from the blowers is lost through the roof." Once the buildings are insulated, Swennes says he may install timed-thermostats and regulate shop temperature to correspond with mechanics' work shifts.

Fuel-saver thermostats, which manufacturers say can cut home-heating costs between 9% and 30%, can work just as well in a fleet maintenance shop temperature-control program, says Honeywell's McDonnell. He points out that vehicle-repair shops in many parts of the country have installed night-setback thermostats or newer micro-electronic types, to program indoor temperature regulation and heat buildings only when occupied.

A once-a-day 10° temperature setback for eight straight hours can result in substantial energy savings, adds McDonnell. For example, at a fleet shop in the Chicago area, the average energy savings would be 11%; in New York City, it would be 12%; and in Portland, Ore., 13%. A twice-a-day temperature setback of 10° would increase energy savings another 75%, says McDonnell. He claims that fuel-saver thermostats can pay for themselves in just one heating season.

Reclaiming waste material for heat

There are several space-heater-type units on the market that utilize waste materials to provide a warm-air flow for interior heating. One type of unit, which works off an air compressor, can be used to duct heated exhaust air to supplement a shop's central-heating system. Other heaters burn waste lubricating oils (as well as standard fuel oil) and are designed primarily to replace fuel-oil or gas-fired forced-heat systems.

DresserWayne's Petroleum Equipment Div., Salisbury, Md., has developed a new rotary-screw air-compressor unit to help shops recover and use heat that previously had been lost. The electric-motor-driven compressor, which comes in 40-, 50-, and 60-hp. models for heat-recovery work, takes the load off the shop's primary heating system and reduces fuel-oil consumption. (The screw-type unit is new in shop applications, replacing the piston-type model; it runs quieter, since piston-hammering noise is eliminated.) Ducts and fans suck hot air from the compressor and feed it into the shop. Units are mounted on channel-steel bases and can be positioned where needed.

Space-heating systems that can burn waste oils from engines, transmissions, hydraulic systems, and machinery, are replacing central-heating systems in some maintenance shops. Two of the newer waste-oil-burning systems are being sold by Dravo Corp.'s Dravo/Hastings Div., Pittsburgh, Pa., and by Heating Alternatives, Manhasset, N.Y.

Dravo/Hastings' Thermoflo Model 45-WO is an automatic and self-contained heavy-duty industrial heater with centrifugal blowers, heat exchanger, and stainless steel combustion chamber. It is designed to burn untreated, unprocessed, and unblended waste oil in compliance with federal and local air-quality standards. Dravo's Martin Giglio says the system offers major savings in shop heating costs.

The 45-WO is rated at 450,000-Btu/hr. output and is designed to heat areas normally requiring between 2,000-gal. and 10,000-gal. of No. 2 fuel oil a year. Two units will heat a conventional 8,000- to 10,000-sq.-ft. shop, says Giglio. He says cost studies, which show waste oil to cost only one-tenth as much as conventional heating oil, indicate that a Thermoflo unit will pay for itself in less than two years. A smaller model (200,000-Btu), the Thermoflo 20-WO, which Giglio says is more adaptable for small-fleet shops, is currently being developed. Its minimum heating efficiency is rated 80%.

The Heating Alternatives waste-oil heater, which is manufactured by Kroll, a West German company, is similar in concept to the Dravo/Hastings model. The Kroll line of industrial heaters ranges from 26,000- to 280,000-Btu; waste oils can be burned without filtering or processing. Blowers within the unit circulate warm air throughout the shop.

It should be pointed out, however, that heaters of the Dravo/Hastings and Kroll variety must be certified by the state in which they are to be installed and used. And fleet operators should be careful not to burn any waste oil that might contain gasoline.

Gas-fired air replacement

Circulating warm air throughout the shop is also being accomplished with gas- or propane-fired heating systems, designed to either replace or supplement existing central-heating systems.

A system developed by the Binks Mfg. Co., Franklin Park, Ill., filters and heats fresh outside air, then delivers it into the shop area through a series of centrifugal blowers. Ralph Neuman, of Binks, says maximum fuel economy is realized with the Directflow Make-up Air Unit because incoming air is heated directly in the burner chamber, not indirectly in a heat-exhanger plenum, as in many conventional heaters. The Directflow is also available in steam, electric, or oil-fired units.

The Binks system originally was developed to replace heated and contaminated air exhausted outside of industrial workplaces. The heater/blower unit can be suspended above the shop floor, with the air-intake hood attached to ductwork passing through the roof or wall of the building. The burner has a maximum modulated turn-down ratio of 30:1.

The air-make-up system is also used in conjunction with shop spray-painting operations. When fume-filled air is exhausted out of the paint booth, heat is lost, as well. The Binks heater/blower unit automatically blows fresh, warm air inside. The air-supply system is activated at the same time the paint booth's exhaust fan kicks on. The unit operates independent of the shop's central-heating system, and requires no additional burning of central-heating fuel.

Still other types of hot-air blowers can be installed above overhead bay doors, and be set to activate automatically when the doors are opened, creating a protective "curtain" of warm air across the entrance.

Solar panels and draft curtains

There are many other space-heat-economy measures being undertaken at truck-fleet maintenance shops throughout the country, as well. Some are as futuristic as the $1.1-million solar-heat-collection panels installed atop the Regional Transportation District bus-maintenance facility in Denver, Colo. or as commonplace as the draft curtains hanging across the loading-dock bays and between shop and warehouse rooms at the Sea-Land fleet terminal in Elizabeth, N.J. ▄

ENERGY RULES A SHOP DESIGN

The Ottawa-Carleton group, who know what energy losses in a cold climate mean, designed a facility that hoards its precious Btus

Moving to keep pace with its rising per capita ridership, now the highest transit usage for any North American city without a rapid-transit rail system, the Ottawa-Carleton Regional Transit Commission, Ottawa, Ont., Can., recently opened the modern Merivale Transit Center. The Merivale garage, which handles and maintains 200 of the fleet's 750 transit buses, follows close behind the Pinecrest garage completed in late 1976 (FO—7/78, p. 102), and its design is heavily based on the Pinecrest facility and lessons learned there.

Thanks to a detailed study of projected population growth patterns and anticipated bus fleet size, OCTRC chose a 12-acre site away from nearby residences in a new industrial park with easy access to main urban streets a half mile in each direction.

Design objectives for the new shop, in addition to providing heated storage for 200 buses (with potential for 260), included maintenance facilities and manpower to handle all running repairs, normal bodywork, and daily servicing and cleaning for up to 260 buses; reduced building operating costs, especially in energy usage; provision of offices and classrooms for consolidation and re-location of OCRTC driver's and mechanic's training schools; and holding construction cost within a tight budget while not compromisng functionality of long term maintenance costs (see drawings).

Planning and design for the new garage involved a smooth working team from OCRTC. Included were

by Jack Lyndall, senior editor

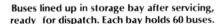
Buses lined up in storage bay after servicing, ready for dispatch. Each bay holds 60 buses.

Hector Chaput, general manager (he had been equipment manager for many years before his promotion to general manager); H.R. Weitzel, equipment manager; and Peter J. Newgard, equipment and plant engineer. The bulk of the design and detail work fell to Newgard, who worked together with J.L. Richards and Assoc. Ltd., Ottawa, the consulting engineers and architects. The general contractor was R.J. Nicol Construction (1975) Ltd., Ottawa.

Construction cost was $3.950,000 (Canadian.) Architectural engineering amounted to $320,000 and land cost was $660,000, for a grand total of $4,930,000.

Lowered construction costs were achieved by several design approaches, Newgard reported in a paper he delivered recently at the annual meeting of the Roads and Transportation Assn. of Canada. For example:

□ Drainage troughs in the storage bay floors were replaced by increased sloping of floors toward catchbasins, which also reduces cleaning costs.

□ While the steel superstructure (instead of poured concrete) reduced costs, the change was actually dictated by soil conditions. In the long run, there will be somewhat higher maintenance costs for painting the steel periodically.

□ A firewall dividing the building into two sections was less expensive than the alternative of insulating all structural steel as required by fire-insurance underwriters. But Newgard notes that proper insulation of the building shell was vital to minimize heat loss.

□ Because of budget considera-

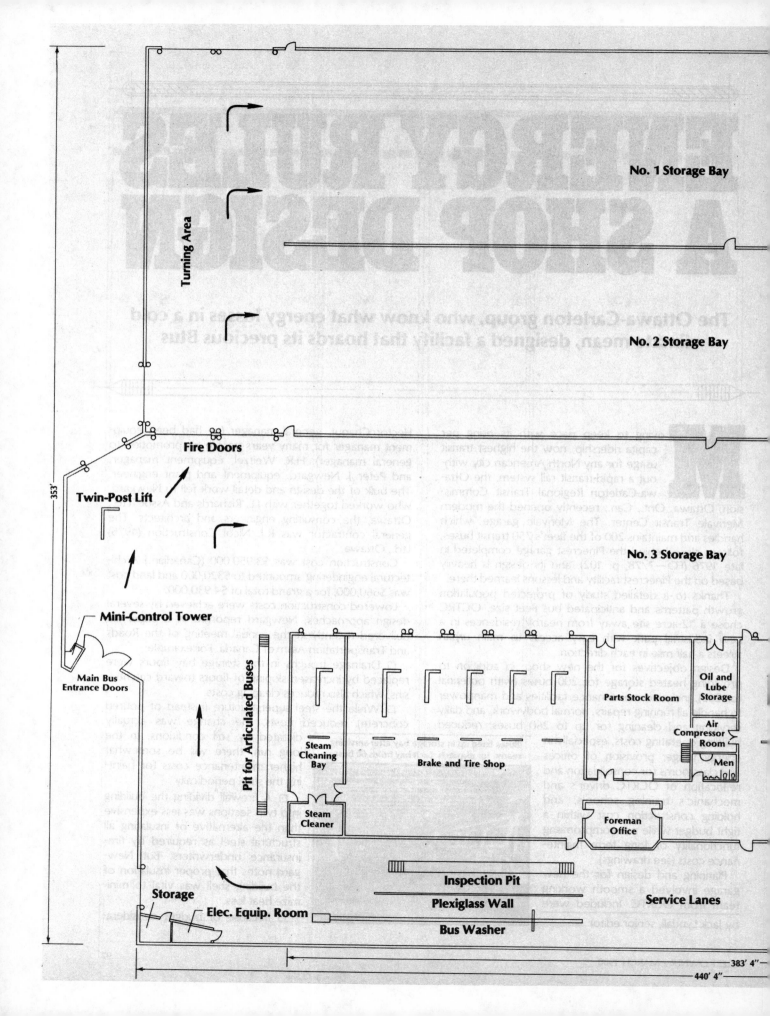

No. 1 Storage Bay

Turning Area

No. 2 Storage Bay

No. 3 Storage Bay

Fire Doors

Twin-Post Lift

Mini-Control Tower

Main Bus Entrance Doors

Pit for Articulated Buses

Steam Cleaning Bay

Steam Cleaner

Parts Stock Room

Brake and Tire Shop

Oil and Lube Storage

Air Compressor Room

Men

Foreman Office

Inspection Pit

Plexiglass Wall

Service Lanes

Storage

Elec. Equip. Room

Bus Washer

353'

383' 4"

440' 4"

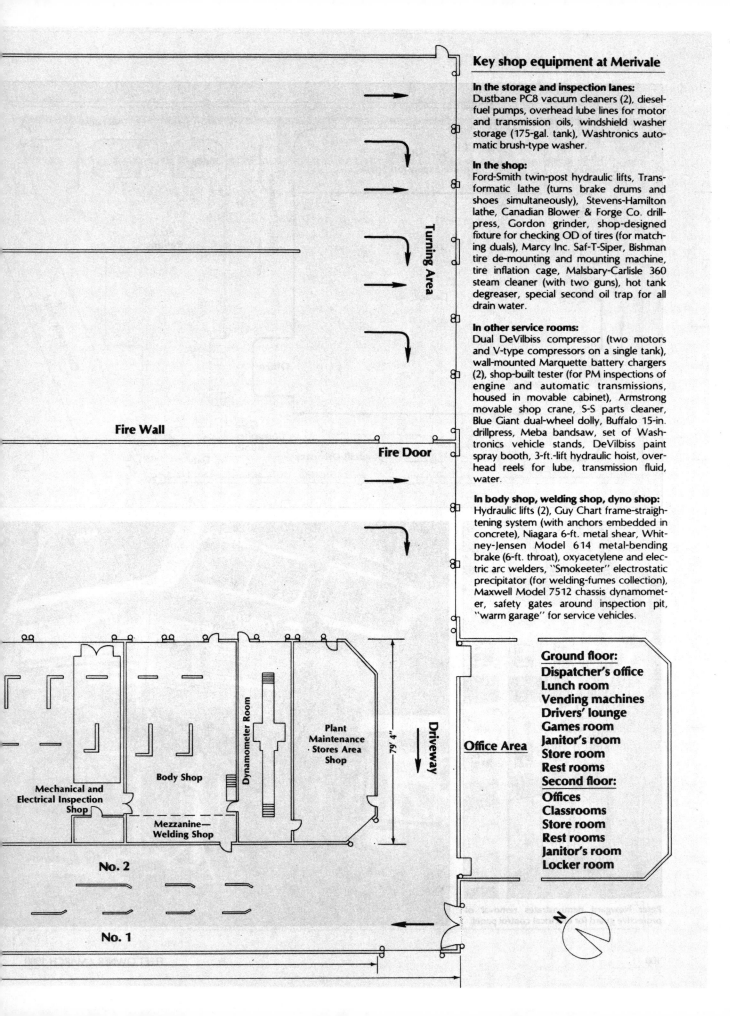

Key shop equipment at Merivale

In the storage and inspection lanes:
Dustbane PC8 vacuum cleaners (2), diesel-fuel pumps, overhead lube lines for motor and transmission oils, windshield washer storage (175-gal. tank), Washtronics automatic brush-type washer.

In the shop:
Ford-Smith twin-post hydraulic lifts, Transformatic lathe (turns brake drums and shoes simultaneously), Stevens-Hamilton lathe, Canadian Blower & Forge Co. drill-press, Gordon grinder, shop-designed fixture for checking OD of tires (for matching duals), Marcy Inc. Saf-T-Siper, Bishman tire de-mounting and mounting machine, tire inflation cage, Malsbary-Carlisle 360 steam cleaner (with two guns), hot tank degreaser, special second oil trap for all drain water.

In other service rooms:
Dual DeVilbiss compressor (two motors and V-type compressors on a single tank), wall-mounted Marquette battery chargers (2), shop-built tester (for PM inspections of engine and automatic transmissions, housed in movable cabinet), Armstrong movable shop crane, S-S parts cleaner, Blue Giant dual-wheel dolly, Buffalo 15-in. drillpress, Meba bandsaw, set of Washtronics vehicle stands, DeVilbiss paint spray booth, 3-ft.-lift hydraulic hoist, overhead reels for lube, transmission fluid, water.

In body shop, welding shop, dyno shop:
Hydraulic lifts (2), Guy Chart frame-straightening system (with anchors embedded in concrete), Niagara 6-ft. metal shear, Whitney-Jensen Model 614 metal-bending brake (6-ft. throat), oxyacetylene and electric arc welders, "Smokeeter" electrostatic precipitator (for welding-fumes collection), Maxwell Model 7512 chassis dynamometer, safety gates around inspection pit, "warm garage" for service vehicles.

Ground floor:
Dispatcher's office
Lunch room
Vending machines
Drivers' lounge
Games room
Janitor's room
Store room
Rest rooms
Second floor:
Offices
Classrooms
Store room
Rest rooms
Janitor's room
Locker room

Office Area

Turning Area

Fire Wall

Fire Door

Mechanical and Electrical Inspection Shop

Body Shop

Mezzanine—Welding Shop

Dynamometer Room

Plant Maintenance Stores Area Shop

Driveway

No. 2

No. 1

79' 4"

N

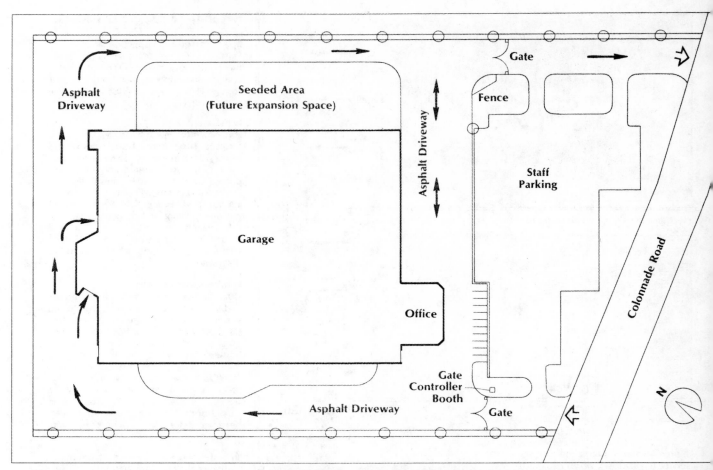

Asphalt Driveway

Seeded Area
(Future Expansion Space)

Gate

Fence

Asphalt Driveway

Staff Parking

Garage

Colonnade Road

Office

N

Gate Controller Booth

Gate

Asphalt Driveway

Peter Newgard demonstrates removal of protective guard for electrical control panel.

Dynamometer room has lower floor level behind the rear of a bus so a mechanic does not have to stoop to make tests or work on an engine.

Unit heater with exhaust fan and heat exchanger (above) reclaims about 70% of heat in stale air being exhausted to the atmosphere in the winter. Hydraulic hoists and axle stands speed work in brake and tire service bay (below), which also has overhead lube, oil, and air reels.

tions, both the Pinecrest and Merivale garages have conventional insulated wall design. The gray ribbed exterior concrete wall panels are 8 in. thick and contain a polystyrene insulating slab in a sandwich design. The approximate insulating value of the wall panels is R 11.

□ However, the Pinecrest roof experience provided the first of the construction "lessons". Before it was a year old, it had already developed ridges in the roof membrane corresponding to joints in the expanded-polystyrene insulating slabs. The ridges will probably crack, eventually, and require costly repairs. Therefore, the Merivale garage roof has conventional fiberglass insulating slabs about 2 in. thick under the built-up roof, giving an over all insulating value of approximately R 9.

Saving 'waste' heat

Because of their high energy consumption, heating and lighting received special design attention. The garage has two types of heating, Newgard explains, both using natural gas. A number of overhead unit heaters around the perimeter of the building keep the temperature from 50-55°F. during weekends and holidays, when building activity is minimal or suspended.

During work hours, a number of overhead make-up air and exhaust fan units draw in new outside air and heat it to replace stale air being exhausted. But, although the stale air is discharged, all the heat is not. A heat exchanger in the units recaptures up to 70% of the heat in the exhausted air and uses it to pre-heat the incoming make-up air, thus reducing the demand for "new" heating of that make-up air.

While the temperature in work area is maintained at approximately 68°F. during working hours, in the repair-bay "island" it is kept at 68°F. around the clock to avoid the long pre-heating time after weekend shutdowns.

To conserve that heat, each of the bus-repair "island" bays has its own roll-up door. The doors also keep out exhaust fumes during periods when buses are entering and leaving the storage bays. In summer the exhaust fans are operated alone.

A wall-mounted control panel in the foreman's office shows the location of each make-up air heater and exhaust unit and has control switches for them. Newgard pointed out that the make-up air heater units are programmed by automatic timers to turn "on" approximately one-half hour before work starts in the unit's area and to operate until a half hour after work ends. The foreman can override the automatic timers up to one hour by a panel of special controls should work periods change suddenly or temporarily. For a long-range change in the unit operating cycles, the main timer must be re-adjusted.

A third heating system is available for operation during snowstorms and freezing rains. Electric heating elements embedded in the concrete slaps and doors clear the approach areas, save on door maintenance, and prevent bus skidding accidents.

A second panel in the foreman's office controls lighting for the various garage area. A skeleton pattern of lights always remains on, even over weekends, and there is an emergency, battery-operated lighting system that comes on automatically should electric power fail.

Although the garage does not have a permanent stand-by electric generator, it does have a connection for the portable stand-by generator that is available on very short notice to any of the OCTRC garages and plugged in to provide minimal lighting and power in an emergency.

For still further energy savings, a power-demand controller was incorporated in the garage's electrical system. "When peak power reaches or exceeds a preset limit," Newgard says, "the controller automatically disconnects power from certain expendable loads. These are disconnected one at a time, in order of priority, until the total demand remains below the limit.

As power demand drops below a differential limit, the loads are automatically reconnected by priority. Expendable loads include the electrified portion of the office multi-zone heater, the in-slab heaters at the overhead doors, and the hot-water heaters."

Heat saving is also designed into the daily operation. For instance, when buses arrive, an attendant in the "control tower" activates a quick-opening, bi-fold-type door that minimizes opening time and heat loss. If an incoming driver reports a defect, the attendant uses an intercom to obtain instructions from the foreman.

Located in the same garage projection is a hydraulic lift. And a stock of mounted tires is stored along the outer wall. With this setup, buses coming in with a soft or flat tire can have the tire taken care of immediately.

One of the major energy- and heat-saving features at Merivale is found in the internal turning areas at the ends of the storage lanes. Traditionally, bus-storage garages have had exterior doors for each lane, and heat loss was high because doors remain open for prolonged periods when buses are switched, or return to and leave the garage. Here, about 95% of the fleet stays inside.

Because of the sharp turning angle, buses parked in the two lanes on the east side of the firewall can not be driven in from the main entrance door. The attendant directs buses assigned to those lanes through a service door in the north wall opposite those lines.

Articulated buses—to come

Planning ahead for a group of 60-ft. articulated buses that will go into service later this year, OCRTC built an extra-long (66 ft.) inspection pit alongside the north wall of the steam cleaning bay, at the end of the repair bay "island", and along the edge of the north turning area.

An unusual feature of the pit, which is equipped with chassis and steering-gear lubricant pumps, plus overhead reels for dispensing motor oil, water and automatic transmission fluid, is an offset extension of the pit near its midpoint. That offset extension, equipped with an easily removable cover, was provided to give mechanics access to the midship-mounted underfloor engines that

will be used in the articulated buses.

Newgard stresses that the placement of the bus repair bay "island" within the building did not hamper efficiency. "Most maintenance work is carried out during the day shift, when at least half of the buses are out of the garage. Buses being placed in the repair bays are turned in the adjacent storage bay which is empty, but which in the late evening is filled with parked buses. Access is required to only a few repair bays in the evening, and those bays are located so that they are the last to become inaccessible," he said.

Merivale has a staff of 41 to service and maintain the 200-bus fleet, which operates on a five-day week, 24 hours per day: 13 automotive (bus) mechanics, 4 body mechanics, 6 servicing attendants, 5 unit-rebuild and tire-repair men, 8 utility men (interior cleaning, tow-truck operation, bus starting, etc.), 1 parts stock man, 1 job planner, and 3 supervisors.

The garage incorporates two novel protective devices, Newgard pointed out during a tour of the shop. One is a row of removable guard posts protecting the main electrical-control panel on the wall of the bus-repair "island", flanking the storage bay. In that location, the control panels are vulnerable to damage by a bus.

In front of the panel, a row of 2½-in.-dia. steel posts are set over dowels anchored in the concrete floor. The upper end of each post fits through a large eyebolt set in the wall. To permit access to the control panel for inspection or repairs, the posts can be quickly lifted from the dowels and set aside, and, equally quickly, replaced.

The second improvement is found in the steel pipes set in the concrete floor at the corner of each roll-up door opening in the repair bay "island". Unlike the usual single pipe filled with concrete, the guards at the Merivale garage are covered with a close-fitting steel sleeve that rotates easily should the post be hit. The sleeves are grease-lubricated and designed to minimize damage to the side of a bus should it scrape against the guard as it enters or leaves a repair bay.

Yet another economy feature planned for dealing with snowstorms (frequent in Ottawa's frigid winters) was pointed out by Newgard: "Paved roadways encircling the building were laid out to accommodate large temporary piles of snow at corners of the property. That 'storage' capability enables us to truck snow away with our own forces during regular working hours rather than hire contractors or pay overtime rates to our employes to haul the snow during the clearing operation."

Future expansion designed in

Because of OCRTC's definite plans for expansion to accommodate an additional 60 buses within a few years, Newgard says that all building systems, bus-repair, and personal facilities were sized for the planned 260-bus capacity.

The east wall can be simply taken down, moved over, and re-erected to provide for construction of an additional bus-storage bay.

On the road to more energy:

A place in the sun for a Denver maintenance shop

by Frank Pitman, McGraw-Hill World News, Denver

Solar energy is supplying nearly half of the total heating requirements for a new 256,510-sq. ft. bus maintenance facility for the Regional Transportation District (RTD) at Denver.

The system, utilizing solar heat collection panels on the roof of the storage section for 252 buses, cost $1.1 million. But the architectural firm, Charles S. Sink & Associates, estimates the savings over a total oil-fired system will repay the cost within 12 years.

Mile-high Denver is especially suited for solar energy. It recently was chosen, in national competition, by the U.S. Energy Research and Development Administration (ERDA) as the site for a $10 million Solar Research Institute. The National Weather Service reports Denver averages 115 clear days, 131 partly cloudy days, and 119 cloudy days each year. Even on many cloudy days the sun shines sporadically.

The solar heat collection system at RTD has a reserve capability for storing three days' supply of solar-heated water, which assists the regular oil-fired system. If stormy weather prevails more than three days—a rare occurrence—the oil-fired system would furnish the required heat.

Original projections showed the solar assist system would provide 34% of the heat needed for the facility. "Actual experience for the first few months now shows it will be more than 50%," Richard Combs of the Sink firm said.

There are 1,400 collector panels, each 8 ft. long and 3½ ft. wide, mounted on sloping frames atop the roof of the bus storage garage. The one-story section occupies 169,439 of the total 256,510 sq. ft. of the facility. The glass collector panels transmit the sun's rays onto a gridwork of galvanized steel pipes that contain a solution of 50% water and 50% glycol antifreeze.

Pumps circulate the solution through the pipe grid, heated by the sun, and into a heat exchanger in the mechanical equipment room. There, the solar heated solution circulates through water in the heat exchanger. The water, at a temperature of 110° F., is pumped into air heating equipment, which maintains temperatures of 45° in the bus garage, 65° in the maintenance and service areas, and 68° in the administration section.

The glycol/water solution, heated by the sun to a temperature of 210-215° F., circulates continuously during daylight hours through the collectors to the heat exchanger.

Excess heat from the solar system also warms an 80,000 gal. storage tank of water underneath the mechanical equipment room. That water is drawn upon for heat on cloudy days. It is maintained at a temperature of 210-215° F., and cooled, by mixing with other water, to 110° before going into the air heating equipment.

The RTD board of directors adopted the solar heating concept after figures presented by the architectural firm indicated considerable savings. The original estimates showed the facility would require 356,000 gal. of fuel annually for a total oil-fired heating system. The solar assist will save a minimum of 121,000 gal. of oil annually. Projecting the cost of the fuel at 58¢ a gal. in 1976, and escalating annually at an inflation rate of 7½%, the minimum savings would be $70,000 annually. However, savings are already far in excess of that. Along with the cost savings, the RTD adopted solar heating as an energy conservation measure. The original estimate was that savings of fuel would total at lest 1.4 million gal. over a 12-year period.

Because of the early success with solar heating on the

project, believed by some the largest in the U.S., RTD recently authorized the go-ahead on an even larger maintenance facility in the east Denver suburb of Aurora for a 380,000-sq. ft. solar-heated facility, estimated to cost about $19 million. RTD authorized an application to the Urban Mass Transportation Administration for 80% of the cost of the Aurora site and structure.

The just-completed Platte Div. facility, also financed with an 80% federal grant, cost slightly less than $10 million.

Final design of the new bus storage and maintenance facility will be completed during 1977 by the architectural firm of Rogers-Nagel-Langhart of Denver. If approved by UMTA, construction would begin in early 1978 with completion planned by early 1979.

The Platte Div. facility is located north of Denver's central business district at 31st and Ringsby Court, alongside the Platte River. The property occupies approximately 17¾ acres of what was previously a landfill.

The structure is divided into three basic areas— 169,439 sq. ft. for bus storage, 78,869 sq. ft. for maintenance and service operations, and 8,202 sq. ft. for administration offices.

Earth berms, 16 ft. high, were placed along three sides of the bus storage area—one side 506 ft. long and two sides each 330 ft.—for thermal insulation and also for appearance.

Bus maintenance and repair is done on the south end of the property. A 78-car parking lot for mechanics is adjacent to the maintenance areas. Adjacent to the administration area, on the north end of the property, is parking for 305 cars belonging to bus operators and visitors.

East of the maintenance area is a fuel tank farm, providing storage for 150,000 gal. of diesel fuel and 100,000 gal. of heating oil. Product and waste oil tanks are located immediately south of the maintenance area. Storage for 50,000 gal. of gasoline is located near the street.

The blown-air curtain at the entry door of the garage keeps the inside air maintained at a temperature of 45°.

The buses exit from the storage garage through 21 telescoping overhead doors, each 24x14 ft., forming the entire west side. The overhead doors are controlled by circulating buses activating sensors buried in the floor. They are equipped with two-minute delay operators which close the doors automatically.

Air curtains also function at the three entrances and three exits for the three fueling-wash lanes. Denver codes require an open area for fueling. The doors are closed during late night hours when the fueling and washing operations are shut down.

Photos by Frank Pitman

Summer sun gleams brilliantly off shiny metal roof panels of new solar heated RTD maintenance garage, Denver, producing big fuel saving.

RTD buses leave maintenance and repair facilities through these exits. Air-curtain doors provide climate control at three wash-fuel bays.

Brake and wheel shop area of new maintenance shop—a total of 78,869 sq.ft.—shows hydraulic bus lifts and covered space heater units.

Bus chassis wash lane (below) features a high pressure cold-water system. RTD points out that 80% of wash water is recycled for conservation and re-use.

Solar heat exchanger in mechanical equipment room (right) transfers sun's heat to fluid in collector pipes that flow into exchanger for air heat transfer.

Entrance to solar-heated bus garage, showing 16 ft. high earth berme (bank) for thermal insulation plus appearance.

Maintenance section of garage showing round brick structure for outside paint storage, insulated for fire protection.

The facility includes:

Fuel-wash area—Three lanes of diesel fueling, bus detail cleaning and vacuuming and automatic bus washing equipment. The fueling areas are protected with a dry chemical fire fighting system. Eighty per cent of the wash water is recycled. The special vacuum cleaning system handles both wet and dry litter inside the buses. There is a separate lane for chassis wash, with a high pressure cold-water system.

Repair shop—Eight running repair bays equipped with automatic overhead exhaust hoods.

Campaign lane—Designed for fleet retrofit operations so as not to disrupt the day-to-day shop activities. Two axle hoists expedite work.

Dynamometer room—The chassis dynamometer is equipped with a strip chart recorder to measure bus performance—a critical need in Denver's high altitude.

Inspection lanes—Two bays include an automatic brake test system with strip chart recorder and vacuum waste oil retrieval systems. Inspections are at 2,000- and 12,000-mile intervals.

Support vehicles—A separate shop maintains trucks, sweepers, supervisors' automobiles, fork-lift trucks and other mobile equipment other than buses.

Tire change—Drive-through tire shop with wheel alignment equipment mounted in the floor, and a lift.

Body shop—Has seven bays with four axle hoists and two service pits; the only pits in the facility. Equipment includes drill presses, rod and tube bender, several shears, gas forge, welding shop and glass shop.

Paint shop—Drive-through paint shop with automatic traveling paint spray booth that can be automatically push-button operated by painters on either side of the bus. Three 40-ft. long buses can be painted simultaneously. Full spectrum lighting for crews working other than in daylight hours. All electrical fixtures are explosion-proof.

Paint storage—A separate circular brick building, 24 ft. in diameter, is adjacent to the paint shop. It houses a small parts painting facility with two hoods. The structure has explosion vents in the ceiling to prevent spread of fire to the main structure.

CF Goes Solar . . .

. . . with installation of sun-power equipment at its Sparks, Nevada terminal, a 33-door facility in the Reno area. The terminal will receive from 50 to 70% of its warmth from a roof-mounted solar heating system. During daylight hours, the sun heats water which circulates through copper tubes in 14 solar collectors. The hot water then goes into insulated storage tanks. Consolidated Freightways will study this process with a view toward using it elsewhere in its system, says Arthur L. Colley, director of terminals. Reno's high percentage of sunny days and its clear air make it an ideal start.

COMPUTER GRAPHICS SPEED SHOP DESIGN

Computer graphics gives shop designers freedom to make many changes in a maintenance facility while it's still on the drawingboard

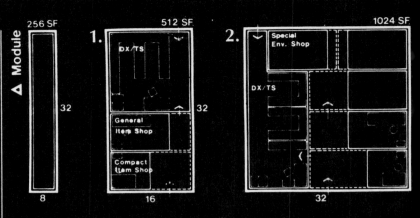

Shop Core Module

Using standard modules, an Army maintenance facility is designed. WAT uses the computer system to create and store modular designs, then to integrate them into a unit.

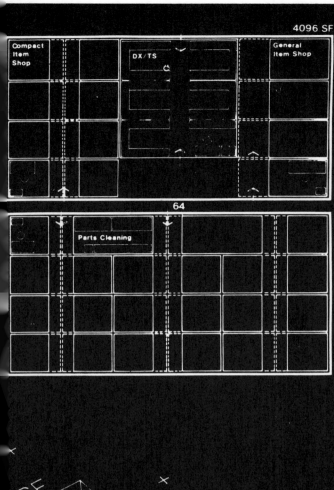

4096 SF

Compact Item Shop

DX/TS

General Item Shop

64

Parts Cleaning

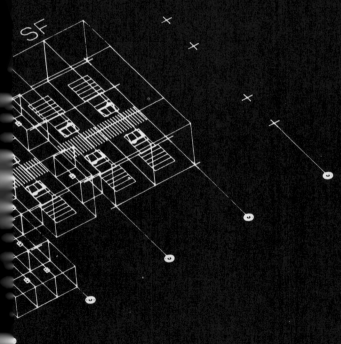

SF

3-Dimensional Plan

Design of the maintenance facility shows computer-graphic's ability to render 3-dimensional diagrams of architectural designs, giving designers freedom to create via freedom from details.

The fusion of architectural art and computer science is being moved closer to completion, and fleets may soon be able to tap that resource to get a complete shop or terminal schematic drawing done in a fraction of the time it normally takes—and at a fraction of the usual cost.

With the advent of computer-aided graphics, complex sets of instructions can be fed into a computer that is linked to an electronically-powered drafting table, such as the unit located in the offices of Morton, Wolfberg, Alvarez, Taracido & Assoc. (MWAT), Miami, Fla.

The system even counts the number of wall outlets, looks for the shortest plumbing route, and squeezes the greatest usable square feet out of any design. It can accomplish 50 hours of such work in just 10 minutes.

David Wolfberg, one of the principals in the Miami architectural firm, says the computer also has the ability to count every nut and bolt that goes into a building, and produce a complete inventory of the items needed to construct a building.

The Miami firm is using the new computer application to help systematize architectural designs for the U.S. Army as part of a $400,000 study.

The Army is so impressed with the merits of the system that it has hired the firm to design prototype vehicle-maintenance facilities that can be used in repeated applications throughout the U.S. Modifications for site and climatic conditions are easily made on the computer, with significant savings resulting on the site-adapted projects.

Denver-based Auto-trol Technology Corp., one of the hardware companies that manufactures computer graphics equipment, says computers are now being used to design everything from oil refineries to trailers. "The advent of computer-chip technology allows firms to store vast amounts of detail from past projects as well as create new designs from scratch," says a spokesman for the firm.

With the ability to remember thousands of details and analyze them simultaneously, the computer gives designers greater freedom to create.

For instance, if an architect wants to move a steel column one foot in either direction, the computer will remember where every plumbing line, electrical line, air-conditioning duct and load bearing wall is within the building and make the proper adjustments. After such modifications, new drawings generate in minutes—something that previously could have required up to 48 hours. Standard details such as doors, windows, etc., can be stored in the computer's memory and called up as needed, thus eliminating repetitive work.

By using the new computer-graphics technique, a fleet manager and his architect can literally take a thorough tour of a new shop building or terminal before it's even built.

UNDERGROUND TANKAGE

Sinking investment or buried treasure?

A tight fuel storage and dispensing system plus regular inventorying will save a fleet money, enhance the safety of workers, and minimize pollution problems.

by Stewart Siegel, assistant managing editor

Many fleets never have to pull into a truckstop or service station to refuel. They fill 'em up at home, drawing on a stock of gasoline or diesel stored in an underground tank on their own premises. With today's high fuel prices, anxiety over future fuel availability, and a deepening need for maximizing all aspects of truck operations, more and more fleets are either expanding on-site tankage, or installing in-ground fuel storage capacity for the first time. Truck operations with enough storage capacity generally purchase fuel from distributors in 8,000-gal. tank-wagon "drops" and pay the bulk price for product. Wholesale or dealer price varies from market to market, but can be 15¢ or more a gallon below retail. A fleet that installs a 10,000-gal. tank can figure the capital recovery on its investment rather easily. Its outlay, which can run $15,000 or more, depending on the nature of the tank and pump, can be recouped out of expected fuel-cost savings. The payback period depends, of course, on the rate of fuel usage and the price advantage of bulk purchases. While fleets with smaller in-ground tanks may not be able to claim a market advantage, there is peace of

In-ground tank installations are generally handled by construction contractors that specialize in such work.

mind in being able to maintain even a modest "strategic fuel reserve" that will carry an operator through a limited supply disruption.

Just the convenience of being able to refuel at home is a significant timesaver. More than one in-ground tank has been installed because the truck operator could no longer afford an hour of truck productivity a day just for driving to a fueling point and waiting to fill up.

Not to be underestimated among the benefits of having your own tank is management control. A fleet manager who regularly inventories tank fuel level in accordance with law is also in a good position to monitor and control fuel use. And, by regularly draining condensate and maintaining tank integrity, he can take a giant step toward keeping fuel quality high and fuel-related vehicle problems low.

Three types of tanks are commonly used to store gasoline and diesel fuel. By far the most common and least expensive are bare-steel tanks, which are manufactured by some 300 fabricators in sizes from 250 to 50,000 gal. But such tanks are most susceptible to corrosion damage and possible leaks.

Tank manufacturers have taken two approaches to help control steel-tank corrosion and possible environmental damage. Buffalo Tank, a subsidiary of Bethlehem-Steel Corp., markets the Buffhide tank, a steel tank coated with an insulating layer of reinforced polyester. The Steel Tank Institute, which has some 70 steel-tank fabricators as members, has developed the "sti-P_3" system of cathodic protection. Activated magnesium anode packs at either end of the tank are electrically connected to the tank body to attract corrosion-causing electrical currents that may be present in the soil. In essence, the anodes sacrifice themselves to the soil currents, thereby protecting the steel tank. The tank is coated with a coal-tar epoxy, and insulated nylon bushings in its flanges help isolate it against stray currents that might be conducted by vent or filler pipes.

Other manufacturers, including Owens-Corning, Century, and Lifetime, have taken a "non-metallic" approach to tank construction. They produce fiberglass-reinforced plastic (FRP) tanks that are immune to corrosion. They are more expensive than other types, but their premium price can be justified, say manufacturers, on lower life-cycle cost based on longer life expectancy.

Many first-time tank buyers are educated to the different types of tanks and requirements for tank maintenance and record-keeping by construction contractors that specialize in installation, repair, and replacement of in-ground tanks.

The installer's job is to deliver a tank that meets Underwriters Laboratory Safety Standard 58 (for steel tanks), or a suitable FRP tank, and install it in compliance with applicable fire and building codes.

The complete job involves more than just burying a tank. For example, a soil resistivity test has to be taken to determine electrical activity in the area. Soil with a resistance factor of 10,000 ohms/cm or less is considered

"active"—corrosive to unprotected steel—and a protected steel or FRP tank may be suggested.

After excavation and debris removal, a sand or gravel bedding is poured. The tank is then positioned, and venting and piping connected. Once a submersible or suction-type pump is readied (pump base poured; pump bumpers set in place; and electrical hookups made) backfilling can proceed. If there is to be traffic atop the tank, a concrete pad will have to be poured to protect the tank from the weight of that traffic.

Herb Lutz, president of Lutz Tank Installation Co., Linden, N.J., says a fleet that's contemplating underground tankage should weigh business needs against tank prices before deciding on a particular tank: "If you intend to remain in your present location for the foreseeable future, it would be best to invest in a quality, longer-lasting tank, such as fiberglass. On the other hand, if you plan to move in the relatively near future, a less expensive bare-steel tank, with a life expectancy of 15 to 20 years, may be the best choice."

Lutz, who claims he can install a 10,000-gal. tank in about a day and have it ready for operation in about two days' time, would charge about $3,400 to install a 10,000-gal. bare-steel tank locally. He figures a fiberglass tank of that capacity would run about $7,000, to which an additional $1,000 worth of pea gravel would have to be added for tank bedding. Both tanks require the same kind of contracting equipment for installation, he says.

Before suggesting a specific tank size, Lutz asks prospective fleet customers how much fuel they use each month. "If a fleet's needs are small, say, 2,000 gal./month, I would suggest it buy a tank of at least 3,000-gal. capacity. That will allow for future growth, and, perhaps most important, allow the fleet's fuel supplier to make regular monthly 2,000-gal. deliveries.

Lutz says that regular fuel deliveries could prove vital if there should be another fuel shortage and allocations are reimposed. "With a tank, you can easily document fuel use and justify your right to a future allocation if another fuel crunch hits." But fleets that fill up at service stations will have to take their chances and depend on dealers' supplies, Lutz cautions. "When there's a fuel shortage, our phone rings off the hook," he says.

In-ground tankage has been a fleet tool for many years, and the American Petroleum Institute (API) estimates there are about a million underground tanks in the U.S. Of those, a vast number are "leakers," older tanks that have either rusted through or been damaged in some way. As a result, water can either seep into the tanks and contaminate fuel, or fuel can leak into the surrounding soil and pollute the environment, create a fire hazard, and, in light of today's fuel costs, prove an expensive profit drain.

The Environmental Protection Agency (EPA), which, among other things, is charged with protecting water quality, is concerned over buried oil-storage tanks,

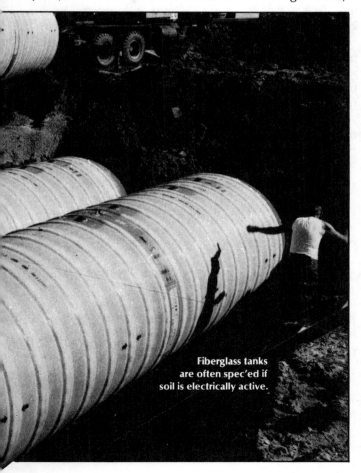

Fiberglass tanks are often spec'ed if soil is electrically active.

because experience has shown that upwards of half the unprotected steel tanks in certain areas of the country leak to some degree.

Several years ago, the EPA developed a Spill Prevention Control and Countermeasure rule (40 CFR 112) that requires large oil-storage facilities with over 42,000-gal. capacity to file spill-prevention plans in case of a leak.

Last May, EPA proposed revisions of the rule that have the effect of requiring new tank installations to have some form of corrosion protection, either cathodic protection, an anti-corrosion coating, or be made of a non-corroding material. The revisions also stress complete adherence to manufacturers' installation instructions. In other words, the instructions must be followed to the letter, for there have been instances where new tanks have been damaged by improper backfilling.

But smaller fuel-storage facilities are within EPA's regulatory reach, too. The agency wants every facility that has experienced a spill of 1,000 gal. or more—regardless of storage capacity—to file a spill-control plan that demonstrates how it will prevent ground-water contamination in case of a leak. The rule revisions also would require any facility that has had two reportable leaks in a year to present a spill-control plan.

In addition, the Occupational Safety and Health Administration (OSHA) requires tank owners to maintain daily inventory records. That requirement, an adaptation of the National Fire Protection Assn.'s Flammable and Combustible Liquids Code 30, is useful on a number of levels. If there is a discrepancy between the number of gallons a fleet pumps and the fuel left in the tank, there is a leak. Also, keeping an accurate record of the fuel in the tank can be of great use to local fire officials in emergencies. But daily "sticking"—inserting a long pole with incremental marks into the tank—also gives a fleet a running "handle" on its fuel-consumption rate.

By applying a dab of water-indicating paste (it turns color in the presence of water) to the bottom of the tank dipstick, a fleet can determine if water is present.

Water that has settled at the bottom of a tank can be "thiefed" with an inexpensive suction pump. By regularly removing unwanted water, a fleet can minimize internal corrosion of steel tanks and just about eliminate accidental introduction of water into vehicle fuel tanks.

Tank manufacturers say water can accumulate even in a sound tank as result of condensation, because the tank vent is open to the atmosphere and the tank "breathes" as the level of fuel inside rises and falls.

Although many leaking and damaged tanks are being excavated and replaced with sound tanks, many older tanks can be given a new lease on life, provided they are not too badly deteriorated and the local fire marshal approves. The process involves draining the tank and inspecting it from within, then sealing small pinhole leaks by spraying with a two-part, chemical-resistant epoxy. The treatment, which is offered by some tank installers, is said to cost about half as much as a replacement tank and is guaranteed for 10 years.

Labor costs are also a big part of total fuel costs for the company fleet. A fuel island attendant standing around waiting for slow-flowing fuel to fill a pair of large vehicle tanks can cost his company a lot of money in wasted man-hours.

Today's technology has helped produce faster and safer fuel dispensing equipment. High speed product pumps push fuel through bulk delivery nozzles like the Model 210, made by the OPW Div. of Dover Corp., Cincinnati, Ohio.

The OPW 210 nozzle has four hold-open notches in the heel of the handle for four different flow rates. For easy opening and topping off, the 210 nozzle utilizes two main poppets with a smaller upper poppet. The small poppet lifts first, to partially relieve the pressure. Then the main lower poppet opens smoothly and easily for full flow.

At the other end of the system, a variety of instruments are available to control, monitor, and move fuel efficiently.

Tokheim Corporation, Ft. Wayne, Ind., markets a high capacity pump, Model 785, for commercial locations that is capable of delivering 15-26 gpm. Standard features include electric power reset, interlock, and hose and nozzle. A positive displacement meter registers up to 1000 gal. and totalizes up to 1 million gal. Suction and remote models are available. The 785 also can be equipped with an electromechanical key control with capability for 24 to 96 keys. Totalizers are used for each key position, and the pump cannot be turned on until a correct key is inserted. Forgotten-key alarm and lockout are standard features.

Once underground storage is decided on, then consideration must be given to the type pumping system to be used, suction and remote or submerged.

Where to put the pump?

Suction pumping calls for a pump at each dispenser on the fuel island, with product suction lines running from each pump to the storage tank. With a suction system, the height that the pumps must lift the product is a critical design factor, according to the American Petroleum Institute (API). With suction, the best results are obtained by keeping tank diameter and piping to a minimum.

Remote or submerged pumping calls for locating the pump in or above the underground storage tank. A single product line from the pump can then branch out to the dispensers on the fuel islands. The system permits reduction in the quantity of buried pipe while allowing the use of more dispensers for each product. An impact valve, level with the top of the island is installed at each dispenser.

If a remote or submerged system is used, a leak detection device is required under NFPA Code 30.

The Bennett (Muskegon, Mich.) Key-Op system for its 12-14-gpm and 22-24-gpm Fleetmaster pumps accommodates up to 60 keys.

New fuel island installations are getting away from long delivery hoses strung across driveways or held up over the truck lane by cables and springs. Instead they are going to remote pumps that record the gallons delivered on a master pump on the driver's side of the fuel island while fuel is being put in the opposite side tank using the remote pump dispenser.

Gilbarco of Greensboro, N.C., manufactures a remote unit that is used in conjunction with its Trimline 625 series standard and its high-gallonage fleet fueling pumps. This unit uses six bladed rotary pumps with integral aluminum air separator for the standard model, while the high-gallonage model uses a rotary gear type with cylindrical air separator.

Wayne pumps, manufactured by the Petroleum Equipment Div., Dresser Industries Inc., Salisbury, Md., also offer high gallonage capacities—up to 30 gpm. The Wayne units use a two-piston meter. The meters are said to be virtually corrosion-proof, with 12 of their 16 precision components made of stainless steel.

Keeping inventory 'at home'

Protecting the fuel from theft while still serving drivers 24 hours a day without a fuel island attendant on-duty around the clock is a problem being faced by more and more companies these days. One solution is the Fleetlock System from Veeder-Root, Petroleum Products Div., Hartford, Conn. Authorized drivers can operate the pump with their own individual key. The system comes in 30 key sections in its basic unit but it can be increased to control up to 90 keys. It features a buzzer alert to notify the driver if he leaves his key in the box, and a separate counter box that can be located at the island or placed in a remote location away from the fuel island. A special feature of the system is its ability to control single or dual product dispensing, such as leaded or unleaded, or gasoline and diesel.

Another important demand in inventory control is actual reading of how much product is in the storage tanks. Most locations will "stick" the tanks at least once a day and convert the inch reading to gallons by use of a conversion chart for the particular tank.

Spenco System, a division of Dresser Industries, Austin, Tex., has developed a system that gives instant control information on every gallon of fuel that enters or leaves the storage tank. Called the Model 330 storage tank inventory gauge, it accurately measures the amount of product in the underground storage tank and displays the reading in either inches or gallons on its display console. Continual monitoring provides closer control of valuable inventory and gives a means for early detection of losses by short deliveries, theft and leakage. Additional indicators monitor water-in-tank and low inventory and automatically alert an operator at set levels of 1⅛ in. and approximately one-fourth tank capacity, respectively. 🚚

SETTING UP SHOP
Small mover serves other fleets

D&J Moving, a four-truck fleet, invested in a shop to do its own repairs, took in work from other small fleets to help cover the overhead, and now appears to have a maintenance 'hit' on its hands.

If you run a small fleet of trucks, there are two typical ways to handle vehicle maintenance and repair: farm work out to dealerships or independent shops, or perform some of the work at home and farm out the rest. But D&J Moving & Storage Co. of Decatur, Ill., a Burnham Van Lines agent, took a different approach.

Dick Doyle, president and owner of the four-truck operation, bought a garage last year and uses the facility not only to perform all work on his own trucks but on other small-fleet vehicles as well.

Outside business is helping cover part of the overhead and may, in the future, help the shop turn a profit.

Doyle's truck-repair facility, which operates under the name of Interstate Auto Mechanics, is a totally separate entity from D&J. It is managed by James Cox, a former millwright, whose skills include welding, machining, and a broad range of automotive and truck repair work.

Like many small movers, Doyle was faced with a maintenance quandary before he bought the garage. "We had to fix our trucks outside," he recalls. "That was okay during the warmer weather. During the winter, however, outside work was impractical, so we tried bringing the trucks inside our storage warehouses. That was some improvement; at least they were protected. But that was no real solution. The warehouses weren't set up for efficient shop work. We had no compressed air, lighting was poor, and just about every piece of shop equipment had to be brought into the particular warehouse where we were working."

Things might have limped along like that for some time had mechanic Cox not returned to the Decatur area to live. When Doyle found out that the skilled mechanic was seeking employment, he hired him, initially on a part-time basis, to take care of D&J's trucks.

But Cox had a dream. "I always wanted to get into my own garage business," he says. Cox had the talent; finances were the only stumbling block.

by Stewart Siegel, assistant managing editor

"I needed a backer," Cox continues, "because the work I like to do is pure mechanics. I want to service companies. The one thing I didn't want to do was run a service station, be distracted with pumping gas and dealing with the general public."

Doyle and Cox had several long talks aimed at solving D&J's need for a better maintenance plan and Cox's deep-seated need to be his own man in a business sense.

It was after those discussions that Doyle began to realize that there might be a way for a small fleet with just a few trucks to justify the expense of setting up a rather elaborate maintenance facility. He started searching for a suitable location.

At just about the same time, Cox was faced with an

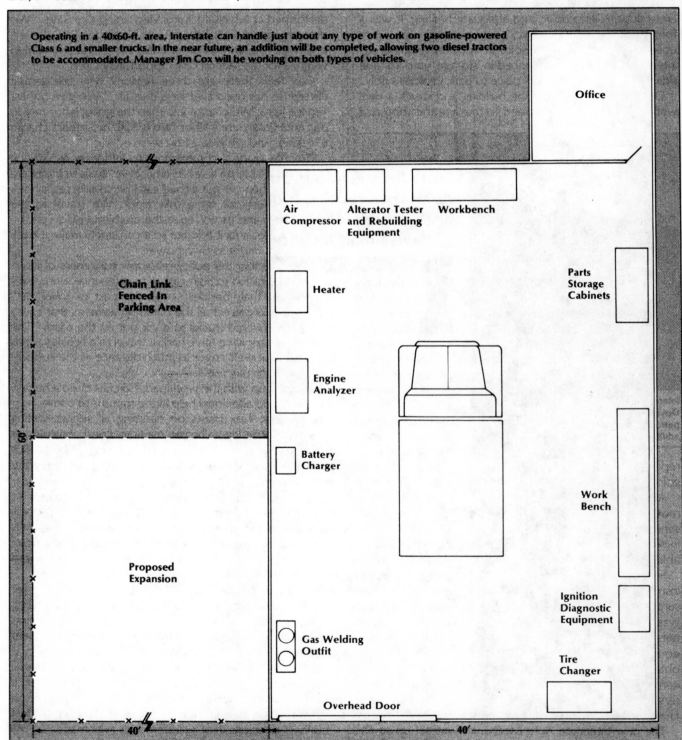

Operating in a 40x60-ft. area, Interstate can handle just about any type of work on gasoline-powered Class 6 and smaller trucks. In the near future, an addition will be completed, allowing two diesel tractors to be accommodated. Manager Jim Cox will be working on both types of vehicles.

important decision, too. He was offered an attractive position with a local salvage yard.

Perhaps the fear of losing Cox is what really pushed Doyle into searching in earnest, because he knew he'd need a qualified manager to handle the shop . . . if he could find the right location.

Several months ago, Doyle found what seemed to be a nearly ideal facility—a 60x40-ft. building with a concrete floor, roll-up door, and adequate heating. It was a former auto "beauty clinic," where used cars were dolled-up before being resold. In addition to generous interior space, it had a fenced-in storage yard to one side, which meant plenty of place to park vehicles safely.

Doyle arranged to buy the building and struck a deal with his mechanic. Cox agreed to manage the shop and

Interstate Auto Mechanics, which is owned and operated by Dick Doyle, president of D&J Moving, helps cover its overhead by performing service and maintenance work for local small fleets in addition to all of D&J's work. This building is headquarters.

repair D&J equipment on salary, with the possibility of going to a commission basis as the business grew.

All existing D&J shop equipment was rounded up and moved to the garage. Since the company was never seriously into truck maintenance, additional investments in shop equipment had to be made so Cox would be able to work efficiently. This was handled in three ways.

Several second-hand items were purchased. Cox inspected that equipment before it was bought to make sure it was in good condition. One of the items obtained was a truck-tire changer, but a number of storage cabinets were also located at a reasonable price. Some other equipment, including a Sun engine analyzer, was obtained on a rental basis. Finally, a limited number of items were purchased new, including a heavy-duty battery charger, because Doyle and Cox wanted to take no chances on their dependability.

The new Interstate Auto Mechanics was set up as an

independent company, and it bills D&J back for all work done on D&J trucks. Naturally, Doyle's moving company benefits from the good service it now gets.

But what really gratifies Doyle is the way the garage business has taken off. As a result of handing out business cards to a select number of fleets, and talking up the new enterprise to operators, several local fleets have elected to have their maintenance and repairs performed at Interstate Auto Mechanics. Cox says, "We recently signed S&R liquors with 12 trucks, P&D Beverages with five, and we service five buses and two station wagons for the Macon City Opportunity Corp.

Cox feels there are three reasons why the garage enterprise has been a success thus far. "We give honest service here. We charge less than the going labor rate in our area (Interstate's labor rate is $20/hr.; others charge $26-$27). And we give 24-hr. service."

Cox has made a commitment to Interstate by making himself available on a seven-day, 24-hr. basis to Interstate clients. "When we get a road call I personally respond— we don't just call for a tow truck. We travel to the breakdown and try to repair the disabled vehicle on the spot, or at least fix it enough so it can safely make it back to the shop under its own power."

Cox feels that this policy reassures customers of Interstate's dedication to high-caliber maintenance work. He's also found that, besides saving the cost of tows, he's been able to correct all the common ailments that cause gasoline-powered trucks to conk out on the road. "The longest distance we have had to travel to a breakdown is 50 miles, but we'll cover as much distance as the customer is willing to pay for."

To keep up with the workload, Cox has hired a helper, and may add additional help in the months to come.

However, Cox insists on handling all service-writing and parts-ordering so he can maintain good control over the shop. The paperwork is then sent to the D&J office for Doyle's review, and Doyle's secretary mails customers their monthly bills.

There are a few drawbacks to the physical layout of the garage, but Cox claims they are not serious and will be corrected shortly. "About the most serious problem is the roll-up door. Only 9 ft. high, it's too low for diesel tractors, although adequate for the gasoline-powered vehicles that represent most of our work."

An extension to the shop will give it two extra stalls for diesel equipment and provide sufficient height for tilting cabs. When that is done, the main portion of the shop floor will be subdivided into six stalls for more efficient work on Class 6 and smaller trucks and minibuses.

Few four-truck operations would take the financial plunge that D&J did in establishing a shop. But when it can be used to do Doyle's work, and make a profit on outside work, it just may be one of the soundest business decisions the Decatur mover ever made.

GETTING ORGANIZED FOR EFFECTIVE PM

Properly organizing a PM effort with correct tools, support equipment, and shop structure will minimize truck downtime, outside repairs

To perform preventive maintenance (PM) most effectively, a fleet needs three things: a place to do the work, basic tools, and support equipment.

Nearly every fleet does some PM—changing oil, lubing chassis, and changing filters. But a solid PM program really goes beyond those basic maintenance duties and extends into regular inspections and minor adjustments of all vehicle components.

If you are interested in cutting downtime and outside repair costs, the trick is to do a better PM job. The question that immediately arises, however, is: "How much will a better PM program cost?"

That's tough to answer. If you've got some tools, already perform a fair amount of PM, and do some light repairs, it shouldn't take that much more of an additional investment.

On the other hand, a fleet with few tools and no facility will have to make a sizeable commitment. It will take a minimum of $4,000 to $5,000 in basic tools and equipment just to get started—and that's not including a shop building.

However, once a shop is established, additional time-saving tools and equipment can be added gradually.

Since a PM shop is a place where inspections, and not major rebuilds, are made, a professional mechanic is not needed to staff it. The small-fleet operator can either do the work himself or appoint someone in his organization to do the work—and hold that person responsible for seeing the job gets done.

by Stewart Siegel, associate editor

A building or structure is needed, unless you happen to be operating in a section of the country where you can work outside year-round. A PM shop building should be a reasonably comfortable structure, well lit, ventilated, and heated. The shop itself will represent your biggest physical PM investment.

The building should have adequate ceiling height so cabs can be raised, and it should have electrical outlets for droplights and whatever electrical equipment you have. Most likely it'll have to be wired for 220-V service.

Because the shop must conform to applicable Occupational Safety and Health Administration (OSHA) standards, it would be well to obtain a copy of OSHA's general industry standards, and familiarize yourself with the requirements. Above all, you want a safe workplace.

In general, the size of your PM shop should roughly relate to the nature of your operation and the number and size of your trucks. For most small fleets, a one-stall shop with enough extra room for storage and moving vehicles in and out with ease is adequate. Since most small fleets use a PM shop for light repairs only, it needn't be overly big. Figure the heaviest job you should be taking on in such a facility is a brake reline.

Once you have a place in which to work, you need certain tools and support equipment for PM and light repairs. Service pros don't go overboard in suggesting a wide variety of tools; however, they do endorse investing in basic, good-quality items.

Since changing oil and lubrication are two basic PM jobs, a shop should be equipped to perform them as efficiently as possible.

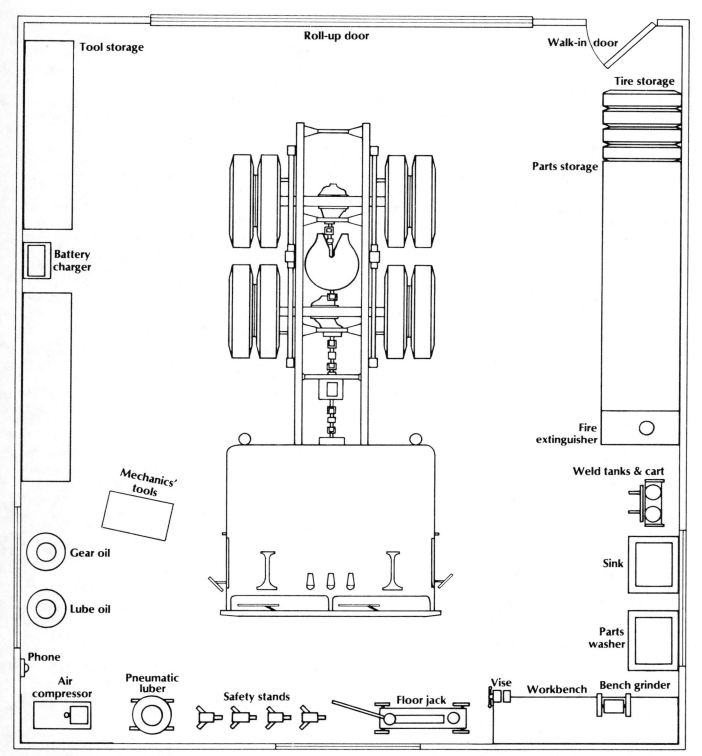

Tool storage

Battery charger

Mechanics' tools

Gear oil

Lube oil

Phone

Air compressor

Pneumatic luber

Safety stands

Floor jack

Roll-up door

Walk-in door

Tire storage

Parts storage

Fire extinguisher

Weld tanks & cart

Sink

Parts washer

Vise

Workbench

Bench grinder

Every small-fleet shop is different, and the layout above should be viewed as an idea-stimulator. It restates the time-saving wisdom of placing shop equipment and tools where you need them. Design allows efficient truck inspection in a safe, comfortable environment.

Hand-operated pumps are a must for transferring transmission, rear axle, and engine oils from drum to vehicle. At the same time, you should seek to comply with Environmental Protection Agency (EPA) requirements for safe effluent disposal, and have some means for storing waste oil until it can be safely disposed of.

Although some fleets get by with a hand-operated grease gun for chassis lubing, it's much faster and easier

to use a pneumatic lube system that runs off compressed air. (In fact, you'll probably find that a air compressor with at least a 5-hp. motor and 80-gal. air tank is your most versatile piece of shop equipment.)

Every small fleet is different. It's important, therefore, to use imagination and improvisation in setting up and improving the PM shop. For instance, you can fabricate your own portable coolant and oil drain pan out of a cutdown 55-gal. drum, mount it on casters, and use it to transfer liquid waste to a larger holding tank.

Top-notch tools are a decided asset. They feel good in your hands and help you do a better, more professional job. A small-fleet operator who does his own PM usually isn't a journeyman mechanic—and therefore has to be extra careful to do a good job. One headache you don't need is to waste time and risk damage by using cheap tools that can strip bolts and skin knuckles. Get a professional-caliber set of wrenches.

It's also advisable to purchase some specialty tools, like a fan-belt tension gauge. If you rely on your thumb for approximation, you may wind up with an improperly tensioned belt that damages alternator bearings.

Should you decide to expand your PM efforts into areas like wheel-seal replacement and bearing work, it's wise to buy specialty tools to make removal and installation virtually foolproof. Don't go overboard and

Getting the shop equipped

If you want to set up a shop and perform your own preventive maintenance—or perhaps broaden the capabilities of an existing facility, it's necessary to have the tools and equipment to do the job right. There's no way to list every piece of equipment, but this checklist will be a handy guide for equipping a small-fleet PM shop with the major items. Certain of these can be purchased rebuilt or second-hand to save additional money.

- [ ] Air compressor (min. 5 hp.; 80-gal. tank)
- [ ] Volt-ohm-amp meter
- [ ] Master mechanic's chassis tool set
- [ ] Cooling-system leak tester
- [ ] Impact wrench (1-in. drive)
- [ ] 10-ton-capacity hydraulic jack (20-ton for heavy equipment)
- [ ] Adjustable safety stands for working beneath raised equipment
- [ ] High-pressure chassis lubricater (mobile)
- [ ] Hand-operated grease gun
- [ ] Portable gear-lube and oil dispensers
- [ ] Battery fast charger
- [ ] Workbench with vise and bench grinder
- [ ] Heavy-duty wheel dolly for dual-wheel removal
- [ ] Battery and coolant hydrometers
- [ ] Small-parts cleaner
- [ ] Oxy-acetylene welding outfit
- [ ] Torque wrenches: 0-300 lb.-in., 0-150 lb.-in., and 0-300 lb.ft.
- [ ] Manometer
- [ ] Tachometer
- [ ] Belt-tensioning gauge
- [ ] Air-pressure gauge
- [ ] Tire-pressure gauge
- [ ] Portable truck-washing equipment

purchase equipment you won't use; invest in tools and equipment that are applicable to your work.

Earlier we mentioned the need for an air compressor. It can do more than supply air for tires. It can operate air tools that make assembly and disassembly faster. An air impact tool to remove fasteners is important and basic. More exotic devices, such as air jacks to speedily lift trucks, are expensive but may be justifiable.

If an air jack is not feasible, a hydraulic jack is a necessity. They come in various capacities. Certainly, if you're running only tractors, a 10-ton jack is the minimum size. If you are running heavier straight jobs, such as dumps or refuse haulers, a 20-ton jack is needed. Don't forget, never trust a hydraulic jack with your life; be sure to use safety stands to protect against accidental jack failure!

Because electrical problems are responsible for the lion's share of truck downtime, a PM shop would do well to have a multitester or volt-amp-ohm meter to help locate minor electrical shorts, voltage drops, and the like. More complicated electrical problems are usually beyond the scope of most small fleets and should be referred to experts.

A portable fast-charger for batteries and a pair of hydrometers (for checking electrolyte specific gravity and antifreeze potency) are most useful.

Additional diagnostic tools are a tachometer and an air-pressure gauge. By using them to check dash gauges you can get an early warning of serious problems. If any of your trucks are equipped with operating antilock braking systems, you might want to consider purchase of a ``121'' tester, since that is the most sensible way to troubleshoot the system.

An additional item that may prove handy in a maintenance shop is a manometer to measure air-cleaner and crankcase-breather restriction.

Cleanliness is important in quality maintenance. A small-parts washing system and a high-pressure washer will be used frequently. Besides making it neater to work on trucks, high-pressure washing of truck exteriors and undercarriages is a positive deterrent to corrosion.

One can talk tools and equipment at great length, but it would be a mistake to give short shrift to the shop's vehicle record system. For, in a very real sense, all your investment in tools, time, and facility is made to develop a set of records that let you spot trouble areas quickly, pinpoint possible unfavorable repair trends, and help decide when it's best to trade a vehicle.

If you merely repair trucks—or perform conscientious PM—and don't keep accurate records, you're defeating an underlying purpose of the shop. Getting organized for PM is a fairly involved job. But if you treat the shop as seriously as any other side of your business, it'll save you a lot of money. Remember, it's easier to systematically set up a shop with the proper equipment, and pull PMs yourself, than to find a good mechanic to do extensive repair work—and then pay the price.

The maintenance shop: A new profit center

by George Snyder, associate editor

When and why would an already functional common carrier maintenance shop take on the added burden of owner-operator and private-fleet repair business? One, when the parent company decides to diversify to generate additional profits and, two, because management arrives at the conclusion that that particular segment of the operation should spread its expertise over a broader area.

Too many common carriers regard vertical expansion by acquiring new rights as the only way to grow. But bigger doesn't necessarily mean better, and many a trucking company balloons in size only to discover that no significant profit increases are forthcoming. Extra revenue taken in is often gobbled up buying and caring for the additional equipment needed.

At least, that's the philosophy of one company officer who seems well on the way toward proving his point. Charles H. "Chuck" Armstrong, vp of Rooks Transfer Lines, Inc. of Holland, Mich., saw his organization reach an economic impasse in 1970 when a Chicago labor situation shut down the operation for three months.

However, instead of becoming a disaster, it proved a blessing in disguise by forcing management to search for supplemental sources of income. The trail eventually led to three-pronged diversification. "We knew," Armstrong told FLEET OWNER, "that we wanted to remain a medium-size short-haul interline carrier operating in the area we'd served for 50 years. We also knew enough to become involved with something with which we were familiar. That, of course, steered us right back to the trucking industry."

At the outset, Chuck Armstrong took a look at what Rooks already had, and what he saw was a subsidiary organization ripe for expansion. In 1947 Overland Industrial Equipment Co. had been established solely to service the Rooks fleet. Why not, Armstrong reasoned, expand it to service small fleets, private fleets and owner-operator vehicles inasmuch as the parent company did not desire to acquire additional authority.

A determining factor was the company's success in maintaining and repairing its own fleet of 55 tractors and 140 trailers. During the early '70s, because of spiraling equipment costs, Rooks philosophy changed from running a truck three years and then trading it, to keeping it in service as long as it remained profitable.

Working under the new philosophy, Keith V. Pas, Rooks fleet superintendent, obtained almost immediate results. Today, only a few years later, every Rooks tractor is expected to log a half-million miles before "majoring," and one GMC unit with a Detroit Diesel 871 has reached the 900,000-mi. plateau without an engine tear-down.

Taking on outside work

Armstrong says, "I had this new shop concept in mind for several years but it was largely Keith's success in establishing long engine tear-down or replacement intervals that convinced me I was on the right track. We both realized if we could do it for ourselves, we could do it for others."

After receiving a go-ahead from the Rooks management team, he surged ahead in expanding Overland Industrial Equipment. Today, 40% of the shop work is done for outside interests.

Armstrong, who also serves as president of OIE, is also convinced that the day of the owner-operator maintaining his own truck is just about over. "Today's truck has become so complicated and sophisticated," he says, "that you can't expect an owner-operator to pound his rig over the highways six days a week and maintain it on the seventh.

"No one is more at home with a truck than the owner-operator, but there just isn't time for him to cope with the complexities of modern machinery, nor does he have the expensive and necessary testing and regulatory equipment. A braking system, for instance, isn't a simple component any more. It's an electrical, computerized entity. And how is he going to get rid of 40 quarts of oil these days and still not run afoul of the EPA?"

OIE operates under the theory that the critical need of the small fleet or owner-operator is to get a repaired truck back on the road and making money as soon as possible. As a result, the outside customer receives a certain priority, but still without affecting the upkeep of the Rooks fleet.

While admitting that the outside work concept is not

brand new, Armstrong feels he's pioneering with an in-depth approach to truck upkeep not previously available to "the little fellow." The approach is based on what he terms "expertise," and OIE has a system designed to provide it.

For example, realizing its main asset is people, OIE employs 12 full-time mechanics and, at the same time, conducts a continuing search for new talent.

On the other hand, finding skilled truck mechanics is easier said than done, so Overland Industrial Equipment literally "grows its own." Working closely with universities and trade schools, it not only provides on-the-job training for their students but sends its own likely prospects to school to increase skills. Ferris State College of Mt. Pleasant, Mich., is one institution that sends students to OIE for six months of training before calling them back to the classroom.

Armstrong considers the major competition in this type of repair and maintenance business to be the ill-equipped one- and two-man shops.

He doesn't feel he's going head-to-head with factory branches or franchised distributors because "They've always been around, and they still have more work than they can handle. What the owner really wants is the assurance that his vehicle is being properly cared for by trained personnel using the proper technical equipment. On that basis we can compete with almost anyone." Here again, of course, it's the one- and two-man shop that usually comes in a poor third by not having the right equipment.

Setting up a parts business

Along with the Rooks venture into outside repair came other diversification that hadn't been counted on in the beginning. For instance, a natural progression from truck service was establishment of a parts business. Today, the OIE Parts Div. stocks a $125,000 component inventory, $25,000 which is allocated to the Rooks fleet, and chalks up yearly sales figures that approach three complete turnovers.

Such lines as Lipe clutches, Synflex and Aeroquip hose, Bower bearings, Stemco wheel seals, Holland hitches, Anchorlok and Chambers brake parts, Abex linings, Bendix-Westinghouse and Seelco brake valves, Monroe shocks, Gould batteries, AC filters and Krylon paints, to name a few lines, are carried. Keith Pas, who also doubles as OIE maintenance superintendent, says, "Any part that isn't stocked can be obtained from Grand Rapids in an hour's time. On the other hand, if we sell a part at least three times a year, we stock it."

In addition to what the company terms its Full Service Garage and the separate Parts Div., another entity has been established—a Materials Handling Div. Formed by Armstrong in 1972, it already rivals the older divisions in activity, sales and potential. The newest division, with three full-time salesmen in the field, distributes the Toyota line of lift trucks but sells parts and service for all makes of lifting, stacking and reach-type equipment.

It currently has 250 new Toyota units in the field and, according to Armstrong, is willing to sell, lease, long term, short term—almost any desirable arrangement. He says, "We're after that market because it ties right in with our over-all truck service concept."

Because lifting equipment is electric-powered about as often as it's gasoline-driven, an industrial-battery department has been integrated into the Materials Handling Div. to sell and service the C & W battery, which is produced in Farmington, Mich. Other truck-related items such as Schreck stackers, dock shelters and conveyors have been added to round out the line.

If an item is compatible with the over-all operation and, most important, profitable, Armstrong doesn't hesitate to add it to the inventory. He's always been extremely growth-conscious, which is probably the main reason for the company's entrance into new fields.

Growing while consolidating

However, growth notwithstanding, Rooks has been contracting at the same time that it has been expanding. The precise word, though, is consolidating.

Rooks was established in 1920 by John Rooks, but by 1942 the greater percentage of the stock was acquired by John Van Dyke Jr., current chairman of the board, who built it into today's livewire short-haul interline operation. Chuck Armstrong came aboard in 1955 as a billing and rate clerk, and worked his way up the corporate ladder through the echelons of traffic and sales management.

After most recently steering the company along the diversification path, Armstrong's next step was to prune dead branches from the trucking operation, initiating the consolidation.

Three terminals in western Michigan were closed and a new freight-handling center was built in Holland to expedite PU & D. Under the new format, freight is sequence-loaded at Holland to reduce breaking and transferring time in Chicago. On the other hand, freight picked up in Chicago is loaded "as is" and "put together" at the Holland freight center.

Rooks also operates a Steel Div. in Harvey, Ill., where a sub-fleet hauls raw product for the manufacture of automobiles and office furniture.

Rooks Transfer Lines' rights extend from western Michigan to a 50-mi. radius around Chicago and into

Chuck Armstrong, left, and Keith Pas, right, confer with mechanic Ray Mokma about teardown of a customer's diesel engine. The Materials Handling Div., which is housed in the building below, operates four service vans and two roll-off trucks.

This modern parts, sales and service facility is incorporated with Overland's 9-bay maintenance shop to serve all types of truck fleets and warehouses.

parts of Indiana. Included in its 140-trailer fleet are vans, open tops, flatbeds and reefers, to provide plenty of hauling versatility.

The reefers are used primarily to haul candy, according to Armstrong, while the company also hauls substantial amounts of office furniture out of Holland and Grand Rapids, numbering among its customers such titans as Herman Miller, Steelcase, Shaw-Walker and Haworth.

Five single-axle GMCs powered by Detroit Diesel 671s are coupled with 35-ft. trailers for city PU & D, the company having substituted that combination for straight trucks over the past few years. According to Keith Pas, 90% of the power units are GMCs with Detroit Diesel 871s, while the rest are Mack COEs or U-Models with the Maxidyne 675.

Linehaul units utilize Fuller RT-910 transmissions and Rockwell rears with 4.11 gear ratios. At present the Spicer 14-in., two-plate clutch is standard, but that will probably change now that OIE is distributing Lipe clutches.

Rooks' 40-, 42-, and 45-ft. linehaul trailers are either Fruehauf, Trailmobile or Ohio Body, but Armstrong and Pas have taken steps to standardize on Ohio Body.

To obtain half a million miles from tractors before a major overhaul, Pas changes differentials and transmissions at 80,000 mi. and filters at 20,000. Oil is changed and the units are lubed at 60,000.

OIE requires completion of a comprehensive "PM Service and Maintenance Inspection Guide" for every company vehicle at every inspection. Drivers' daily vehicle inspection reports are also SOP. The maintenance inspection guide has over 135 points to be checked. An engine, for instance, requires a 19-point check. A volume of these reports not only serves to show how a unit is performing, but more important, how it's wearing.

When asked if outside customers receive the benefit of this elaborate checklist, Armstrong replied, "They don't, because the cost of preparing them would probably be prohibitive. But we'd do it if they asked. That's the point I'm trying to make; we're ready and willing to provide truck service at any depth."

One bay of the modern OIE 9-bay facility is used solely for tire storage and to house heavy-duty truck scales, used chiefly by outside customers. Although the company standardizes on Dunlop tires, the rubber inventory appears somewhat depleted. "You bet it is," Chuck Armstrong said. "Like just about every other trucker, we have learned not to tie up our money needlessly in tires. Buy only what you need."

Because Rooks is an interline hauler, the OIE shop inherits a considerable number of trailer problems from other lines and often has to put its two-man trailer-repair team to work on a comparatively non-profit basis. "If they break down when we've got them," Pas says, "we fix them. But some of them simply give you fits. You'd be amazed at some of the poor trailer maintenance we encounter. Some of the rubber we come across is also incredible."

Pas blames excessive speeds for many of the tire problems. Rooks Transfer Lines is remarkably safety-conscious and, over the years, has captured several national safety awards for fleets its size. In this vein, Pas noted that Rooks established a 55-mph speed limit long before it became law because "we knew it was better for the equipment."

Today, Rooks Transfer Lines is a $5-million-a-year operation, with Overland Industrial Equipment hovering at the $2-million mark and coming on strong. Rooks currently employs 155 persons; Overland 27.

Looking ahead

When asked to elaborate on future plans for the 58-year-old company, Armstrong replied, "We're going to continue to hammer away at 'expertise,' because as equipment becomes more complicated, our services will be more in demand. We get the tough jobs, and every time we're successful the word spreads a little bit farther. Our immediate goal is to double the number of outside customers during the next 12 months."

Armstrong is convinced that to run an operation such as his, a company must be of a certain size and have a definite empathy with the small fleet and the owner-operator. According to him, most large-fleet shops have all they can do to take care of their own equipment, and many smaller ones don't care to be identified with outside work. "Nevertheless," he concludes, "we expect competition if only because success attracts all those eager to get in on a good thing."

OIE shop hours are from 6:00am to 10:30pm. So far, the company hasn't found it necessary to open on weekends. Pas says he sees a vehicle approximately 26 times a year for preventive maintenance and perhaps another three or four times for repairs. "We haven't had to operate weekends," he told FLEET OWNER, "because all of our 50 customers have become conditioned to our hours and know they can bring their truck in at the end of the day for PM and they'll have it back by 10:30 the same evening. Major repairs, of course, are a different matter and are scheduled as needed."

If, as planned, the customer figure doubles, OIE can go either of two ways: It can operate the shop around the clock or increase existing facilities.

Rooks Transfer Lines, the parent company, is headquartered in the building at right, while OIE parts, sales, and service center can be seen at left, partially hidden by the linehaul unit.

Truly a winter fleet, Rooks is located near the eastern shore of Lake Michigan. Quite often, the only thing units in the OIE shop (right) have in common is that they're trucks. Here, an FWD transit mix chassis comes in for repairs alongside. a company Mack COE.

SHOP SAFETY
OSHA rules for fleet shops

From the moment you walk through the front door of a shop until you walk out the back, OSHA is with you. But shops that use good common sense and practice good housekeeping have little to fear.

If there's one area of concern common to truck-fleet maintenance-shop managers across the country, it's OSHA—the much maligned and often dreaded acronym for the Dept. of Labor's Occupational Safety and Health Administration—whose general-industry and safety and health standards govern more than 5-million workplaces and 60-million workers throughout the United States.

The rules are voluminous and complex, and cover virtually every aspect of life in the fleet shop—from location of doorway exits and lavatory facilities to air quality and mechanical safeguards. The standards are legally enforceable and compliance is mandatory. Violations are punishable by fines of $1,000 a day or more and, in flagrant cases, imprisonment.

So, like it or not, it is imperative that every maintenance-shop manager know the rules and comply with them. Inspections by OSHA compliance officers are made without warning and, theoretically, nearly every fleet shop in the country is a potential target for a visit.

Although the scenario sounds ominous, OSHA says its "black hat" reputation is largely undeserved. "We're trying to promote safety, not punish people," says Larry E. Gromachey, ass't. administrator for OSHA Region IX, based in San Francisco. "Most truck-fleet workshops will never see an OSHA inspector; we aren't lurking behind every bush." Instead, the agency is encouraging businesses to work with local OSHA officials if safety questions or problems arise. In most areas, on-site safety and health consulting services are provided free of charge, upon request.

"But mainly, we urge employers to keep channels of communication open between themselves and their workers, then listen and respond to what the employees are saying about their working environment," adds Gromachey. "Let's face it, other than reports of imminent-danger conditions or serious on-the-job accidents, it's employee complaints that get us into a workplace."

OSHA also relies on data from the U.S. Bureau of Labor Statistics to help

by Thomas W. Duncan, Western editor

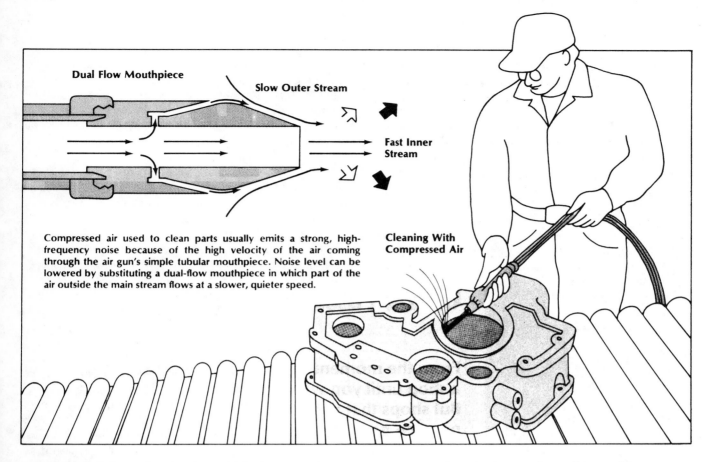

Dual Flow Mouthpiece

Slow Outer Stream

Fast Inner Stream

Cleaning With Compressed Air

Compressed air used to clean parts usually emits a strong, high-frequency noise because of the high velocity of the air coming through the air gun's simple tubular mouthpiece. Noise level can be lowered by substituting a dual-flow mouthpiece in which part of the air outside the main stream flows at a slower, quieter speed.

determine high-hazard industries, which then are given priority slots on regional compliance inspections schedules. According to Gromachey, trucking and freight-forwarding have "reportable injury incident" rates above the national industry mean.

(Note: Although OSHA is authorized to inspect a workplace without giving advance warning, a 1978 U.S. Supreme Court ruling in *Marshall vs. Barlow's Inc.* says OSHA cannot make warrantless inspections without the employer's consent. If OSHA is denied access, a search warrant based on probable cause must be obtained before the inspection can legally proceed.)

Changing the nature of the rules

As part of its effort to function more efficiently and effectively and to make compliance less burdensome, OSHA is changing the nature of the rules themselves. Since OSHA was created 11 years ago, the regulations have existed as specification standards, which set forth the myriad safety and health goals to be achieved. They are now being rewritten as performance standards, which, according to Gromachey, "tell you how to achieve compliance, instead of just specifying what the end result has to be."

OSHA hopes industry responds favorably to its standards revision project. One fleetman who thinks maintenance-shop managers will welcome the change is Timothy N. Burbrink, manager of hazardous-materials activities for Consolidated Freightways, Menlo Park, Calif. "If the rules are rewritten as performance standards, it should make it easier for us to understand what OHSA

wants us to do to be in compliance," he explains.

The rules change won't happen overnight, though. "It's taken six years just to rewrite the section on noise," says Gromachey. "It may be another 20 or 30 years before we're completely finished."

At the same time, obsolete regulations will be deleted from the standards, as well. More than 900 obsolete sections were removed in a revocation project several years ago. Many of those standards had been unchanged for years, and were in existence long before Congress passed the Occupational Safety and Health Act (OSHAct) in 1970.

OSHA standards are intended to form the framework for a safe, hazard-free workplace. Input instrumental in formulating many of the safety and health rules is funneled to OSHA through the National Institute for Occupational Safety and Health (NIOSH), an agency of the U.S. Dept. of Health and Human Resources (HHS). NIOSH was created by the OSHAct to conduct research into safety and health problems and provide technical assistance and rules recommendations to OSHA (with particular emphasis on toxic substances).

Expertise needed to interpret the rules

Dealing with OSHA rules (on top of the steady stream of safety and health-related standards being handed down by the various agencies of the Dept. of Transportation and the Environmental Protection Agency) has become such a major involvement for fleet operators that many larger carriers have departments or regulations-specialists who deal with nothing else.

It's a full-time job," agrees CF's Burbrink. "OSHA published one massive set of workplace standards; it doesn't break them down on an industry-by-industry basis. You've got to go through the whole book to find those sections that pertain to the maintenance shop. Burbrink spends much of his time traveling throughout the CF system, training and updating fleet shop personnel on OSHA and other regulatory requirements.

Unfortunately, most trucking maintenance and repair facilities are being run without the benefit of such in-house expertise. For that reason, FLEET OWNER asked OSHA's Gromachey and Mel Okawa, NIOSH western region program consultant, to offer advice on what a fleet maintenance manager should know and do to make sure his shop does not run afoul of the law. The information they provided cuts through much of the "legalese" of OSHAct and covers many (but by no means all) of the important OSHA-regulated aspects of shop operation.

Welding standards mandate protection

According to OSHA, welding is a typical truck-repair-shop operation that exposes workers to potential safety hazards. In arc welding, for instance, a worker can be exposed to infrared or ultraviolet radiation and risk eye injury or skin burns. Compliance with OSHA welding standards requires the following:

☐ Regular equipment inspections, adequate ventilation, and immediate replacement of worn, leaking, or burned gas hoses (gas welding), damaged cables and connections (electrical arc welding).

☐ No welding near flammable liquids or explosive vapors, dirty gas tanks, oil barrels, or open drums.

☐ Welding should be done behind flame-resistant screens or inside booths. A protective apron, rubber gloves, and helmet with face shield must be worn.

In gas welding operations, tank-storage areas must be protected, ventilated, kept dry, and isolated from heat sources. Oxygen tanks and welding gas tanks must be stored at least 20 ft. apart or separated with a flame-resistant barrier at least 5-ft. high. Oxygen tanks must be at least 35 ft. from oil and grease pits. Tank caps must be in place and valves closed when tanks are not in use. Acetylene should not be used with regulator pressure of more than 15 psig. Shutoff wrenches should be left on the valve stems, and all tanks should be secured with a chain or strap to prevent falling.

For electrical arc welding, cables should be spread out while welding is in progress. Ground and electrode cables should be joined by special connectors. No splices are allowed in the cables within 10 ft. of the electrode holder. Welding should not be done in damp or wet conditions. Electrode holders must be stored away from objects that conduct electricity.

Hand tools, grinders must be safe

OSHA standards cover many types of mechanics' hand tools—electric, hydraulic, and pneumatic-powered, and manually operated. Basically, the rules require the proper use and care of the tools. For example, electric tools must not have frayed or worn power cords and must have a ground connection or be double-insulated to prevent shock. Cords are not to be dragged through or left lying in spill spots on the shop floor.

For pneumatic tools, cracked or worn air hoses must be replaced immediately, and air-pressure reducers, gauges, and moisture/dirt traps kept clean. All compressed air used for cleaning must be reduced to 30 psi when the nozzle is dead-ended. Operators should wear goggles and masks.

OSHA rules cover all machine safeguarding. Grinders

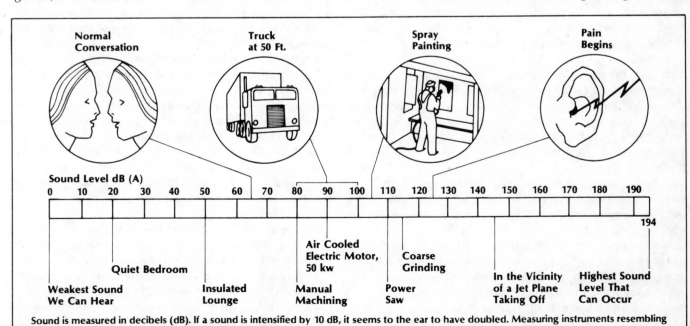

Sound is measured in decibels (dB). If a sound is intensified by 10 dB, it seems to the ear to have doubled. Measuring instruments resembling the human ear in sensitivity to noise of varying frequencies record the "A-weighted sound level" in units called dB(A).

must be guarded to prevent injury should the grinding wheel break. A bench- or pedestal-grinder must have safety guards that cover at least 75% of the wheel. An adjustable work- or tool-rest must be kept within ⅛ in. of the wheel, and the tongue guard must be within ¼ in.

Portable grinders should have top and side guards. In some cases, local ventilation may be required and a respirator worn. Goggles or face shield are required, unless the tools or workbench have built-in vacuums.

Air-contaminant levels specified

Many contaminants can be found in the air of a truck-repair facility. Mechanics frequently may be exposed to fumes, dust, and vapors that arise from welding, cutting, grinding, cleaning, painting, or engine-idling situations. OSHA standards are aimed at maintaining a healthy quality of air inside the shop. Specific worker exposure limits for many potentially dangerous materials and substances are listed. Some of the more common airborne contaminants found in truck-fleet shops are carbon monoxide, asbestos, diesel vapors (oxides of nitrogen), and other metal oxides.

Because engine exhaust and space heaters, two sources of deadly carbon monoxide gas, are often found in repair shops, good ventilation must be provided. In many indoor facilities, exhaust fumes from idling engines may need to be ducted to the outside.

OSHA standards specify that no worker is to be exposed to more than 50 parts of carbon monoxide per million parts of air in an eight-hour workday. Exposure above the 100-parts-per-million level are considered serious violations, and exposures over the 500-ppm level are treated as imminent-danger situations. A proposal from NIOSH that would lower the average daily permissible exposure level to 35 ppm and forbid any exposure over 200 ppm/day is under study by OSHA.

OSHA also is updating its standards covering asbestos dust, which can be encountered during brake repairs or brake-drum lining work. Recent studies have linked asbestos with lung disease. Asbestos dust must be vacuumed, not blown, from brake drums and floors. The vacuum should have a high-efficiency filter; dry-sweeping and cleaning are prohibited. Good ventilation must be provided or a filter-respirator must be worn.

Spray painting must be controlled

Spray painting of vehicles can be dangerous because solvent vapors and fire hazards are created. Again, good ventilation must be provided. If a spray booth or paint room is used, the ventilation system must sufficiently remove contaminated air so that an operator can work without a respirator. (In practice, however, few workers go without them.) The exhaust system should pull vapors away from, not toward, the painter. A contaminant-level sensor is required to warn of a drop in air supply. Exhaust filters must be inspected and replaced regularly. Paint

and lacquer supplies must be kept away from heat sources, as well. Welding, power-tool operation, and smoking are not allowed near vehicle-painting areas. No more than one-day's supply of paint should be stored near the spraying area at any given time.

Solvent fumes also can be encountered when chemical solutions are used for parts cleaning and degreasing. Solvent vapors can cause internal harm if inhaled, and the solutions can cause skin and nerve damage. Proper ventilation is required, as are protective gloves.

In some shops, paint, lacquer, thinner, or solvents must be drawn from bulk storage into portable containers. OSHA regulations also cover the transfer of flammable liquids. In such operations, static electricity can build up and sparks can cause an explosion. According to NIOSH, the most important rule to remember is to make sure the storage drum or tank is grounded and that a bond wire connects the drum to a portable safety container.

Shops that do body-repair work will also be involved with epoxy-plastic compounds, primarily body filler. Respirators may be needed when grinding or sanding epoxy compounds, and protective gloves should be worn.

Radiator, air-conditioner, and fuel-tank repairs

In radiator and air-conditioning repair work, pressurized liquid coolants and/or gases can be encountered. OSHA rules require the wearing of protective clothing to guard against hot-coolant spray, caustic epoxy leak-filler compounds and chemical-cleaning solutions, as well as jagged metal edges of damaged sections. Repair work should be done in ventilated areas, or using respirators, to guard against harmful fumes from solder or flux.

Other OSHA regulations apply if a vehicle's fuel tank is being repaired. If the tank is leaking and still mounted on the truck, the vehicle must be moved outside the shop. A syphon tank must be attached and grounded, and the remaining fuel pumped out into a safety container. If the tank requires welding or other hot work, all traces of fuel and vapors must be removed.

OSHA specifies noise-exposure limits

The regulation of noise in the workplace is a major part of the OSHA standards. Under the OSHAct, every employer is legally responsible for providing a work environment free of excessive noise hazards. The law limits worker noise exposure to 90-dB(A), averaged over an 8-hr. period. Shorter exposure time limits are specified for higher dB(A).

OSHA's most recent rulemaking, which will take effect Apr. 15, requires that a hearing-conservation program be established for all employees (except agricultural and construction workers) who have occupational noise exposure equal to or exceeding 85 dB(A), averaged over eight hours. Noise monitoring must be completed by Oct. 15. (Recent speculation in Washington is that the Apr. 15 date will be postponed.)

FLEET OWNER DATA SHEET

	Halon 1211	Carbon dioxide		Water
Class A fires. Paper, wood, cloth, and trash	Not recommended.	Not recommended.		Yes. Excellent. Water saturates; prevents rekindling.
Class B fires. Gasoline, oils, paints, greases, other flammable liquids	Yes. Excellent. Halon leaves no residue; does not damage equipment.	Yes. Excellent. Carbon dioxide leaves no residue; does not affect equipment or foodstuffs.		No. Water will spread fire, not put it out.
Class C fires. Live electrical equipment: motors, switches, appliances, etc.	Yes. Excellent. Halon is a non-conductor; leaves no residue; does not damage equipment.	Yes. Excellent. Carbon dioxide is a non-conductor; leaves no residue; does not damage equipment.		No. Water, a conductor, should not be used on live electrical equipment.
Extinguisher operation. Always direct discharge at the base of flame.	Same as dry-chemical type. Pressurized Halon discharges 13 ft.	Pull ring lock pin out of handle. Aim horn at base of fire. Squeeze handles together and spray agent in side-to-side, sweeping motion. Compressed CO_2 gas discharges 4 to 6 ft.	Same as the 150-lb. dry chemical. Discharge: 15 ft.	Hold upright, pull locking pin. Raise hose and squeeze lever, directing water into fire. Range: up to 40 ft.
Net wt./vol. of agent	2¾ lb. 5 lb.	5 lb. 10 lb. 15 lb. 20 lb.	50 lb.	2½ gal.
UL rating of extinguisher	5-B:C 10-B:C	5-B:C 10-B:C 10-B:C 10-B:C	20-B:C	2A
Approvals, standards	UL,DOT UL,DOT	UL,OSHA, UL,OSHA, UL,OSHA, UL,OSHA, FM,DOT FM,DOT FM,DOT FM,DOT	UL,OSHA, DOT	UL,FM,OSHA
Periodic maintenance	Same as dry-chemical extinguishers.	Inspect monthly or more frequently. Weigh semi-annually. Hydrostatic test every 5 years. (Sooner if extinguisher shows evidence of corrosion or mechanical damage.)		Inspect monthly or more frequently. Hydrostatic test every 5 years.

Class D fires. Combustible metals: Magnesium, titanium. Apply special extinguishing powder by scoop or shovel.

How to choose the right extinguisher

Tri-Class (ABC) dry chemical		Regular dry chemical	
Yes. Excellent. Chemical forms a fire-retardant blanket to prevent reflash.		Not recommended.	
Yes. Excellent. Chemical powder smothers fire. Screen of dry chemical shields the extinguisher operator from heat.		Yes. Excellent. Chemical powder smothers fire. Screen of dry chemical shields the extinguisher operator from heat.	
Yes. Excellent. Chemical is a non-conductor. Screen of dry chemical shields the extinguisher operator from heat.		Yes. Excellent. Chemical is a non-conductor. Screen of dry chemical shields the extinguisher operator from heat.	
Pull ring lock pin out of handle. Aim nozzle at base of fire. Squeeze handles together and spray powder in side-to-side, sweeping motion. Stored compressed air or nitrogen discharges powder 12 to 20 ft.	Unwind hose, pull locking pin, open valve on cylinder. Open nozzle lever, sweep agent across fire. Discharge: 40 ft.	Pull ring lock pin out of handle. Aim nozzle at base of fire. Squeeze handles together and spray powder in side-to-side, sweeping motion. Stored compressed air or nitrogen discharges powder 12 to 20 ft.	Unwind hose, pull locking pin, open valve on cylinder. Open nozzle lever, sweep agent across fire. Discharge: 40 ft.

2½ lb.	6 lb.	10 lb.	18 lb.	150 lb.	2¾ lb.	6 lb.	12 lb.	22 lb.	150 lb.
1-A, 10-B:C	2-A, 40-B:C	4-A, 60-B:C	10-A, 80-B:C	40-A, 160-B:C	10-B:C	40-B:C	60-B:C	80-B:C	160-B:C
UL,OSHA, BMCS,DOT	UL,OSHA,FM, BMCS,DOT	UL,OSHA, DOT,FM	UL,OSHA, DOT,FM	UL,OSHA, FM,DOT	UL,OSHA, BMCS,DOT	UL,OSHA,FM BMCS,DOT	UL,OSHA, FM,DOT	UL,OSHA, FM,DOT	UL,OSHA, FM,DOT

Tri-Class (ABC) dry chemical	Regular dry chemical
Inspect monthly or more frequently. Hydrostatic test every 12 years. (Sooner if extinguisher shows evidence or corrosion or mechanical damage.)	Inspect monthly or more frequently. Hydrostatic test every 12 years. (Sooner if extinguisher shows evidence of corrosion or mechanical damage.)

Abbreviations: UL—Underwriters' Laboratories Inc.
OSHA—Occupational Safety & Health Adm.
BMCS—Bureau of Motor Carrier Safety
FM—Factory Mutual Research Corp.
DOT—U.S. Department of Transportation

Chart adapted from material supplied by Kidde Belleville, div. of Walter Kidde & Co.

INDEX